Deleuze, Guattari and the Schizoanalysis of Post-Neoliberalism

Schizoanalytic Applications

Series Editors: Ian Buchanan, Marcelo Svirsky and David Savat

Schizoanalysis has the potential to be to Deleuze and Guattari's work what deconstruction is to Derrida's – the standard rubric by which their work is known and, more importantly, applied. Many within the field of Deleuze and Guattari studies would resist this idea, but the goal of this series is to broaden the base of scholars interested in their work. Deleuze and Guattari's ideas are widely known and used, but not in a systematic way and this is both a strength and weakness. It is a strength because it enables people to pick up their work from a wide variety of perspectives, but it is also a weakness because it makes it difficult to say with any clarity what exactly a 'Deleuzo-Guattarian' approach is. This has inhibited the uptake of Deleuze and Guattari's thinking in the more willful disciplines such as history, politics and even philosophy. Without this methodological core, Deleuze and Guattari studies risk becoming simply another intellectual fashion that will soon be superseded by newer figures.

The goal of the Schizoanalytic Applications series is to create a methodological core and build a sustainable model of schizoanalysis that will attract new scholars to the field. With this purpose, the series also aims to be at the forefront of the field by starting a discussion about the nature of Deleuze and Guattari's methodology.

Titles published in the series:

Deleuze and the Schizoanalysis of Feminism, edited by Janae Sholtz and Cheri Carr

Deleuze and the Schizoanalysis of Literature, edited by Ian Buchanan, Tim Matts and Aidan Tynan

Deleuze and the Schizoanalysis of Religion, edited by Lindsay Powell-Jones and F. LeRon Shults

Deleuze and the Schizoanalysis of Visual Art, edited by Ian Buchanan and Lorna Collins

Deleuze, Guattari and the Schizoanalysis of Trans Studies, edited by Ciara Cremin

Deleuze, Guattari and the Schizoanalysis of Postmedia, edited by Joff P. N. Bradley, Alex Taek-Gwang Lee and Manoj N. Y.

Deleuze, Guattari and the Schizoanalysis of the Global Pandemic, edited by Saswat Samay Das and Ananya Roy Pratihar

Deleuze, Guattari and the Schizoanalysis of Post-Neoliberalism

Edited by

Saswat Samay Das, Ananya Roy Pratihar
and Emine Gorgul

BLOOMSBURY ACADEMIC
LONDON · NEW YORK · OXFORD · NEW DELHI · SYDNEY

BLOOMSBURY ACADEMIC
Bloomsbury Publishing Plc
50 Bedford Square, London, WC1B 3DP, UK
1385 Broadway, New York, NY 10018, USA
29 Earlsfort Terrace, Dublin 2, Ireland

BLOOMSBURY, BLOOMSBURY ACADEMIC and the Diana logo are trademarks
of Bloomsbury Publishing Plc

First published in Great Britain 2024

Copyright © Saswat Samay Das, Ananya Roy Pratihar, and Emine Gorgul,
and Contributors, 2024

Saswat Samay Das, Ananya Roy Pratihar, and Emine Gorgul have asserted their right under
the Copyright, Designs and Patents Act, 1988, to be identified as Author of this work.

Cover design by Charlotte Daniels
Cover image: Abstract landscape background
(© StudioM1 / iStock / Getty Images Plus)

All rights reserved. No part of this publication may be reproduced or transmitted
in any form or by any means, electronic or mechanical, including photocopying,
recording, or any information storage or retrieval system, without prior permission
in writing from the publishers.

Bloomsbury Publishing Plc does not have any control over, or responsibility for, any
third-party websites referred to or in this book. All internet addresses given in this
book were correct at the time of going to press. The author and publisher regret any
inconvenience caused if addresses have changed or sites have ceased to exist,
but can accept no responsibility for any such changes.

A catalogue record for this book is available from the British Library.

A catalog record for this book is available from the Library of Congress.

ISBN: HB: 978-1-3503-7156-9
ePDF: 978-1-3503-7157-6
eBook: 978-1-3503-7158-3

Series: Schizoanalytic Applications

Typeset by Deanta Global Publishing Services, Chennai, India

To find out more about our authors and books visit www.bloomsbury.com
and sign up for our newsletters.

Contents

List of Contributors	vi
1 Introduction: Grounding Post-Neoliberalism *Saswat Samay Das, Ananya Roy Pratihar and Dipra Sarkhel*	1
2 The Invisible Hand: Deleuze, Serres and Platform Capitalism *Brent Adkins*	21
3 From Deleuze and Guattari's Interregnum to Our Own, or How to Navigate the Coming Post-Neoliberal Age *Samuel Weeks and Evan Lyons*	35
4 Postcapitalist Surplus Value: Humans, Machines, Information *Claudio Celis Bueno*	55
5 A Critique of the Post-Neoliberal Techno-Utopia of Transhumanism Drawing on Deleuze and Guattari's Philosophy *Francisco J. Alcalá*	75
6 Analog and Digital Power *Jens Schröter*	93
7 Agroecology and *Zoë*: Beyond the *Bios* of Neoliberalism *Adrian Konik*	109
8 A Radical Ecology to Believe in This World *Aline Wiame*	127
9 An Infantile-Image in Latin America: A Memory for the World *Marcus Pereira Novaes and Antonio Carlos Rodrigues de Amorim*	143
10 Schizoanalysis and Neoliberalism: Philosophy as Revolutionary Praxis for a People-to-Come *Tony See*	161
Index	175

Contributors

Brent Adkins is Professor of Philosophy at Roanoke College in Salem, Virginia, USA. His primary interests are nineteenth- and twentieth-century European Philosophy, Modern Philosophy and politics. His books include *Death and Desire in Hegel, Heidegger and Deleuze* and *True Freedom: Spinoza's Practical Philosophy* and with Paul Hinlicky *Rethinking Philosophy and Theology with Deleuze: A New Cartography.* More recently, he published *Deleuze and Guattari's A Thousand Plateaus: A Reader's Guide and Critical Introduction* and *A Guide to Ethics and Moral Philosophy.*

Francisco J. Alcalá is a postdoctoral researcher of the CIAPOS programme at the University of Valencia (Philosophy Department, Area of Metaphysics and Theory of Knowledge). His research interests focus on contemporary French philosophy, particularly on Gilles Deleuze, the author around whom he has articulated the different lines of his research, demonstrating a particular interest in the intersection of the strictly theoretical or metaphysical side and the socio-political and cultural side of philosophical thought. One of his latest articles in this regard is 'A Pedagogy of Generosity: On the Topicality of Deleuze and Guattari's Thought in the Philosophy of Education' (*Educational Philosophy and Theory*, 2022).

Antonio Carlos Rodrigues de Amorim is a full professor in the Faculty of Education at University of Campinas, Brazil, and a researcher in its Laboratory of Audiovisual Studies. Amorim is the author of many articles and a few books' chapters in Portuguese, Spanish and English, focusing on themes about curriculum, philosophy of difference and images into post-structural methodologies.

Claudio Celis Bueno is an assistant professor in New Media and Digital Culture at the University of Amsterdam and co-director of the AI and Cultural Production research group at the Amsterdam School for Cultural Analysis. He is the author of the book *The Attention Economy: Labour, Time and Power in*

Cognitive Capitalism. His research focuses mainly on the relationship between digital technologies, capitalism and labour.

Saswat Samay Das is an associate professor in the Department of Humanities and Social Sciences, Indian Institute of Technology, Kharagpur, India. He has jointly authored *Taking Place of Language* (2013). He has jointly edited *Technology, Urban Space and the Networked Community* (2022), *Deleuze and the Global Terror* (2021), *Deleuze and the Global Pandemics* (Deleuze Series, forthcoming, 2023). He has published in well-known international journals such as *Philosophy in Review, Deleuze Studies, Cultural Politics, Environmental Politics, Contemporary South Asia* and *EPW*.

Adrian Konik is a professor in Cultural Studies at Nelson Mandela University, South Africa. He is the author of *Buddhism and Transgression: The Appropriation of Buddhism in the Contemporary West* (2009) and other related articles, and his fields of research include film, philosophy and ecology. His work has appeared in journals such as *Environmental Communication, Angelaki: Journal of the Theoretical Humanities, Discourse: Studies in the Cultural Politics of Education, Phronimon: Journal of the South African Society for Greek Philosophy and the Humanities* and the *South African Journal of Philosophy*.

Evan Lyons is a recent graduate from Thomas Jefferson University in Philadelphia, Pennsylvania, USA. He received his BS in Law & Society and plans to further his education in the upcoming years. His research focuses on interdisciplinary analysis of juridical, political and philosophical topics.

Marcus Pereira Novaes has a PhD in Language and Arts in Education (State University of Campinas) and Vice-president at the Brazilian Reading Association (2022–24). Novaes is interested in writing with an emphasis on Education, Latin American cinema, childhood and Deleuze's philosophy.

Ananya Roy Pratihar is an assistant professor in Communication Studies at the Institute of Management and Information Science, Bhubaneswar, India. She has jointly edited *Technology, Urban Space and Network Community* (2022) and is currently coediting *Deleuze, Guattari and the Global Pandemics* and *Deleuze, Guattari and Inquiry into the Postneoliberal*, both forthcoming in 2023 with Bloomsbury in the series Schizoanalytic Applications. Her book reviews and articles have been published in *Philosophy in Review,*

French Studies, Environmental Politics and *Exchanges: The Interdisciplinary Research Journal.*

Dipra Sarkhel is a research fellow at the Indian Institute of Technology, Kharagpur, who works in a broad area concerning recent continental thinking and critical theory, under the supervision of Prof. Saswat S. Das. He has been awarded a research fellowship by the University Grants Commission for securing one of the highest ranks in the National Eligibility Test. He is currently guest-editing a special issue titled *Deleuze, Planetarity and Decoloniality* for Deleuze and Guattari Studies, Edinburgh University Press. His research interests include Planetary Studies, Ecophenomenology, Deleuze Studies, Process Philosophy, Cosmic Humanities and other interrelated fields of inquiry. He has recently published in the journal *Environmental Politics.*

Jens Schröter has held the chair for media studies at the University of Bonn since 2015. He directs the DFG research project 'Van Gogh TV' and leads the VW foundation's 'Society after Money' project. He is also involved in the 'How is Artificial Intelligence Changing Science?' grant. His diverse fellowships and numerous publications highlight his contributions to the field of media studies. His recent publications are *Medien und Ökonomie* (2019); (together with Christoph Ernst) *Media Futures: Theory and Aesthetics* (2021); (together with Julia Eckel, Christoph Ernst, eds.) Tech/Demos (Navgationen 1, 23).

Tony See is a lecturer in Philosophy in the School of Humanities at the Nanyang Technological University in Singapore. His research interests are in Continental Philosophy and Comparative Religions. He was appointed Research Scholar in Deleuze and Guattari Studies at Osaka University in Japan (2016), and he has published *Deleuze and Buddhism* (2017) and *The Wisdom of the Lotus Sutra: A Philosophical Exposition* (2023).

Samuel Weeks is Assistant Professor of Anthropology at Thomas Jefferson University in Philadelphia, Pennsylvania, USA. He received an MA from the University of Lisbon and a PhD from the University of California, Los Angeles. During 2017–18, Dr Weeks was an affiliated researcher at the Ecole des hautes études en sciences sociales in Paris. His research has been published in the journals *Deleuze and Guattari Studies*, *Dialectical Anthropology*, *Review of Radical Political Economics*, among others.

Aline Wiame is an associate professor of Arts and Philosophy at the Philosophy Department and the research team ERRAPHIS of Université Toulouse – Jean Jaurès (France), and a member of the Institut Universitaire de France. Her research draws on contemporary French philosophy and Anglo-American humanities and social sciences and focuses on arts and ecology, as well as on speculative philosophy. She wrote one monograph in French (*Scènes de la défiguration*, 2016) and frequently publishes in French and English about Gilles Deleuze, ecology and the arts (e.g. 'Shame as a Geophilosophical Force', *Subjectivity*, vol. 15, no. 3, September 2022, pp. 119–34).

1

Introduction

Grounding Post-Neoliberalism

Saswat Samay Das, Ananya Roy Pratihar and Dipra Sarkhel

Are we in a *post-neoliberal* world?

Is there a need to postize neoliberalism at all (Springer 2014)? The special issue of *Theory Culture & Society* on post-neoliberalism expresses the impossibility of doing so.[1] It does not approach the 'post' of post-neoliberalism as a definite historical bloc or a particularity. On the contrary, it represents it as a mobility at once caught up in and amplifying the dynamics of neoliberal capitalism. The point is contemporary theorization doesn't merely reconstruct the utopian postist grammar by equating 'post' with pure mobilities, but also renders the latter as an affectual force field. However, mobilities produced by the market dynamics stand for many as a site of disturbing ambivalences. Such mobilities no longer breed excitations of precarity or open up passages for liberation. On the contrary, they lead us to multiple dead ends, reterritorializing institutional apparatuses of coding, interpellating and controlling by representing them as neoclassical trends.[2] Further, such mobilizations cannot be seen as creatively displacing the ethical grammatology of de/reterritorialization provided by Deleuze and Guattari. On the contrary, they reflect how markets manipulate radical intellect into becoming a ground for transforming their profit-making machinations into praxis.

More importantly, while radical intellect opens up a world of dialogical interplay between multiple perspectives, profit-centred movements of all kinds work with a politics of indifference[3] towards dialogical circuits. This is why we get to encounter a parallel exclusivity of new existential worlds opened up by the market economy. These worlds coexist, yet never appear caught up in processes of co-becomings. On the contrary, they produce patterns of repulsive flights and withdrawal from each other. For instance, with intensification of economic inconsistencies, the link between the world of scientific revolutions and masses is at its weakest. While billions of dollars are being spent by the diverse corporate agencies to sustain the world of medical engineering that promises humanity a dis-utopia of techno-humanistic immortality in the form of 'nanobots technology' and 'cell therapy' this world stands disjuncted from and remains intangible to the worlds of hunger, poverty, war and suffering that the neoliberal economy generates with flamboyant disregard for human life (Coburn 2004; Jagannathan and Rai 2021). Therefore, for us, the post of post-neoliberalism opens a problematic zone where mobility generates stasis by releasing intensities of fear, paranoia and suspicion, and the absence of dialogical interplay between diversity of worlds only leads us to a plethora of suicidal dead ends.

Foucault and the (post) neoliberal machine

However when it comes to creatively mapping post-neoliberalism, writings rest upon Michel Foucault and Gilles Deleuze's parallax insights into the emergence of neoliberalism. Therefore, what we need at this moment is a close reconstructive reading of these insights, a process that may reveal the extent to which the post-neoliberal condition eludes these insights. In the undelivered section of his lecture notes on the post-war German political economy, Foucault had stated that 'Germany's real miracle was to have made the jurisdiction of the state derive from the veridiction of the market' (2004, 96). By doing so, Foucault did not merely indicate the interplay between the state and the market in the context of Germany. Rather, he ended up showing how the shift towards neoliberalism made market dynamics, the empirical rise and fall of its prices, the constitutive essence of state jurisdiction.[4] The question is whether the current post-neoliberal scenario structurally stands foursquare with or deviates from Foucault's description of the state's subservience to market forces. One may argue that with the massive rise of right-wing powers, grounded on the decline of Leftist ideologies and Centrist positions, we get to encounter a disconcerting situation. This is a situation that abruptly makes contemporaneity structurally analogous to Germany's post-war political economy. Of course, we cannot deny that examples showing how state gets colonized or puppeteered by market forces are on the rise. Yet, we think with the unprecedented rise of right-wing partisan ideology we also get to meet a process of ambivalent ideological restructuring of the state. To put it differently, the state exists, but not as an interventionist or agentic reasoning power set to ensure calibration of market performance, setting up an interplay between the spontaneity of market flows and its performative ethicality, based on sociocultural stratification, but as an ideological apparatus, aiming to carry out self-serving negotiation with markets.[5] However, such negotiations stand as an exercise in trenchant double articulation. This is because while the right-wing governmentality invites its marketization by encouraging massive privatization of its zones of ownership, selling everything that is considered to be 'of and by the state' to private players and market mandarins, it sets off an ambivalent process of critiquing the marketization of its ideology and conviction (Newman 2020).[6]

Therefore, what stands out is global markets turning towards treating right-wing ideology as a kind of grist to the mill of its reckless profiteering. Such marketization remains remarkably unique. In the past, liberalism had upheld the market as the ultimate source of truth, extending far beyond mere human understanding and immune to questioning, serving as the benchmark against which all government interventions, policies and practices were to be evaluated.[7] However, the contemporary commodification of right-wing ideology within the market landscape, along with its constituent components, signals the emergence of morally dubious and lumpen markets, mirroring patterns of what Henry Giroux calls *gangster capitalism*.[8] As markets relate to right-wing's ultra-conservative fascist policies directed towards nurturing ideas of nationalism, localism, religious fanaticism, ethno-centrism, identity politics, populism, gender divides, caste and racial configuration, not as threats or bottlenecks in relation to their smooth functioning, but as objective resources to be exploited for generating excess profit or surplus value, as one may call it, they do not stand as what Deleuze called 'smooth spaces' (1987, 371), but as mutant anti-productive colonial mechanisms wedded to ethics of capturing, seizing, selling and buying just about everything. Such lumpen profit-centric market ethics of buying and selling everything may be seen as generating the 'haecceities' (Deleuze 1987, 261) of a post-neoliberal condition. This is a condition that does not yield lines of flight towards greater liberty and emancipation. Rather, it generates deadlocking grids of contradictions or stultifying forms of hermetism by selling and buying status quoist ultra-conservative values alongside critical opposition to such values with equal gusto. Moreover, this turns out to be a process that makes post-neoliberal organization of our being vary from the classical neoliberal ones.

In his lectures, Foucault lays bare the processes of neoliberal subject formation. The mechanisms of neoliberalism for Foucault partakes of bio-political engineering, producing what he calls *homo economicus* or rationally calculating subjects[9] (2004, 147). Such subjects for him are not so much what he calls partners of exchange (2004, 225) engaged in social processes. Instead, Foucault views them as entrepreneurs of themselves, concerned only with maximizing their human capital, as a source of revenue (2004, 226). As entrepreneurs, these subjects count, calculate and deploy their economic, cultural, technical and physical resources, including their body and genetic composition, only to become not so much a fact or gift of nature, but variables to be manipulated[10] (2004, 270). Such bio-political strategies by mechanisms of neoliberalism, as Foucault argues, work well beyond liberalism's familiar reinforcement and redeployment of market mechanisms and privatization of social services. Such strategies redefine human experience, replacing the liberal subject with what Dillon and Reid call the 'bio-human' (2009, 20–1).[11] Foucault argues that with neoliberalism one even gets to encounter *virological* mutations of biopolitics, evident in techno-capitalistic stratifications of vibrating and pulsating masses, a stratification that divides and classifies these masses into multiple exclusive sets as per their positional and situational vulnerabilities (Chandler and Reid 2016). As Laurence McFalls and Mariella Pandolfi state:

> A host of new social technologies for preventing or alleviating potential or actual vulnerabilities and for encouraging resilience and adaption have proliferated, with eligibility for programs for depending on the self-labelling of particular individuals as vulnerable by virtue of their identification with any number of the countless socially, demographically or biologically constructed and targeted categories of vulnerability (migrants, the elderly, pregnant women etc.). (2016, 52)

No doubt, in the post-neoliberal condition these mutations persist. Both bio-political and techno-capitalistic engineering continue to drill into each one of us a vulnerability only to classify us in terms of that. With such an engineering, post-neoliberalism stands committed to tailoring not exactly what Foucault understands as bio-human (Dillon and Reid 2009, 20–1), but 'vulnerable beings', by subjecting them not merely to an interplay of discipline and control, but making them reliant upon techno-capitalist industries of care.[12] Moreover, for persuading masses to see themselves as vulnerable or disabled, this engineering invents a new grammatology, sharply distinct from ones that classical neoliberalism had employed. This grammatology stands directed towards lending capitalism a human face. As Wanda Vrasti states:

The moralizing Stories of Enron, Lehman brothers and Goldman Sachs teach us that economic conduct based solely on rational choice and cost-benefit calculations to the exclusions of all other social and moral considerations can actually be bad for business. Instead, flexible accumulation requires new political animals, such as the social entrepreneur, the creative workers ... actors who use social corporate responsibilities, continuing education, ethical consumption or charitable contributions to lend capitalism a human face. (2011, 3)

Further, post-neoliberalism doesn't merely set up credible affective structures, carrying out exercises in a kind of patipolitics or 'a governance of suffering' (Millar 2021), as one may call it, to ensure that we passionately attach ourselves to therapeutic industries of care, formations that turn out to be ultimately exploitative and unsustainable, rather it creates such attachments by eclipsing durations of intellectual dialogue making with that of populist anti-intellectualism. It does so by marketizing the former, a process that culminates in providing intellect's reconstructive machinism a populist turn. In the light of this, one may subject Boltanski and Chiapello's claim that capitalism today feeds on self-criticism sometimes by way of bypassing them via appropriations (2007, 36–40).[13] However, post-neoliberal markets even produce horrific economic inconsistencies by standing as the breeding ground of forms of corporate oligarchy which creates new stratifications. Hayek advocated for the dismantling of traditional sources of authority, including the church, state and family, in favour of allowing the free market's spontaneous forces to eliminate obstacles to growth, while also promoting a new internationalism centred on the unimpeded movement of capital and labour across national boundaries (Davies and Gane 2021). Even Foucault had argued in the same vein:

When you allow the market to function by itself according to its nature, according to its natural truth, if you like, it permits the formation of a certain price which will be called metaphorically, the true price, but which no longer has any connotations of justice. It is a price that fluctuates around the value of the product. (2004, 31)

With the hegemonic influence of few corporations upon the market spontaneity, post-neoliberal markets do not stand as a rhizosphere or a force field yielding a line of breakthrough networks or kinetic divergences; rather, markets become emblematic of a disturbing stabilizing dynamism, betraying in its movement a certain kind of concentric allegiance to facial coordinates of such corporations. Such a process ensures that ethics of care and futurity stand as resources that only a few could buy from offspring of dominant corporations while the majority stands vulnerable to natural cycles of death and disasters. With the interplay of all these trends, we encounter divergences in the realm of bio-political engineering of subjects. The subjects that post-neoliberal condition produces are not merely those that the marketocratic state machinery can readily puppeteer; rather, these subjects stand as perversely hybrid, a combination of what the diverse exploitative political dynamics seeks to make them: vulnerable, disabled, ideological yet ethically committed to techno-modelled future of immortality.

Deleuze and (post) neoliberalism

However, the populist marketization of radical intellect that post-neoliberalism carries out, reducing its undefinable heurism to a set of instrumental guidelines, becomes sharply evident in its populist reworking of Deleuze's philosophy, a process that aims at inventing forms of 'populist' Deleuzism. In her essay 'Extinction, Deterritorialisation and End Times: Peak Deleuze' (2020) Claire Colebrook connects with Andrew Galloway's view that claims that populist reworking of Deleuze's philosophy is at its peak. Colebrook observes in her essay while going on to stress the impossibility of such reworkings:

> The signs of this glut are apparently everywhere with 'Google Deleuzians', 'Carl Sagan Deleuzeans' and 'wet diaper' Deleuzean enthusiasms being bound up and complicit with late capitalism and neoliberalism, Galloway targets a widespread valorisation of excess for its own sake, and adopts Annie McCarthy phrase 'Red Bull sublime' in order to tie theoretical enthusiasms for unboundedness with uncritical celebration of intensity. (2020, 327)

However, what we need at this juncture is a reengagement with views representing Deleuze's philosophy as the germinal ground for the operations of neoliberalism alongside Deleuze's critique of neoliberal trends. This would be an exercise that attempts to show how post-neoliberalism works by vigorously popularizing radical intellect in order to ethically bind masses to its operations while stressing that it is only radical intellect that could stand as an effective war machine against such workings. Deleuzeans indicate that Slavoj Žižek's much-quoted statement that 'there are . . . features that justify calling Deleuze an ideologist of late capitalism' (2004, 183–4) is a product of his misreading of Deleuze – a misreading that smacks of neoliberalism's populist misreading of radical intellectual formations. This cannot be denied, as there is no attempt by Žižek to supplement his statement by teasing out dimensions from Deleuze's philosophy to show how they serve as fragments of neoliberal

Introduction   7

trends. In contrast, Dany-Robert Dufour produces a sample of what may be called 'engaged misreading' of Deleuze's philosophy:

> Deleuze failed to see was that, far from making it possible to get beyond capitalism, his programme merely predicted its future. It now looks as though the new capital-ism has learned its Deleuzean lesson well. Commodity flows must indeed circulate and they circulate all the better now that the old Freudian subject, with his neuroses and the failed identifications that always crystallize into rigidly anti-productive forms, is being replaced by a being who can be plugged into anything and every-thing. (2008, 11)

Such critiques of Deleuze's philosophy project an interplay between neoliberal capitalist productionist logic and the former, while Deleuzeans treat such critiques as based on 'grave misinterpretation of Deleuze's ideas or that they only apply to vulgar simulations of his philosophy' (Schleusener 2020, 42). Undoubtedly, with their roots in immanence of desiring production, Deleuzean subjects are not schizophrenic neoliberal personas plugged into 'everything and anything'. Rather, subjects for Deleuze are pure multiple caught in co-becomings of diverse temporalities, whereas neoliberal personas oscillate between multiple rigid contradictions reflecting neurotic attachments to each one of them. Further, aberrant movements of subjects in Deleuze's philosophy mirror cosmological patterns – the swerves and flights of atoms – while precarity exhibited by neoliberal personas is a product of capitalocentric external agencies of profit-making.

Yet, such critiques stand as a site of reference for neoliberalism's populist operationality. This is because while such critiques fail to distinguish between neoliberal personas and Deleuze's restructuration of subjects in terms of machinism or transversalism, they lay down some kind of deterministic cartography for the neoliberal populist reconstruction of Deleuze's idea of subjectivity. Commentaries that rely upon statements made by Deleuze in *Anti-Oedipus* to stress his accelerationist attitude towards neoliberalism have been subjected to critique by Deleuzeans (Shaviro 2015). However, a reengagement with this statement may be required in order to show how many have ended up misreading this statement only to make it vulnerable to, or available for, neoliberal strategies of populist reductionism. In *Anti-Oedipus*, Deleuze states:

> But which is the revolutionary path . . . to withdraw from the world market, as Samir Amin advises the third world countries to do, in a curious revival of fascist economic solution? Or might it to go in the opposite direction? To go still further, that is in the movement of the market, of decoding and deterritorialization? For

perhaps the flows are not decoded enough, from the view point of theory and praxis of a highly schizophrenic character. Not to withdraw from the process, but to go further, to accelerate the process as Nietzsche put it (1983, 239–40).

However, what we encounter as we subject these lines to multiple reconstructive readings is not Deleuze's romanticization of capitalism. Instead, these lines expose how, in order to view the market as a mechanism of decoding and deterritorialization or as a plane of consistency, Deleuze creatively reworks the Hayekian idea of the market. Moreover, such readings may prompt us to stress the historical context of this statement. We must not forget that Deleuze attempted such reconstruction during the 1970s – given that *Anti-Oedipus* was published in 1972 – a time which made the deterritorializing capacity of the market even more precarious (Schleusener 2020). The effortless free flow of productionist desire in the form of commodities had brought the market to a point of collapse or to the point of natality (Harvey 2007). Standing on the ethics of laissez-faire markets was an ensemble of liberatory routes and passages, beyond the crampy ideological confinements and prison house of humanist biases. And nothing corroborates this more than the aggressivity of desire among the postcolonial developing nations or world outside Europe to embrace the ethics of laissez-faire that bore proximal concomitance with Deleuzean view of the market as a great deterritorializing force.

Moreover, Deleuze was equally critical of capitalist markets' behavioural dynamics. For him, they stood as poor mimicries of his projection of immanent workings of the cosmos. Deleuze not only represented such workings by his non-conceptual grammatology of deterritorialization and reterritorialization, but he claimed that such workings were driven by energies of *thanatos* or a death drive immanent to them (Adkins 2007; Deleuze and Guattari 1987). On the other hand, the excess capitalist production stood as impoverished deducted abstractions. There was no such death drive that was immanent or innate to such production. Rather, these productions were governed by external agencies of profit-making.[14] The capitalists stood distanced from the immanent rhizomatic expansion of nature as they did not allow their production to reach a point of natural exhaustion or entropy.[15] Rather, these capitalists both endlessly and forcibly recycled such productions into an annoyingly messy excess while subjecting their previous productions to a violent process of artificial rejection (Vandenberghe 2008). Forms stultifying ecological waste and cycles of reckless consumption that we encounter in current times exemplify this. And as we know, it is the abstract humanist greed for production of this excess that drove evils such as colonialism, imperialism and fascism and resulted in what we call anthropogenic disaster. In this sense, the hallmark of neoliberal operationality lay in replacing our natural death drive with neurotic attachment to sites of capitalist accumulations.

However, more than artificially engineered deterritorialization, it is unwavering focus on profit-centred reterritorialization that expresses the operativity of post-neoliberalism. Deleuze and Guattari indicate this in *Anti-Oedipus* by stating that 'Capitalism institutes or restores all sorts of residual and artificial, imaginary and Symbolic territorialities. . . . Everything returns or recurs: States, nation, families' (1983, 34). Though Deleuze and Guattari tend to 'favour deterritorialization over reterritorialization, the forces of movement over those of stasis' (1987, 44), under post-neoliberal conditions one gets to see an ambivalent normativization of mobility, a process that culminates in making it yet another site of neurotic attachment.[16]

In his *Critique of Cynical Reason* (1988) Peter Sloterdijk indicates the irony of movement in our times. It is this irony that holds the key to understand the current post-neoliberal condition. Sloterdijk argues 'that which first appeared to be a controlled departure towards freedom has turned out to be a slide into catastrophic and uncontrollable hetero-mobility' (1989, 24).[17] This extremism of movement mutates it into what Deleuze and Guattari in their *A Thousand Plateaus* call a line of pure destruction and abolition. Schleusener corroborates this as he argues 'under the conditions of global capitalism, mobility thus seems to have lost its cultural value as a means to escape from repressive social assemblages and overstep rigid boundaries, since mobility itself has become the general rule to which almost anyone now has to conform' (2020, 46).

However, not only does the post-neoliberal condition produce forms of anti-mobility, it also subjects us to newer mechanisms of control. These mechanisms work with processes of continuous modulation that Deleuze views as a key constituent of what he calls a control society. Frieda Beckman notes: 'One of the key features of control society as Deleuze theorises it is the instant but continuous adjustment and manipulation of affect that makes the arduous disciplining of the subject moving from one institution to the next increasingly redundant' (2018, 4). In his 'Postscript on Control Societies' Deleuze argues:

> In disciplinary societies you were always starting all over again (as you went from school to barracks, from barracks to factory), while in control societies you never finish anything – business, training and military service being coexisting metastable states of a single modulation, a sort of universal transmutation. (1992, 179)

Beckman states, what 'emerges in the place of the long-term training of the individual body is the *dividual* of control society that is parts of selves, affects, desires, which are identified, addressed and controlled by means of samples and data' (2018, 4). Beckman argues that 'Sovereign societies relied on simple machines such as levers and clocks, disciplinary societies on machines of energy and production, and control societies on computers. The most recent stage is a move from analogical to digital' (2018, 4). However, for naturalizing its sustenance of control society, post-neoliberalism doesn't merely provide a populist turn to radical philosophy or create credible affective structures to fashion the ability of masses to derive genuine pleasure from such apparatuses of control. Rather, by funding academic or knowledge-creating centres, it affects their operationality, reorienting them frequently towards supplementing its naturalization of such exploitative structures. Such funded reorientation manifests in two different ways. On the one hand, we get to encounter populist reductivization of critical academia. Thinkers such as Paul Patton register how, with post-neoliberalism, universities no longer remain zones of re-structurative thinking or a chaotic battlefield of ideas, but become service providers to extra-academic apparatuses. It is such neoliberal restructuration of academic institutions that puts pressure on philosophers to be of relevance to the real-world policy, economic and political issues and various entrepreneurial and practical ends (Patton 2018, 193–207).[18] However, the contributors of this volume attempt to map divergences in neoliberal operationality that lead us to the post-neoliberal condition while showing how Deleuze's philosophy still stands as a cornucopia of reconstructive possibilities when it comes to finding new weapons for addressing this condition and producing a new assemblage for the futurity.

In Chapter 2, 'The Invisible Hand: Deleuze, Serres and Platform Capitalism', Brent Adkins discusses the limits of post-neoliberal reconstructions of Deleuze and Guattari's ideas of deterritorialization or despecialization. For Deleuze and Guattari, it is not merely the biological expansion of humans, but their cultural and historical diversification as well, that at once expresses the gradual process of despecializing. Deleuze and Guattari maintain such a stance, for they view the immanent workings of cosmos as a process of productive despecializing. In the case of the biological expansion of humans, this process captures the manner in which human organs diversify their functions by delinking from the territoriality of their primary functions. The cultural and historical diversification of humans follows a similar pattern, delinking from their singular line of development to form fresh combinations. In light of this, capitalocentric reconstruction of Deleuze and Guattari's idea of despecialization stands as an exercise in perverse displacement that leads to new modes of domesticating the revolutionary flights of our being. The capitalist mode of despecialization is based on axiomatization. This is a process that ends up creating new combinations for controlling the masses as per norms of marketization inclined towards excess profit-making. Further, as a process indicating cosmic rhythm of desiring production, de-specializing stands as the breeding ground of differences or univocity, while capitalist driven de-specialization only effects repetition of the same. This is because, with its ethics of connecting and interacting, it only brings about an interplay that repeats differences into domesticable sameness rather than yielding a rhizomatic network of differences. Weeks and Lyons connect with the parallel line of thinking in Chapter 3, 'From Deleuze and Guattari's Interregnum to Our Own, or, How to Navigate the Coming Post-Neoliberal Age'. They show how minor political movements deflate attempts by post-neoliberal apparatuses to fashion a populist consumerist version of such movements. In order to stress the effectiveness of minor movements, they show how Deleuze and Guattari's thinking stands as a potential zone for initiating political restructuration. Weeks and Lyons end their chapter by claiming that persisting engagement with Deleuze's ideas could open up a futurity pregnant with possibilities beyond post-neoliberal framings. Claudio Celis Bueno connects with Adkins, and Weeks and Lyons, by arguing that it is Deleuze and Simondon's intellectual grammatology of amplification that could unsettle post-neoliberal appropriation of information technology. While McKenzie Wark's *Capital Is Dead* and Paul Mason's *Post-capitalism* view information technology explosion as generating a process of overcoming capitalism based on extracting surplus value, Claudio Celis Bueno in Chapter 4, 'Postcapitalist Surplus Value: Humans, Machines, Information' argues that such a boom makes way for a postcapitalist mode of production that stands equally committed to extracting surplus value for gaining excess profit. While Marx views the extraction of surplus value as a process that leads to the exploitation of human labour, the postcapitalist mode of extracting surplus value leads to broader exploitation because it entails both human and non-human agents. Bueno eventually positions Deleuze and Guattari's notion of machinic surplus and Simondon's theories of amplification not only as the new grammar for understanding surplus value in postcapitalistic scenarios, but as new weapons to deflate post-neoliberalism's subsumption of experimental technological growth within capitalistic concerns.

Francisco Alcalá, in Chapter 5, 'A Critique of the Post-Neoliberal Techno-Utopia of Transhumanism Drawing on Deleuze and Guattari's Philosophy', views transhumanism as an expression and a product of post-neoliberal populist processing of Nietzschean idea of overman. Alcalá argues that, with its urge to transcend the limits of human body, transhumanism not only builds up a revulsion for the biological foundation of humanity, but also ends up creating a genetic supermarket, based on the idea of selective breeding. While he distinguishes transhumanism from cultural posthumanism, indicating that the latter deepens the humanist ideals of emancipation while acknowledging the biological foundations of humanity, his main objective lies in showing the capitalocentric workings of the transhumanist genetic supermarket. Working by a process of limiting the production of genetic engineering technologies, post-neoliberal economy only makes such engineering available to a few, in particular elites, at an exorbitant price. By such a process, post-neoliberal economy perpetuates inequality instead of promoting collective well-being and equality. Bueno argues that powerful corporations, already exerting their influence to the detriment of states, may monopolize these technologies, further deepening social inequalities. The chapter supports these claims by referencing sources that discuss the rise of corporate influence and unequal access to technology.

Similarly, Jens Schröter in Chapter 6, 'Analog and Digital Power' shows how post-neoliberal dispositive invents technologies of control while deconstructing the categorical distinction between analog and digital technologies, reiterating. He argues that post-neoliberal society domesticates the revolutionary desires of masses by using a mixture of analog and digital technologies and claims that the transition from the former to the latter cannot be seen in absolute terms by showing that use of modulation technologies by the post-neoliberal control society can also be employed by analog technologies. In order to drive his point home, he refers to the distinction between analog and digital technologies that Deleuze provides in his 'Postscript on Control Societies'.

Correspondingly, Adrian Konik in Chapter 7, 'Agroecology and Zoë: Beyond the Bios of Neoliberalism', engages with Deleuze's postscript to control societies to show how with its reduction of individual corporeality to a form of dividual incorporeality, post-neoliberal digitalization assimilates the revolutionary potential of the Deleuzean idea of becoming minor. With his idea, Deleuze shows how by withdrawing from institutionalized majoritarian identities and moving towards a process of becoming imperceptible, one may resist neoliberal stratagems of assimilating identitarian organization and molarities. However, Konik shows how post-neoliberal operationality works out an arresting cartography of imperceptibility by reducing individuals to dividuals. This is a reduction that captures individuality by turning it into a site of imperceptible electronic waves and intensities. For post-neoliberal apparatuses, individuals are not bordered organisms, but a collection of electrical data, signals and intensities. Therefore, for Konik, it is only by going beyond post-neoliberal digital economy that we may resist this economy. Konik shows that agroecological movements bear the potential of unsettling corporatized agrobusiness. He shows how these movements showcase a perpetual process of withdrawal from the large agrobusiness agency driven by post-neoliberal schemes and agendas for generating surplus value. He ends his chapter by showing how by necessitating an interplay between their decision to remain cut off from the profit-driven corporatized agrobusiness and their ethical commitment to producing life-enriching raw organic foods, they stand veridical to infinite life's commitment to maximization of its own potential.

Aline Wiame also connects with Konik's thought patterns in the chapter *A Radical Ecology to Believe in This World*. She shows how post-neoliberal mass media affects new technologies of control while arguing that Deleuze's non-conceptual grammatology of minor films nurtures a revolutionary potential that will eventually deflate post-neoliberal controlling mechanisms. Wiame engages with Deleuze's diagnosis of contemporary disbelief to claim that by repeatedly generating affectualities of disbelief and bewilderment, post-neoliberal mass media produces and arrests contemporaneity in folds of anti-intellectualism, preventing it from executing creative thought experiments or transforming established patterns of thought into flows of thinking. Wiame claims that by continuously working with a mimetic or representationalist framework, post-neoliberal media refines established understanding of our world, creating disbelief rather than facilitating encounters with the real. On the other hand, she thinks that by persistently entrapping us in interminable circuits of information rather than generating affective ideas, post-neoliberal media creates bewilderment. However, she relies on the potential of cinema to work out an affective ecology. She argues that films can excite a rebellious tone and temper of Donna Haraway's take on Anthropocene/Capitalocene/Plantationocene rather than treating what Latour calls 'objective knowledge' as the logic of supplementing its populist operationality. She goes on to foreground the double-pincered potentiality of cinema. Despite popular cinema's production of clichés that, according to Deleuze, function as shields, hindering individuals from genuinely engaging with reality and reducing the world to a cesspool of lethal clichés, Wiame posits that cinema carries the potential to defy ecological catastrophe and provide a subtle means of escaping our state of disbelief. She desires production of minor films in a schizoanalytic framework rather than production of majoritarian populist cinema, for she thinks the former could produce affects bearing the revolutionary potential to disrupt clichés, dullness and normative subjectivation. For her, such a disruption stands as the ground for transforming subjects puppeteered by representationalist populist cinema to *super-jects* who might bear the potential to create a new world order.

In Chapter 9, 'An Infantile-Image in Latin America: A Memory for the World', Amorim and Novaes connect with Wiame's thought processes by engaging with Deleuze's philosophy of Cinema to stress the machinism of minor films. They carry out schizoanalysis of *The Wolf House* (2018), an experimental animated film, to show how it challenges the continuation of fascist discourses, based on stabilizing established truths, by producing a machinic assemblage of minor images. For them, it is the machinism of such films, based on potentially mimicking the immanent workings of the real, that produces the required agency to subvert the post-neoliberal production of post-truth discourses. While post-neoliberal industries produce profit-centred axioms by which they can govern the masses, minor cinemas view truth as possessing the power of the real. In this sense, these authors blur the dichotomy between truth and false. For them, while it is the artist who is often accused as the creator of false images, it is such images that carry the power of the real against the hegemonic regimes of established truths. Further, with their schizoanalysis of *The Wolf House*, they show how it screens the forces of time, precepts and affects that compete with the moral and judgemental discourse. Highlighting the artistic creations, the authors argue that such films teach us to see other perspectives, escape judgement and perceive the powers of life and creation. It highlights the ethical choice of connecting with forces that increase potency and build an assemblic common, rather than diminishing existence and subsuming affects. Both authors generate possibilities of thinking radically in a post-neoliberal world.

Chapter 10, 'Schizoanalysis and Neoliberalism: Philosophy as Revolutionary Praxis for a People-to-Come' by Tony See serves as a concluding section of the collection where he not only reiterates the revolutionary potential of minor becomings that Deleuze and Guattari stress, but also critiques such becomings by adopting a paradoxical approach towards Deleuzean schizoanalysis. First, he foregrounds the critical diagnostic potential of the Deleuzean schizoanalytic framework, positioning it as a perfect machine for mapping neoliberal capitalism's operationality, in particular the manner in which it produces mental illness. He does this by claiming that by indicating the failures of psychoanalytical approach in mapping the relationality between operations of neoliberal capitalism and mental illness, thinkers such as Berardi and Fisher stress the indispensability of

Deleuze's schizoanalytic approach in the post-neoliberal context. While Berardi and Fisher consider mental illness as a product of neoliberalism capitalist restructuration of desire, these thinkers claim that the psychoanalytic process of diverting attention from the workings of neoliberal capitalism by yielding exclusive attention to subject-centred interiority of the unconscious makes it an ally of such workings. Second, See positions Deleuzean schizoanalytical framework as a potential war machine against the neoliberalization of the Freudian psychoanalysis while claiming that the former necessitates the generation of new radical philosophies rather than standing as a paramount weapon of resistance against neoliberal functionality. See claims that it is the schizoanalytic reconstruction of the libidinal economy of the unconscious, based on viewing it as the genetical ground of political economy, that makes it problematic. He argues that if schizoanalysis of the unconscious makes it a germinal ground of political economies, how can it be restructured to serve as a line of flight from our existential entrapment in neoliberal capitalism?

With this one may view post-neoliberalism as a process disjunctively allied with rather than as a process collapsing into or entangled with neoliberalism. What constitutes and articulates the latter's disjunctive alignment with the former are processes such as populist marketization of right-wing ideology, populist reductivization of radical intellectualism, the rise of industries of care, based on promising us a futurity of techno-humanist immortality, and the ethical entrapment of bio-political *homo economicus* in such industries. Such processes make post-neoliberalism an epistome of dead ends. To put it differently, post-neoliberalism opens up a new duration where we only get to sense the impossibility of taking a flight towards new emancipatory openings. Thinkers theorize this impossibility in new ways while showing how a collective betrayal of the post-neoliberal condition may be worked out by exploiting Deleuze and Guattari's philosophy.

Notes

1 By contemplating the post-Covid-19 deviation from market-based policies and discussing threats posed by ideologies such as paleoconservatism, neoreactionary politics, ordonationalism, libertarian paternalism in determining post-neoliberalism, the special issue engages with this (im)possibility. For details, see Davies and Gane (2021).

2 In other words, this is what Davies and McGoey call 'epistemological ambivalence of neoliberalism' (2014, 89). See also Peck, Theodore and Brenner (2009) and Springer (2014).

3 This system's reliance on 'innate individual differences and acquired traits' (Bettache, Chiu and Beattie 2020) overtly legitimizes social hierarchies. For more on its politics of indifference, see Giroux (2008), Kyriakopoulos (2016) and Huzar (2019).

4 In this context, McFalls and Pandolfi elaborate: 'Thus, when the veridiction – or capacity to speak relativistic, empirical, pragmatic truth – of the human sciences replaced the jurisdiction – or capacity to articulate absolute, ideal, dogmatic truth – of the episteme of representation, liberalism dealt a not-quite fatal blow to reason of state' (2017, 223).

5 To understand this newfound statist discourse, see Luiz Carlos Bresser-Pereira (2009) and Robison (2006).

6 See the discussion of what Ray Kiely (2018) calls 'the neoliberal paradox' and refer to Gudavarthy and Vijay (2020) to understand these double articulations under right-wing ideologies.

7 For a detailed historical account, see Engartner (2012).

8 This is characterized by 'its attack not only on all vestiges of the social contract, but its culture of cruelty in which more and more individuals and groups are considered excess, waste, contaminated, and subject to forms of racial and social cleansing' (Giroux 2019, 8).

9 Citing economist Gary Becker, Foucault, in this context interestingly writes: 'We should not think at all that consumption simply consists in being someone in a process of exchange who buys and makes a monetary exchange in order to obtain some products. The man of consumption is not one of the terms of exchange. The man of consumption, insofar as he consumes, is a producer. What does he produce? Well, quite simply, he produces his own satisfaction' (2004, 226).

10 Foucault elaborates: 'homo œconomicus . . . appears precisely as someone manageable, someone who responds systematically to systematic modifications artificially introduced into the environment. Homo œconomicus is someone who is eminently governable. From being the intangible partner of laissez-faire, homo œconomicus now becomes the correlate of a governmentality which will act on the environment and systematically modify its variables' (2004, 270–1).

11 Elaborating on the biopoliticization of humanitarianism, Julian Reid identifies: 'Reducing the human to the biohuman, developing and installing practices with which to regulate human conduct so that it functions to constitute humans as biohumans, and ultimately waging war on the human to institute the biohuman, are all features of how liberal regimes of governance, in particular, have served to promote their own accounts of biohumanity historically' (2010, 393–4).

12 For a detailed discussion on *caring capitalism* or *benevolent biopolitics*, see Vrasti (2011) and Prozorov (2007).

13 See also what Jim McGuigan defines as 'the incorporation, and thereby neutralization of cultural criticism and anti-capitalism into the theory and practice of capitalism itself' (2009, 38) in his *Cool Capitalism* (2009).

Introduction

14 Vandenberghe's elaboration is useful to note here: 'With Deleuze and Guattari, we can conceptualize the colonization of the life-world in terms of a progressive generalization of machinic control beyond the sphere of production and a concomitant interiorization of domination by the subject. When the machinic production of capital captures the subjects to control them from within, "enslavement by the machine" mutates into "subjection to the machine"' (2008, 884).

15 Thus, Bruce Braun succinctly puts it: 'The problem with capitalism is not that its logic is bent on nature's destruction – for all human labour plays that role – but rather that its imperative towards growth means that it will radically foreshorten the earth's "best before" date. To be sure, Altvater imagined the possibility of establishing economic systems that could reduce the rate of entropy, but ultimately these merely postponed the final day of reckoning' (2006, 198).

16 For a detailed speculation on these ambivalences of mobility, see Schleusener (2011, 2017).

17 In this context, Sloterdijk importantly develops his three axioms for a critique of kinetics: 'First, that we are moving in a world that is moving itself; second, that the self-movements of the world include our own self-movements and affect them; and third, that in modernity, the self-movements of the world originate from our self-movements, which are cumulatively added to world-movement' (1989, 30).

18 Paul Patton further develops these ideologies of institutional neoliberalism as follows: 'This "postmodern" or neoliberal university shares many of the characteristic features of social and economic institutions in Deleuze's societies of control. Universities are no longer expected to mould the intellect and character of students. They are viewed rather as service providers as well as centres of knowledge-production and knowledge-transfer that are supposed to be responsive above all to the economic needs of the community. Their role is not only to provide a skilled labour force but also to generate the knowledge bases of new technologies susceptible to commercialisation. In this context, philosophy and other liberal arts face a profound challenge' (2018, 203).

References

Adkins, Brent (2007), *Death and desire in Hegel, Heidegger and Deleuze*, Edinburgh: Edinburgh University Press.

Beckman, Frida, ed. (2018), *Control Culture: Foucault and Deleuze after Discipline*, Edinburgh: Edinburgh University Press.

Bettache, Karim, Chi-yue Chiu and Peter Beattie (2020), 'The Merciless Mind in a Dog-Eat-Dog Society: Neoliberalism and the Indifference to Social Inequality',

Current Opinion in Behavioral Sciences, 34: 217–22. https://doi.org/10.1016/j.cobeha .2020.06.002.

Boltanski, Luc and Eve Chiapello (2007), *The New Spirit of Capitalism*, London: Verso.

Braun, Bruce (2009), 'Towards a New Earth and a New Humanity: Nature, Ontology, Politics', Essay, in Noel Castree and Derek Gregory (eds.), *David Harvey: A Critical Reader*, 191–222, Malden: Blackwell.

Bresser-Pereira, Luiz Carlos (2009), 'Assalto Ao Estado E Ao Mercado, Neoliberalismo e Teoria Econômica', *Estudos Avançados*, 23 (66): 7–23. https://doi.org/10.1590/s0103 -40142009000200002.

Chandler, David and Julian Reid (2016), *The Neoliberal Subject: Resilience, Adaptation and Vulnerability*, London: Rowman & Littlefield International.

Coburn, David (2004), 'Beyond the Income Inequality Hypothesis: Class, Neo-Liberalism, and Health Inequalities', *Social Science & Medicine*, 58 (1): 41–56. https:// doi.org/10.1016/s0277-9536(03)00159-x.

Colebrook, Claire (2020), 'Extinction, Deterritorialisation and End Times: Peak Deleuze', *Deleuze and Guattari Studies*, 14 (3): 327–48. https://doi.org/10.3366/dlgs .2020.0407.

Davies, William and Linsey McGoey (2014), 'Rationalities of Ignorance: On Financial Crisis and the Ambivalence of Neo-Liberal Epistemology', Essay, in by Linsey McGoey (ed.), *An Introduction to the Sociology of Ignorance: Essays on the Limits of Knowing*, 75–96, London: Routledge.

Davies, William and Nicholas Gane (2021), 'Post-Neoliberalism? An Introduction', *Theory, Culture & Society*, 38 (6): 3–28. https://doi.org/10.1177/026327642110 36722.

Deleuze, Gilles (1992), 'Postscript on the Societies of Control', *October*, 59: 3–7. https:// doi.org/http://www.jstor.org/stable/778828.

Deleuze, Gilles and Félix Guattari (1983), *Anti-Oedipus: Capitalism and Schizophrenia*, trans. Robert Hurley, Mark Seem and Helen R. Lane, Minneapolis: University of Minnesota Press.

Deleuze, Gilles and Félix Guattari (1987), *A Thousand Plateaus: Capitalism and Schizophrenia*, trans. Brian Massumi, Minneapolis: University of Minnesota Press.

Dillon, Michael and Julian Reid (2009), *The Liberal Way of War: Killing to Make Life Live*, London: Routledge.

Dufour, Dany-Robert (2008), *The Art of Shrinking Heads: On the New Servitude of the Liberated in the Age of Total Capitalism*, Malden: Polity.

Engartner, Tim (2012), *Silent Conversion to Anti-statism: Historical Origins of the Belief in Market Superiority*. No. 28, ZÖSS Discussion Paper.

Foucault, Michel (2004), *Naissance de la biopolitique: Cours au collège de france (1978– 1979)*, Paris: Seuil/Gallimard.

Giroux, Henry A. (2008), 'Beyond the Biopolitics of Disposability: Rethinking Neoliberalism in the New Gilded Age', *Social Identities*, 14 (5): 587–620. https://doi .org/10.1080/13504630802343432.

Giroux, Henry A. (2019), 'Neoliberal Fascism as the Endpoint of Casino Capitalism', *Fast Capitalism*, 16 (1): 7–24. https://doi.org/10.32855/fcapital.201901.002.

Gudavarthy, Ajay and G. Vijay (2020), 'Social Policy and Political Mobilization in India: Producing Hierarchical Fraternity and Polarized Differences', *Development and Change*, 51 (2): 463–84. https://doi.org/10.1111/dech.12581.

Harvey, David (2007), *A Brief History of Neoliberalism*, Oxford: Oxford University Press.

Huzar, Timothy J. (2019), 'A Politics of Indifference: Reading Cavarero, Rancière and Arendt', *Paragraph*, 42 (2): 205–22. https://doi.org/10.3366/para.2019.0299.

Jagannathan, Srinath and Rajnish Rai (2021), 'The Necropolitics of Neoliberal State Response to the COVID-19 Pandemic in India', *Organization*, 29 (3): 426–48. https://doi.org/10.1177/13505084211020195.

Kiely, Ray (2018), *The Neoliberal Paradox*, Cheltenham: Edward Elgar Publishing.

Kyriakopoulos, Leandros (2016), 'Establishing Indifference: The Affective Logic of Neoliberalism', Essay, in Kostas Athanasiou, Eleni Vasdeki, Elina Kapetanaki, Maria Karagianni, Matina Kapsali, Vaso Makrygianni, Foteini Mamali, Orestis Pangalos, and Charalampos Tsavdaroglou (eds), *UniConflicts in Spaces of Crisis: Critical Approaches in, against and beyond the University*, 88–101, Thessaloniki: Encounters and Conflicts in the City Group.

McFalls, Laurence and Mariella Pandolfi (2017), 'Too-Late Liberalism: From Promised Prosperity to Permanent Austerity', Essay, in Philippe Bonditti, Didier Bigo and Frédéric Gros (eds), *Foucault and the Modern International Silences and Legacies for the Study of World Politics*, 219–35, New York: Palgrave Macmillan.

McGuigan, Jim (2009), *Cool Capitalism*, London and New York: Pluto Press.

Millar, Isabel (2021), *The Psychoanalysis of Artificial Intelligence*, Basingstoke: Palgrave Macmillan.

Newman, Janet (2020), 'Living with Ambivalence: Bureaucracy, Anti-statism and "Progressive" Politics', *New Formations*, 100 (100): 146–60. https://doi.org/10.3898/newf:100-101.10.2020.

Patton, Paul (2018), 'Philosophy and Control', Essay, in Frida Beckman (ed.), *Control Culture: Foucault and Deleuze after Discipline*, 193–210, Edinburgh: Edinburgh University Press.

Peck, Jamie, Nik Theodore and Neil Brenner (2009), 'Neoliberal Urbanism: Models, Moments, Mutations', *SAIS Review of International Affairs*, 29 (1): 49–66. https://doi.org/10.1353/sais.0.0028.

Prozorov, Sergei (2007), 'The Unrequited Love of Power: Biopolitical Investment and the Refusal of Care', *Foucault Studies*, 53–77. https://doi.org/10.22439/fs.v0i4.894.

Reid, Julian (2010), 'The Biopoliticization of Humanitarianism: From Saving Bare Life to Securing the Biohuman in Post-Interventionary Societies', *Journal of Intervention and Statebuilding*, 4 (4): 391–411. https://doi.org/10.1080/17502971003700985.

Robison, Richard, ed. (2006), *The Neo-liberal Revolution: Forging the Market State*, Basingstoke: Palgrave Macmillan.

Schleusener, Simon (2011), 'Sovereignty at Sea: *Moby Dick* and the Politics of Desire', in Winfried Fluck, Katharina Motyl, Donald E. Pease and Christoph Raetzsch (eds), *REAL: Yearbook of Research in English and American Literature*, Volume 27: *States of Emergency – States of Crisis*, 121–42, Tübingen: Narr Verlag.

Schleusener, Simon (2017), 'The Dialectics of Mobility: Capitalism and Apocalypse in Cormac McCarthy's *The Road*', *European Journal of American Studies*, 12 (3): 1–14.

Schleusener, Simon (2020), 'Deleuze and Neoliberalism', *Coils of the Serpent*, (6): 39–54. https://doi.org/https://coilsoftheserpent.org/category/issue-6-2020/.

Shaviro, Steven (2015), *No Speed Limit: Three Essays on Accelerationism*, Minneapolis: University of Minnesota Press.

Sloterdijk, Peter (1989), 'Eurotaoism', Essay, in Tom Darby, Bela Egyed, and Ben Jones (eds), *Nietzsche and the Rhetoric of Nihilism: Essays on Interpretation, Language and Politics*, trans. Michael Eldred, 99–116, Montréal: McGill-Queen's University Press.

Springer, Simon (2014), 'Postneoliberalism?' *Review of Radical Political Economics*, 47 (1): 5–17. https://doi.org/10.1177/0486613413518724.

Vandenberghe, Frédéric (2008), 'Deleuzian Capitalism', *Philosophy & Social Criticism*, 34 (8): 877–903. https://doi.org/10.1177/0191453708095696.

Vrasti, Wanda (2011), '"Caring" Capitalism and the Duplicity of Critique', *Theory & Event*, 14 (4). https://doi.org/10.1353/tae.2011.0041.

Žižek, Slavoj (2004), *Organs without Bodies: On Deleuze and Consequences*, New York: Routledge.

2

The Invisible Hand

Deleuze, Serres and Platform Capitalism

Brent Adkins

Deleuze's work is filled with references to animals and animal behaviour: rats and birds, territorial markings and becomings of all kinds. The figures of the serpent and the mole from 'Postscript on the Societies of Control' loom large in this bestiary as totems of disciplinary and control societies. The importance of these figures is solidified by Deleuze's enigmatic closing line: 'The coils of the serpent are even more complex than the burrows of a molehill.' One can almost imagine that Deleuze is referring to a once well-known fable involving a snake and a mole that has since been lost to the mists of time.

The thrust of Deleuze's opposition between serpent and mole is that the disciplinary society so aptly described by Foucault in *Discipline and Punish* is being replaced by a control society, and that these two societies differ in both means and ends. The disciplinary society *moulds* individuals by enclosing them in institutions, and Foucault articulates the analogical relation among these institutions. A control society, on the other hand, arises as the locus of power shifts away from institutions towards continuous *modulation*. Here, the object of control is no longer the individual but the dividual. Whereas the mole can only produce enclosures that mould, the coils of a serpent are infinitely variable.

Within the context of distinguishing discipline and control societies, Deleuze turns to the relation between technology and capitalism. As technology shifted from simple machines to industrial machines, disciplinary society was best able to channel power through the factory. Capitalism kept pace by rewarding increasing efficiency in production. The processes of production were increasingly harnessed by the factory through Taylorization, and the success of the factory was likewise measured by what it produced. In contrast to this, the introduction of computers inaugurated a tendency away from production to marketing. The goal was no longer to produce as many widgets as possible but to take widgets produced elsewhere in order to capture as much market share as possible. 'This technological evolution must be even more profoundly a mutation of capitalism' (Control, 6). The shift from the logic of institutions to the logic of markets characterizes the shift to neoliberalism. Within the context of Deleuze's work, particularly his work with Guattari, this chapter explores whether the serpent remains an apt totem for post-neoliberalism.

Background

Although Deleuze and Guattari do not use the term 'neoliberalism' to discuss capitalism, they very clearly identify the tendencies within capitalism that thinkers such as Foucault, Harvey and Brown label neoliberal.[1] For these thinkers, what characterizes neoliberalism is a shift away from a distinction between economics and government to the subordination of government to market imperatives. Deleuze and Guattari summarize this nicely when they suggest that, under global capitalism, '[i]n principle, all States are isomorphic; in other words, they are domains of realization of capital as a function of a sole external world market' (ATP, 464). They arrive at this point through an analysis of desire in *Anti-Oedipus* and the state/war machine dynamic in *A Thousand Plateaus*. Although these analyses, which span both volumes of *Capitalism and Schizophrenia*, are not entirely commensurate with one another, the fundamental logic remains consistent.

To put the matter briefly, while *Anti-Oedipus* articulates capital as the decoded, deterritorialized body without organs that subtends capitalism, *A Thousand Plateaus* places capitalism in direct opposition to the state as a war machine. As is well known, the war machine is first introduced in *A Thousand Plateaus* and functions differently from the body without organs of *Anti-Oedipus*. What remains constant, though, is the notion of capitalism dealing directly with decoded and deterritorialized flows. In *Anti-Oedipus*, this takes the form of the rather conventional narrative in which serfs detach themselves from their ancestral lands in order to sell their labour in newly arising industrial centres. This flow of labour is accompanied by a flow of capital that seeks to maximize profit by minimizing labour costs. As Foucault notes, these are the conditions under which the disciplinary society arises and deploys its power in institutional form.

In contrast to this, *A Thousand Plateaus* does not treat capitalism as sui generis but as a possible expression of the war machine. Other examples of war machines include nomadic societies, Kleist's literature, metallurgy and non-woven fabrics such as felt. What's at issue in the invention of the war machine as a concept is its tendency towards the new. The war machine is Deleuze and Guattari's way of talking about what disrupts the status quo, in short, what decodes and deterritorializes. This decoding and deterritorialization occurs in different registers of the status quo, whether it be political, social, literary, material, spatial and so on. Thus, in the vocabulary of *A Thousand Plateaus*, there is no pure war machine, just as there is no pure state. The objects under analysis in *A Thousand Plateaus* are assemblages or arrangements (*agencement*) composed of differing ratios of stasis and change. Capitalism is a war machine because (on balance) it tends towards change rather than stasis.

Despecialization

In order to further expand on Deleuze and Guattari's insights in *Capitalism and Schizophrenia*, I'd like to return to what both *Anti-Oedipus* and *A Thousand Plateaus*' analyses of capitalism have in common: decoding and deterritorialization. My contention is that thinking through these notions in their biological and anthropological senses will not only help us understand capitalism better, but also allow us to distinguish among different kinds of capitalism. The ultimate result of this analysis will be the identification of the current state of capitalism and the ways that it exceeds neoliberalism.

While acknowledging that code and territory have distinct meanings in the work of Deleuze and Guattari, for ease of exposition I want to talk about the tendency of each to stabilize or change under the umbrella of specialization or despecialization. Here I'm drawing on the work of Michel Serres, but I believe it's commensurate with the overall thrust of Deleuze and Guattari's work. To begin with, let's return to a source that Deleuze and Guattari share with Serres, André Leroi-Gourhan. What these thinkers focus on from Leroi-Gourhan's work is the importance of the hand in human biological and cultural evolution. Indeed, he argues that human cultural evolution is a direct result of the biological evolution of the hand.[2] For Deleuze and Guattari, this provides a very clear illustration of deterritorialization. Through the process of evolution, the forepaws of our ancestors literally become detached from the earth – deterritorialized. This has two salutary effects. First, it frees up the hands for grasping. Second, it also frees up the mouth, which is now no longer needed for grasping. This paves the way for the development of language and with it the development of culture and its rapid spread.

For Serres, the hand is also crucial in anthropogenesis or to use his term 'hominization', but he focuses on the way that the hand becomes 'despecialized'.[3] Here Serres is playing with the relation between the words 'species' and 'specialization'. Going all the way back to Aristotle, things are defined by their 'specific difference'. That is, within a given kind or genus, things are distinguished by how they differ within that kind. This, of course, is the kind of thinking that informs Linnean taxonomy. Within this context, biological evolution can be seen as a process of specialization.[4] Darwin's finches, for example, in adapting to varying environments across the Galapagos Islands, developed specialized beaks best suited to their particular conditions. This process of specialization ultimately results in speciation, in which the descendants of a single kind of finch branched into multiple distinct species.

In contrast to this typical story, Serres notes that human evolution is not marked by this kind of specialization. Rather, human evolution is marked paradoxically by despecialization. In the case of the hand, for example, the shift from quadrupedality to bipedality is characterized by the forepaws becoming less specialized. Instead of being adapted for locomotion and balance, and then further specialized according to the animal's environmental niche, say, digging in the case of moles, the human hands are not adapted to any particular task or environment. The phalanges and metacarpals are not curved to facilitate arboreal locomotion. The human hand does not possess claws for better predation. It seems as if every hand in the animal kingdom is better suited to some particular task than the human hand. That is, the human hand is despecialized rather than specialized. It has general use, not special use.

The difficulty with despecialization is that it is not immediately clear how the despecialized animal can adapt to its environment and flourish. For Serres, at this point, the object of evolution shifts from biology to culture. Human adaptation no longer follows the long and tortuous path of trial and error across the genome, which can take hundreds or thousands of generations to accomplish. It instead follows the path of cultural adaptation, or what Serres calls 'exo-Darwinism'. Humans can stay warm in inhospitable environments not because over thousands of years we become increasingly hirsute, but because we invent technologies (fire, weapons, hunting, sewing) that allow us to use the warmth of animals and, perhaps most importantly, bequeath that knowledge to our descendants. Here we see the myth of Epimetheus and Prometheus recapitulated. Epimetheus is tasked with 'specializing' all of the animals and, after dispensing flight to birds and claws to lions, discovers that he's forgotten to reserve any gifts for humanity. At this point, Prometheus steps in. Fearing that humanity will be cast into the world naked and defenceless, he steals fire from Zeus and thus sets humanity on the course of cultural specialization rather than biological specialization.[5]

On Serres's reading, then, biological despecialization necessitates cultural and technological specialization. Humans are obligate tool users, and historically we have invented specialized tools. Furthermore, human cultural and technological diversity is the direct result of cultural and technological evolution. Here, cultural diversity is analogous to biological diversity. However, whereas the mechanisms that produce biological diversity create ultimately incommensurate species, cultural diversity can further diversify by interacting with other cultures.

Technological despecialization

The majority of human history is thus characterized by a biologically despecialized body that specializes and diversifies culturally. The fact of biological despecialization, however, raises the possibility of technological despecialization. That is, are there technologies that are despecialized rather than specialized? Ultimately, I want to show that capitalism itself can be characterized in terms of degrees of despecialization and that post-neoliberal capitalism marks the greatest degree of despecialization achieved so far.

Hominization is dotted with technological despecializations that proved to be inflection points. For example, the despecialization of the hand led to the invention of the hand axe. Interestingly, as Eliade notes, a cutting tool is not directly analogous to claws or teeth; the blade neither punctures nor tears, it cuts.[6] We might think of this as a despecialization of traits related to hunting, preparation and consumption. Along the same evolutionary path, the use of fire to cook food increased caloric intake, reduced the caloric cost of digestion and further despecialized the jaws, teeth and facial muscles of palaeolithic hominids. In short, biological and technological despecialization can be mutually reinforcing.

In most cases, though, technological despecialization is followed by cultural specialization. That is, in the language of Deleuze and Guattari, despecialized technologies are recoded and reterritorialized on a given socius. We can imagine, for example, that early hominid communities in different parts of the world had rules about how tools were made and who could make them (code), as well as naming the proper location and material for their production (territory). Indeed, this is the typical rhythm of human history, oscillating between despecialization and specialization.

In contrast to this typical rhythm, Deleuze and Guattari argue that capitalism works differently in two ways. First, capitalism works directly on decoded and deterritorialized flows. Second, it does not work on these flows by recoding and reterritorializing them but by axiomatizing them. The fundamental referent for Deleuze and Guattari's use of 'axiom' is the work of the Bourbaki group in mathematics and not Euclid's use in the *Principles of Geometry*. In *Anti-Oedipus*, for example, they write, 'Bourbaki says as much concerning scientific axiomatics: they do not form a Taylor system, nor a mechanical game of isolated formulas, but rather imply "intuitions" that are linked to resonances and conjunctions of structures, and that are merely aided by the "powerful levers" of technique' (AO, 251). Guattari in the *Anti-Oedipus Papers* connects this notion of axiom directly to capitalism, 'The idea of a scientific task that no longer passes through codes but rather through an axiomatic first took place in mathematics toward the end of the nineteenth century. . . . One finds this well formed only in the capitalism of the nineteenth century' (22 February 1972). For the Bourbaki group, axioms establish sets. For Deleuze and Guattari, axioms are emblematic of the kind of consistency that can be created without codes or territories.

Precisely because capitalism endlessly invents axioms rather than codes, it is inherently despecializing. For it is the code that specializes. In the case of biological specialization, the genetic code specializes. In the case of cultural specialization, the code is ritual, gestural and linguistic. In *Anti-Oedipus*, this specialization is articulated in terms of a strict division between alliance and filiation. This division codes kinship relations and determines not only who may marry but those who determine who may marry. There can be no equivalence or direct exchange between alliance and filiation. Neither is reducible to the other, and their relation is always mediated by coding. The way that these relations are coded distinguishes one socius from another. In contrast to this, capitalism makes everything directly exchangeable. Money is the universal solvent that dissolves all the codes and gives everything a direct equivalent. This is the work of axiomatization. My contention, however, is that axiomatization like despecialization is not binary but comes in degrees. Thus, while capitalism functions differently from other social formations, it does not axiomatize everything all at once. Axiomatization/despecialization is a tendency towards which capitalism tends. Different kinds of capitalism will evince different degrees of despecialization.

The hand of capital

If we look at this history of capitalism, we can see this increasing despecialization at work. Industrial capitalism, for example, is characterized by decoding and deterritorializing flows of energy and labour, but also by the specialization of the means of production. In order to produce at a scale sufficient to extract surplus value, new machines were invented to more efficiently channel energy and labour. The machines for weaving textiles were of necessity distinct from the machines for producing steel rails for trains. Furthermore, while there was a tendency to simplify the tasks of workers in a factory, this same specialization distinguished workers in each industry. At the same time, however, (and this returns us to Deleuze's 'Postscript') the geometry of the factory becomes despecialized. That is, even if the machines and procedures differ from industry to industry, the factory itself is homogenized. As Foucault shows, factory geometry maximizes visibility to ensure the greatest possible utility. Furthermore, this geometry is indicative of all institutions across a disciplinary society. This is why factories, hospitals, prisons and schools bear a striking resemblance to one another.[7]

In its initial stages, industrial capitalism was free from state interference, especially as long as the industry was focused on domestic markets. The state, however, became increasingly involved when industries became entangled with other countries through trade, acquisition of raw materials or in seeking to lower labour costs. Indeed, the solitary use of 'the invisible hand' in Adam Smith's *Wealth of Nations* concerns this very point. In responding to the objection that laissez-faire capitalism will lead to the flight of capital as each industry seeks to lower its operating costs in order to maximize profits, Smith writes,

> By preferring the support of domestic to that of foreign industry, he intends only his own security; and by directing that industry in such a manner as its produce may be of the greatest value, he intends only his own gain, and he is in this, as in many other cases, led by an invisible hand to promote an end which was no part of his intention. (4.2.9)

For Smith, there is no danger that domestic industry will seek greener pastures. One's own provincialism will naturally and unconsciously keep business at home without any need to concern oneself with the greater good.

Smith's minor (and perhaps overly optimistic) point, of course, gets expanded to become a general principle of human behaviour and thus economics itself, namely that value is increased when people are allowed to pursue their self-interest. The corollary here is that when people take the common good as their focus rather than self-interest, value is decreased. The neoliberal appropriation of Smith's observation is that markets should be free from any kind of controls, and that to impose controls in relation to prices or wages hinders the market's ability to maximize the production of value.

It is precisely at this point that conceiving of markets as information processors arises. Friedrich von Hayek famously argues in his 1946 paper 'The Use of Knowledge in Society',

> We must look at the price system as such a mechanism for communicating *information* if we want to understand its *real* function – a function which, of course, it fulfills less perfectly as prices grow more rigid. (Even when quoted prices have become quite rigid, however, the forces which would operate through changes in price still operate to a considerable extent through changes in the other terms of the contract.) The most significant *fact* about this system is the economy of knowledge with which it operates, or how little the individual participants need to know in order to be able to take the right action. In abbreviated form, by a kind of symbol, only the most essential information is passed on and passed on only to those concerned. It is *more than a metaphor* to describe the price system as a kind of machinery for registering change, or a system of telecommunications which enables individual producers to watch merely the movement of a few pointers, as an engineer might watch the hands of a few dials, in order to adjust their activities to changes of which they may never know more than is reflected in the price movement. (526–7, Emphasis added)

Here, the interests of the state in keeping domestic industry domestic are entirely absent. The hand of providence in Smith becomes a machine that relays the minimal sufficient information needed in order to adjust one's behaviour accordingly. This behaviour then becomes new information that's processed by the 'machinery for registering change' and so on.

While there's much to be said about Hayek's prescience here in linking markets and information, for our purposes here I want to focus on this shift away from industrial production to markets as a kind of despecialization. Smith's image of the hand remains profoundly territorialized. He does not imagine a global marketplace. Rather, he imagines each country with its own domestic industries, and the best way to prevent those domestic industries from going abroad. The tempting argument is to simply make moving domestic industries abroad illegal. This is a clear instance of seeking the common good rather than individual interest. Smith proposes instead that we avoid appeals to the common good and let individual (but unconscious) patriotism accomplish the same end. The invisible hand thus preserves the national interest, not the interest of a global market.

In contrast to this, Hayek proposes a machine that processes information, a machine that works best when it is not subject to (price) controls.[8] Here, it might seem that Smith and Hayek are proposing the same thing; no controls are better than some controls. But, Hayek is arguing for the deterritorialization of markets. The goal is not to preserve national industries but to create a global 'telecommunications' machine that processes pricing information. The function of markets, then, in Hayek's view is hindered if pricing controls are put in place, but at the same time, the free flow of information does not reinforce national industries. Thus, far from individual action supporting domestic industry, it encourages the rapid globalization of industries.

Smith was not quite at the point where he could imagine global industry or multinational corporations. From his perspective, economies were properties of nation-states and the 'invisible hand' would keep them that way. Hayek is writing in the aftermath of global conflict and in the midst of a new world order establishing itself. On his view, the economy is no longer the property of individual states, and thus cannot be regulated on that level. Additionally, attempts to control prices on an international scale are bound to be inefficient and cause disruptions in the flow of information. The only solution from Hayek's perspective is to deterritorialize and decode markets so that they can function according to axioms. That is, rather than depending on a national spirit or traditional values to code and territorialize information, information is axiomatized and reaxiomatized every time a decision is made, which then ramifies throughout the system. Here, Hayek is imagining a despecialized market that is infinitely variable and performs its function precisely by not having a predefined telos.

Neoliberalism and beyond

Hayek's vision became the effective economic policy of the world when Reagan and Thatcher came to power in the United States and the United Kingdom. Cultural hegemony replaced political hegemony. Or, better, cultural hegemony became political hegemony as the spread of Western, particularly American, culture began to dominate. Interestingly, the culture was a commodified, corporate culture, not analogous to past dispersions of culture such as the wheel or agriculture. That is, it is no longer the state seeking to expand its influence

30 *Deleuze, Guattari and the Schizoanalysis of Post-Neoliberalism*

through diplomacy; it is a corporation trying to increase shareholder value by opening new markets for its products.

The opening of new markets or the exploitation of new resources typically follows crisis. Following the 2008 economic crisis, companies increasingly turned to data as an underutilized resource. This precipitated a shift to what Nick Srnicek calls 'platform capitalism':

> What are platforms? At the most general level, platforms are digital infrastructures that enable two or more groups to interact. They therefore position themselves as intermediaries that bring together different users: customers, advertisers, service providers, producers, suppliers, and even physical objects. More often than not, these platforms also come with a series of tools that enable their users to build their own products, services, and marketplaces. (30)[9]

Srnicek goes on to argue that there are five basic types of platform: advertising, cloud, product, industrial and lean. For my purposes here, the distinctions among these platforms are less important than how they function. One of the key characteristics of platforms is their reliance on 'network effects'. Srnicek writes,

> the more numerous the users who use a platform, the more valuable that platform becomes for everyone else. Facebook, for example, has become the default social networking platform simply by virtue of the sheer number of people on it. If you want to join a platform for socialising, you join the platform where most of your friends and family already are. Likewise, the more numerous the users who search on Google, the better their search algorithms become, and the more useful Google becomes to users. But this generates a cycle whereby more users beget more users, which leads to platforms having a natural tendency towards monopolisation. It also lends platforms a dynamic of ever-increasing access to more activities, and therefore to more data. Moreover, the ability to rapidly scale many platform businesses by relying on pre-existing infrastructure and cheap marginal costs means that there are few natural limits to growth. One reason for Uber's rapid growth, for instance, is that it does not need to build new factories – it just needs to rent more servers. Combined with network effects, this means that platforms can grow very big very quickly. (30–1)

Two important shifts take place here that we'll characterize in terms of despecialization. First, platform capitalism collapses the distinction between product and production. Under earlier forms of capitalism, the process of production was distinct from the product. Companies needed to buy the equipment and labour to produce something for the market. This something was then taken by a distinct marketing and sales arm and presented to the public as a consumable in a way that completely obscured the production process. With platform capitalism, there's no product per se. Rather, what's being sold is connectivity or interaction. These connections then produce more connections in what becomes a self-refining process that in turn allows more connections to be made. The platform becomes the capitalist dream whereby capital directly produces more capital without the mediation of a commodity. Marx's Money–Commodity–Money cycle simply becomes a Money–Money cycle as the platform becomes an ouroboros. The platform becomes a despecialized hand that forgoes the specialization of the commodity and simply produces money by facilitating the exchange of money.

The second shift is a shift from a geometric space to a topological space. As Serres notes in his discussion of time, the traditional view of time is metric and linear. The pastness of events is precisely measurable and events themselves constitute a static ordinal series. Thus, not only are older events 'farther away' than more recent ones, this order can never change. An event that happened twenty years ago will always be seven years earlier than an event that happened thirteen years ago. In contrast to this geometric view of time, Serres proposes that time is better thought of as a crumpled handkerchief. While it is possible to smooth out the handkerchief and establish clear distances among points on it, when we fold it up, relations among these points become continuously variable. In Serres's view, this image of time much more closely fits with our experience. I may wear events from twenty years ago like armour, while events of two weeks ago are kept in the fading distance. Reading a book about Ancient Rome might collapse two millennia of 'distance' and keep current news at bay. For Serres, then, time is topological, turbulent and in continuous variation.[10]

I would like to suggest that something similar is going on with platform capitalism. Not only are platforms despecialized in relation to commodities, they are despecialized in relation to time and space. In Deleuze and Guattari's language, platforms are the shift away from striated space to smooth space. In contrasting textiles and felt as exemplars of striated and smooth space, they write concerning felt,

> An aggregate of intrication of this kind is in no way homogeneous: it is nevertheless smooth and contrasts point by point with the space of fabric (it is in principle infinite, open, and unlimited in every direction; it has neither top nor bottom nor center; it does not assign fixed and mobile elements but rather distributes a continuous variation). (475–6)

32   *Deleuze, Guattari and the Schizoanalysis of Post-Neoliberalism*

In contrast with textiles that utilize a matrix of warp and weft that striates universally, felt effectuates a topological space of continuous variation composed of aleatory and turbulent local connections. In *Hominescence*, Serres is explicitly arguing that the tool-making that characterized most of human cultural development has shifted away from local teleology and become despecialized, universal. 'This is why I readily say that unlike any other tool, always by definition specialized, that is to say, finalized, a computer can be defined as a universal tool, an expression that, itself, can be taken to be an oxymoron. It allows one, surely, to do anything' (50). I am arguing here that platform capitalism, facilitated by computing power and telecommunications, is precisely the same kind of despecialized tool as the computer. It's not 'for' anything and, as a result does everything.

Conclusion

We began this chapter with a brief look at Deleuze's essay 'Postscript on the Societies of Control'. What we discovered there was a clear dividing line between the industrial capitalism of the disciplinary society and the kind of capitalism that arises in a control society. The key characteristic of the shift was the tendency towards modulation. The question explored by this essay was whether this modulation only characterizes neoliberalism, or if it might also clarify the nature of post-neoliberalism. That is, are the coils of a serpent sufficiently complex to account for post-neoliberalism? The answer is yes, at least tentatively. What the coils of the serpent describe are continuous variability, or a smooth space, or a topological space. Within this context, we can see that the tendency towards control and markets as information processors is accelerated by technologies of data collection and analysis to produce platform capitalism. These newer technologies are 'despecialized' in Serres's sense of the term, and, in turn, produce a new despecialized technology.

I do not, however, see platform capitalism as an end point or goal of capitalism. Despecialized technologies will continue to produce additional despecialized technologies now that the economy has become increasingly unmoored from commodities. We can see additional evidence of this in recent inventions such as cryptocurrency or NFTs. Despecialized technologies will continue to cannibalize their own digital productions, such that commodities are increasingly marginalized. I do not think this economic tendency (or any smooth space for that matter) can save us. Indeed, I think this tendency can only magnify the

The Invisible Hand

exploitative nature of capitalism as these tools become universal and seek to convert natural resources into digital resources. The perfect illustration of this tendency can be found in the recent trend in the United States of cryptocurrency companies buying decommissioned power plants and bringing them back online with the sole purpose of providing uninterrupted power for their cryptocurrency mining. All mediation is erased. Nature is directly axiomatized. Space is smoothed. Energy itself is despecialized. The serpent consumes its own tail.

> One day a mole came out of its burrow and found a snake suffering in the cold. In compassion the mole invited the snake into its burrow. The snake was so long that its coils filled every inch of the burrow, and there was no longer room for the mole. So, the mole began to dig. Every new passage was immediately filled by the snake. The more it dug, the more the snake filled the burrow. Eventually the mole became lost in its own burrow. It could only find the middle of the snake, never its head or tail. The snake, for its part, found that the passages of the burrow were so tight that it could no longer move.

Notes

1 Foucault (2008), Harvey (2005) and Brown (2015).
2 Leroi-Gourhan (2018).
3 Though it is a recurring theme in Serres, see Serres (2019).
4 Simondon's work on individuation is no doubt crucial for both Serres and Deleuze. See Simondon (1964).
5 See Stiegler (1998).
6 Eliade (1981).
7 Foucault (1995).
8 Hayek is writing in the wake of the price-control debate that followed World War II. See Mirowski and Nik-Khah (2017).
9 Srnicek (2017).
10 Serres (1995).

References

Brown, Wendy (2015), *Undoing the Demos: Neoliberalism's Stealth Revolution*, New York: Zone Books.
Deleuze, Gilles (1992), 'Postscript on the Societies of Control', *October*, 59 (Winter): 3–7.

Deleuze, Gilles and Félix Guattari (1983), *Anti-Oedipus*, trans. Robert Hurley, Mark Seem and Helen R. Lane, Minneapolis: University of Minnesota Press.

Deleuze, Gilles and Félix Guattari (1987), *A Thousand Plateaus*, trans. Brian Massumi, Minneapolis: University of Minnesota Press.

Eliade, Mircea (1981), *History of Religious Ideas, vol. 1: From the Stone Age to the Eleusinian Mysteries*, trans. Willard Trask, Chicago: University of Chicago Press.

Foucault, Michel (1995), *Discipline & Punish: The Birth of the Prison*, trans. Alan Sheridan, New York: Vintage Books.

Foucault, Michel (2008), *The Birth of Biopolitics: Lectures at the Collège de France, 1978–1979*, trans. Graham Burchell, New York: Picador.

Guattari, Félix (2006), *The Anti-Oedipus Papers*, ed. Stéphane Nadaud, trans. Kélina Gotman, Cambridge: Semiotext(e).

Harvey, David (2005), *A Brief History of Neoliberalism*, New York: Oxford University Press.

Hayek, F. A. (1945), 'The Use of Knowledge in Society', *American Economic Review*, 35 (4): 519–30.

Leroi-Gourhan, André (2018), *Gesture and Speech*, trans. Anna Bostock Berger, Cambridge, MA: MIT Press.

Mirowski, Philip and Edward Nik-Khah (2017), *The Knowledge We Have Lost in Information: The History of Information in Modern Economics*, New York: Oxford University Press.

Serres, Michel (1995), *Conversations on Science, Culture, and Time: Michel Serres with Bruno Latour*, trans. Roxanne Lapidus, Ann Arbor: University of Michigan Press.

Serres, Michel (2019), *Hominescence*, trans. Randoph Burks, New York: Bloomsbury.

Simondon, Gilbert (1964), *L'individu et sa genèse physico-biologique (l'individuation à la lumière des notions de forme et d'information)*, Paris: Presses universitaires de France.

Smith, Adam (2000), *The Wealth of Nations*, Books IV–V, New York: Penguin.

Srnicek, Nick (2017), *Platform Capitalism*, Cambridge: Polity Press.

Stiegler, Bernard (1998), *Technics and Time 1: The Fault of Epimetheus*, trans. Richard Beardsworth and George Collins, Palo Alto: Stanford University Press.

3

From Deleuze and Guattari's Interregnum to Our Own, or How to Navigate the Coming Post-Neoliberal Age

Samuel Weeks and Evan Lyons

If Deleuze and Guattari were alive today, what would they make of the signs of the incipient post-neoliberal age all around us? A decidedly mixed balance sheet, we can imagine. On the one hand, the pair would surely have lauded the recent moment of 'pandemic Keynesianism' as a long-overdue departure from generalized austerity and monetarism – a programme which, in their native France, dated from the mid-1980s. Of far greater interest to them would likely have been the post-neoliberal 'pink tide' experiments initiated throughout Latin America from the 2000s – in countries from Venezuela and Ecuador, to Bolivia and Argentina, and more recently, Mexico and Chile.

Yet, on the other hand, Deleuze and Guattari would undoubtedly find bleak most of the developments of our emerging post-neoliberal age. Multinational corporations, which Deleuze famously likened to a terrifying gas (1992, 4), have only become more concentrated and monopolistic, penetrating further into still-more realms of human existence, to say nothing of artificial intelligence, outer space or the genome of biological life. In politics, while neoliberalism's fall has given rise to a handful of promising leftist movements in the Global North and South – along the lines of those long supported by Guattari – the resulting political space has largely been occupied by openly illiberal, ultra-nationalist and xenophobic politicians. Add into this volatile mix a planetary climate crisis, rampant inequality and the Covid-19 pandemic – meaning that any shift to a post-neoliberal age will, in all likelihood, bring with it even more confusion and precariousness.

Before addressing *post*-neoliberalism, however, we will first reflect briefly on the troubling rise of neoliberalism as an intellectual and politico-economic project – which, no doubt to their dismay, corresponded to the second half of

Deleuze and Guattari's political and scholarly lives.[1] As they witnessed throughout the 1980s and early 1990s in countries such as France and the United States, the neoliberal project consisted of two connected initiatives. The first of these implied the use of state power to expand the mechanisms and competitive forces of the market into society more broadly. In France, after the end of his Common Programme in 1983, which saw allied ministers from the French Communist Party leave the government, then-president François Mitterrand enacted a number of macroeconomic 'reforms' along these neoliberal lines – including a tighter monetary policy to combat inflation, tax cuts on higher incomes and capital gains, the privatization of public enterprises and reductions to welfare and other forms of social spending.

A second general tendency – noted by Foucault as early as 1979 – is that, in addition to being a set of policy prescriptions, neoliberalism also entails a 'a mode of subjectivity, operating via networks of capillary power inside and outside the state, taking particular root in those technocratic para-state institutions of central banks, quangos, outsourcers, and multilateral agencies' (Davies and Gane 2021, 5). In 'Postscript on the Societies of Control', Deleuze notes the emergence of a similar nexus of technocratic forms that span both corporations and schools: 'just as the corporation replaces the factory, *perpetual training* tends to replace the *school*, and continuous control to replace the examination. Which is the surest way of delivering the school over to the corporation' (1992, 5; italics in the original).[2] Taken together, and in light of their vast scope and deep roots, the above two dimensions – as a political economy and as a generalized approach to life – mean that neoliberalism is unlikely to be displaced in the short term via a mere shift in policy consensus.

The intellectual force behind neoliberalism was undoubtedly the Austro-British economist Friedrich Hayek (1899–1992), born a generation before Deleuze and Guattari. With help from colleagues at his Mont Pèlerin Society, Hayek sought to re-invent post-World War II liberalism not via Smithian laissez-faire neoclassical economics but rather via government interventions in the service of markets – which would subsequently come to serve as the primary regulation mechanism for states, societies and persons. In *Individualism and Economic Order*, Hayek asserts that 'competition can be made more effective and more beneficent by certain activities of government than it would be without them' (1948, 110). From a vastly different ideological vantage point, Deleuze and Guattari nonetheless noted a similar process at work:

> There is a tendency within capitalism continually to add more axioms. . . . Keynesian economics and the New Deal were axiom laboratories. Examples of the creation of new axioms after the Second World War: the Marshall Plan,

forms of assistance and lending, transformations in the monetary system. . . . What makes the axiomatic[3] vary, in relation to the States, is the distinction and relation between the foreign and domestic markets. There is a multiplication of axioms most notably when an integrated domestic market is being organized to meet the requirements of the foreign market. (1987, 462)

Thus, to Hayek and his fellow neoliberals – as noted by Deleuze and Guattari – a main role of states is to extend market dynamics into societal realms not previously organized by capitalist principles. Herein lies, according to Martin, a paradox at the heart of neoliberalism: that the state must 'clear the ground for the growth of the market by aggressively removing rival apparatuses from the field of economic organisation, including itself' (2018, 206).

Even though Hayek and his colleagues were most interested in the economic dynamics of the post-World War II Global North, it was not long before neoliberal policies were applied to political economies in the previously colonized world. To quote Deleuze and Guattari: 'central capitalism needs the periphery constituted by the Third World, where it locates a large part of its most modern industries; it does not just invest capital in these industries, but is also furnished with capital by them' (1987, 465). In the aftermath of the early 1980s petrodollar-fuelled debt crises in Mexico, Brazil, Argentina and elsewhere, the so-called Washington Consensus institutions – the World Bank, International Monetary Fund and US Treasury – implemented a brutal series of structural adjustment programmes in country after country. Analogous to Mitterrand abandoning his Common Programme in 1983, these neoliberal 'reforms' obliged recipient governments to eliminate price controls, reduce public expenditures, privatize state-owned enterprises, expand market forces and open domestic economies to foreign investment and competition. Perhaps not unsurprisingly, however, the legacy of neoliberal intervention in Latin America was, for the most part, one of disappointment; from the 1980 to 1998, the halcyon days of neoliberalism in the region, GDP growth amounted to a paltry 6 per cent, as opposed to an impressive 75 per cent in the pre-neoliberal era of 1960–80 (Macdonald and Ruckert 2009, 4).

A post-neoliberal turn?

Deleuze and Guattari both died early (and tragically) in the first part of the 1990s, a few years before a 'pink tide' of South American countries – first Venezuela, then Argentina and Brazil and later Bolivia and Ecuador – began to mark their breaks from the previous two decades of neoliberal policymaking.

Indeed, by the turn of the century, neoliberalism's obvious failure to develop the region's political economies had opened a political space for governments to pursue governance alternatives. In the language of Deleuze and Guattari's *A Thousand Plateaus* (1980), these progressive experiments are akin to 'war machines' – that is, 'revolutionary devices [operating] at the periphery *en plein air* with whatever resources happen to be at hand, rather than adhering to the supposed [neoliberal] "laws" or "science" formulated by the sedentary states and their apparatuses of capture at the core of the world system' (Weeks 2019a, 99).

Throughout the 2000s, these post-neoliberal 'war machines' appeared with frequency across large parts of Latin America. In Venezuela, the government of Hugo Chávez massively expanded the country's public-health infrastructure, with the help of oil receipts and Cuban doctors; the Workers' Party government of Luiz Inácio Lula da Silva implemented the *Bolsa Família*, a popular cash-transfer programme to millions of working-class and -poor families in Brazil; in Argentina, in the wake of a 2001 sovereign-debt crisis, movements of militant 'picketers' (*piqueteros*) wrested control of factories from their owners and continued production under the principles of 'worker self-management'. In implementing these and other 'war machines', 'pink tide' politicians and activists throughout Latin America largely succeeded in challenging the ideological and policy hegemony previously enjoyed by the neoliberal Washington Consensus institutions.

Scholars such as Canessa (2014) and Martin (2018) debate, however, the extent of these 'turns' away from neoliberalism. Riofrancos (2020) details the vital importance of high global commodity prices during the mid-2000s in underpinning the mostly modest post-neoliberal experiments of the 'pink tide' governments. In Bolivia, for example, the 2009 passage of a constitution championed as both anti-colonial and post-neoliberal coincided with ecologically destructive infrastructure projects and resource extraction, often carried out in collaboration with foreign multinationals. As such, then-president Evo Morales's government would ride roughshod over much of the opposition to these projects, which often originated from the very same indigenous peoples who had just been recognized for the first time in the country's constitution.

In the Global North, the 2008–9 financial crisis originating in the sub-prime US housing market (Tooze 2018), and the subsequent sovereign debt crises on the Eurozone periphery (Weeks 2019b), seemed to put the fate of neoliberalism very much in doubt. Many large banks and insurers in the United States and Western Europe that had become 'too big to fail' required multibillion-dollar taxpayer-funded bailouts, while individual citizens in these countries faced generalized austerity or, worse, unemployment and evictions. Due to the drop in aggregate demand, political economies throughout the Global North experienced painful multiyear recessions, even depressions – and unemployment rates ballooned as high as 25 per cent in countries such as Spain and Greece. Were he alive during 2008–9 global financial crisis, Deleuze might say, 'the [neoliberal] administrations in charge never cease announcing supposedly necessary reforms. . . . But everyone knows that [the Washington Consensus] institutions are finished, whatever the length of their expiration periods. It's only a matter of administering their last rites and of keeping people employed until the installation of the new forces knocking at the door' (1992, 4).

And yet, reports of neoliberalism's death (e.g. Posner 2009; Stiglitz 2016) have proved premature. Martin describes this tension succinctly: 'despite the near collapse [in 2008] of an economic system based on neoliberal assumptions that could only be saved by the abandonment of those very assumptions, once the crisis had passed we seemed to move straight back into the framework that had brought us to the brink of disaster' (2018, 205). While such statements make it seem as if we live in a world in which breaking free of neoliberal constraint has become nigh impossible – that the only remedy for neoliberalism's various afflictions is seemingly more neoliberalism – any objective analysis would nonetheless point to the ways in which political economies throughout the world are moving away from neoliberalism. To quote Deleuze, we are currently living through another 'mutation of capitalism' (1992, 6), similar to the 1980s displacement of Keynesianism by neoliberalism that he so presciently analyses in 'Postscript on the Societies of Control' (1990).

While many of its critics (Harvey, Klein, Piketty, Brown and undoubtedly also Deleuze and Guattari) wish that the drift from neoliberalism would proceed in a leftward direction, this is – for the most part – not the case. Even a cursory look at global politics – from Brazil, to India and Russia and even the United States – reveals that the most powerful 'war machines' against neoliberalism are those originating on the right or far-right. A common feature to the extant right-wing alternatives to neoliberalism is their rejection of Hayek's faith in the deterritorializing nature of capitalist competition and his disinterest vis-à-vis the outcomes of this process. Instead, rightist critics of neoliberalism are committed 'to protecting and nurturing the "right" producers, lifestyles and demographics. . . . The state is [thus] repurposed . . . to one that acts with explicit cultural, ethnic and economic biases' (Davies and Gane 2021, 19). To accomplish this goal, strongmen such as Trump, Putin, Modi, Erdoğan and Bolsonaro[4] seek to recentralize the sovereign powers that they claim have been 'stolen' by the liberals

40   *Deleuze, Guattari and the Schizoanalysis of Post-Neoliberalism*

and 'globalists' who run the world's technocratic, multilateral and financial institutions. Given that these right-wing experiments in post-neoliberalism are very much ongoing, it remains to be seen whether such efforts amount to a wholesale break from neoliberalism or simply represent another dystopian mutation in its logic and modes of practice.

From Deleuze and Guattari's interregnum to our own

The transmogrification of neoliberalism going on around us thus begs the question: How would Deleuze and Guattari navigate our current post-neoliberal interregnum? To undertake such a thought experiment, we look for clues in how the pair approached the main interregnum of their time: one that took them from May '68; to the oil embargo, steel crisis and end of the *Trente Glorieuses*; to the election of Mitterrand; and finally to the Maastricht Treaty and the arrival of neoliberalism as a *pensée unique*. As such, this chapter details five episodes from Deleuze and Guattari's political thinking and engagement from the above period that can serve as guideposts for our own uncertain trek into a post-neoliberal age.

The first event we discuss is Deleuze's mid-1970s calls for solidarity with Palestinians, which is a powerful reminder of the continued importance of aiding the struggles of the world's many marginalized peoples. Second, the pair's opposition to the 1977 extradition of lawyer Klaus Croissant – deemed a 'terrorist' by the French authorities for his legal representation of West German Red Army Faction militants – is a call to defend those who suffer at the hands of predatory states. Third, Deleuze's unflinching late-1970s combat against the so-called *nouveaux philosophes* ('New Philosophers') is an exemplar of how to denounce the deluge of 'fake news', faulty logic and pseudo-intellectualism in our midst. Fourth, in *A Thousand Plateaus* (1980), Deleuze and Guattari hint at some new and promising forms of political economy that could potentially find applications in the wake of neoliberalism's slow death. Fifth, already in the essay 'Postscript on the Societies of Control' (1990), Deleuze foretells the dominance that Big Tech has come to attain and, in doing so, makes calls *avant la lettre* for much-needed programmes of technological democratization and anti-surveillance. Indeed, as we ask, can these examples from Deleuze and Guattari's 'late' thinking and engagement provide a potential way through what is likely to be the morass of post-neoliberalism?

Our intention for this chapter, therefore, is linear and sequential – admittedly not very Deleuzo-Guattarian – and is inspired by Jameson's well-known call to counter the 'weakening of historicity' (1984, 58) in political and scientific realms. As such, we are convinced that the thought experiment herein amounts to an important assessment of the continued relevance of Deleuzo-Guattarian thought in a context of emerging post-neoliberalism. It does not pretend to be a totally comprehensive account of Deleuze and Guattari's thinking and political engagement from '68 until their deaths in the 1990s. In a similar fashion, the pair's oeuvre, it should be stressed, does not represent 'a unified corpus of abstract ontological ideas and principles' (Schleusener 2020, 40); it does offer, we believe, some methodological and conceptual guideposts for responding to developments and challenges arising in this post-neoliberal world – what, in *What Is Philosophy?*, they might refer to as 'the now of our becoming' (Deleuze and Guattari 1994, 112).

Return to the Third World

The first guidepost offered to us by Deleuze for the post-neoliberal age comes from his long-held calls for solidarity with the Palestinian people and denunciation of the Israeli occupation, which he saw as a wholesale settler-colonial project predicated on 'geographical evacuation' (Deleuze 1983). Medien (2019) situates Deleuze's criticism of Israeli settler-colonialism within an emerging neoliberal logic premised on the systemic dispossession, exploitation and erasure of indigenous peoples. She argues that Deleuze's critique offers a re-animation of Palestinians' identity and affirmation of their existence via resistance to Israeli occupation, a 'line of flight' that enables them to advance towards a 'multiplicity of what is possible' (Deleuze and Sanbar 2006, 200).

Given that Deleuze's repeated call for solidarity with Palestinians affirmed their existence at the same time that it denounced Israel's settler-colonial state apparatus, one can apply the same logic to the post-neoliberal processes that continue to reterritorialize entire territories, peoples and cultures. In such a context, Deleuze and Guattari would identify the attendant axioms of post-neoliberalism not as simple theoretical propositions, but as operative statements, born from 'gropings in the dark, experimentation, [and] modes of intuition' that come about in novel conjunctures (Deleuze and Guattari 1987, 461). In concert with the arrival of post-neoliberal axioms comes the creation of new war machines, which operate within a smooth topography outside the control of states (Deleuze and Guattari 1987, 466–7). Axiomatics such as post-neoliberalism, they would contend, contain the seeds of their own destruction and thus allow for the '[recreation of] unexpected possibilities for counterattack [and] unforeseen initiatives determining revolutionary, popular, minority, [and] mutant machines' (Deleuze and Guattari 1987, 422).

To get a sense of some of the promising war machines in our midst, we again look to South America; since the late 1990s, many countries in this region have witnessed massive protests in reaction to the Washington Consensus policies adopted by their governments. In 2019, over a million Chileans took to the streets for a general strike in response to subway-fare increases, generalized economic precarity and an illegitimate constitution and political order. As these protests gained support, their social base grew sufficiently to enable the protestors to shut down critical infrastructure and halt commercial activity (Pérez and Osorio 2021). In Argentina, at the same time, widespread worker mobilizations led the resistance to the neoliberal policies and austerity measures enacted by then-president Mauricio Macri. Farías (2018) and Sobering (2021) detail the methods of Argentines' resistance to this intensified neoliberalization – specifically via their *asambleas populares* ('people's assemblies') and through *empresas recuperadas* ('recovered companies'). As Deleuze and Guattari might have noted, it is the Global South that will likely provide us with inspiring examples of progressive alternatives to the quagmire of post-neoliberalism. Whether these take place in Argentina, Palestine or elsewhere in the Global South, the 'struggles of the Third World' – as the pair asserts – are 'the struggles of the oppressed masses and minorities [everywhere]' (1987, 471).

Against predatory states

The second guidepost offered by Deleuze for our post-neoliberal age is a call for vigilance against predatory states. Fortified by the experience of May '68, a number of French public intellectuals – including Deleuze and Foucault – organized to bring attention to the 'travesty of justice that is the prison' with the 1971 formation of the Groupe d'information sur les prisons, which aimed to 'let those with experience [in] prison speak' (Harcourt 2021, 65). Through the group, Deleuze calls out the 'deliberate and personified provocations by means of which this [prison] system functions and ensures its order, by means of which the system creates its excluded and condemned in conformity with a politics shared by Power, the police, and the administration' (Deleuze and Defert 2004, 246). Also during this time, Deleuze and Guattari sought to counter the widely held and reactionary attitudes towards homosexuality in French society by contributing to the 1973 volume *Trois milliards de pervers: Grande encyclopédie des homosexualités*, which represented one of the first opportunities for LGBT persons to speak in light of new avenues of thought, desire and expression brought about by May '68. Upon its publication, copies of the volume were seized by authorities, and Guattari was fined for an 'affront to public decency' (Dosse 2010, 273–4).

Deleuze and Guattari further spoke out against predatory states in their 1977 *Le Monde* op-ed 'Le pire moyen de faire l'Europe' – which criticized the extradition of Klaus Croissant, a defence attorney at the Red Army Faction's 1975 trial in Germany (Patton 2010, 91). For the pair, the extradition of Croissant at the bequest of German authorities meant sending a political dissident into the clutches of a predatory legal apparatus that was in a 'state of exception' (2006, 149). Deleuze and Guattari also saw the German government's demands for Croissant's extradition to be a means of forcibly exporting the country's legal and security models, becoming thus a 'qualified organizer of repression' (2006, 147). Their concerns along these lines proved prescient; Croissant's subsequent extradition displayed the speed with which states like Germany can resort to emergency judicial powers – through which it becomes politically necessary to secure convictions, no matter how flimsy the basis (Portelli 1985).

Forty-five years later, we can take these interventions of Deleuze and Guattari to be a model for how to resist predatory authorities and denounce states of exception. In our post-neoliberal era, there is perhaps no clearer example of predatory state action than the broken and cruel systems of granting (or not) political asylum to those fleeing war, occupation, violence and persecution. Aradau and Canzutti propose looking at the processes of asylum as 'technologies of cruelty' (2022), whereby continuities of violence seek to undo the individual subjectivities of asylum seekers. Indeed, in Germany, Mexico, the United States and other countries, detention centres act as the chosen state apparatus to intercept displaced persons, thus reterritorializing individuals coded as 'refugees' while forcing them to internalize 'appropriate subject positionings' to satisfy the bureaucratic requirements of asylum seeking.

Combating anti-intellectualism

The third guidepost Deleuze offers us regards the resurgence of anti-intellectual currents in the post-neoliberal interregnum. In his 1977 polemic 'On the

New Philosophers and a More General Problem', Deleuze laments the rise of 'intellectual marketing' in the French media landscape, criticizing the recent attention showered on the anti-Marxist *nouveaux philosophes* such as Bernard-Henri Lévy (BHL),[5] André Glucksmann and Alain Finkielkraut. He argues that this shift began with the realization of journalism's event-creating power, the discovery of its own 'autonomous and sufficient thought within itself' (Deleuze 2006, 142).

Oskar Negt details how the *nouveaux philosophes* were integrated into a network of mass-distributed content, with French media companies having 'bent over backwards to profit from this unexpected gold mine' (1982). The marriage between the likes of BHL and Glucksmann and the profiteers of their work seemed 'more akin to the marketing of film-stars or pop-singers than the diffusion of serious ideas' (Reader 1987, 108). If Deleuze and Guattari's philosophical project was to create an environment whereby ideas could circulate as lines of flight, the *nouveaux philosophes* 'rebuilt a stuffy, airless room . . . [negating] all forms of politics and experimentation' (Dosse 2010, 378).

As Negt adds, the phenomenon of the *nouveaux philosophes* was not just a cause for anti-intellectualism and reactionary propaganda, but also a symptom of disenchanted thought fostered by a climate of retreat and resignation from political change (1982). In this light, the *nouveaux philosophes* might be better described as corporate intellectuals, or those who are imbricated into a 'system of power that blocks, prohibits, and invalidates' popular discourses and knowledge (Foucault and Deleuze 1977, 207). Today, as in 1977, the corporate intellectual is once again, at the forefront of contemporary knowledge production – which is guided and promoted by market forces regardless of the quality of the ideas that are being proposed (Di Leo 2006, 193–4). Social media are rife with anti-intellectualism of this sort – from the harassment of journalists and academics, to the spread of harmful conspiracy theories, to the knee-jerk rejection of public policies backed by expert consensus.

Again, Deleuze and Guattari provide us with examples to combat the morass of anti-intellectualism in this post-neoliberal age. In the early 1980s, Deleuze and Guattari (along with Derrida) were instrumental in creating the Paris-based Collège international de philosophie to rethink the teaching of philosophy in France as well as liberate the discipline from its existing institutional bonds in lycées and universities. Concurrently, and in a similar vein, Guattari created a series of independent or 'pirate' radio stations,[6] a 'transversal rhizomatic system that breaks with State- and market-based vertical logics' (Dosse 2010, 304). Guattari was himself introduced to the subversive power of pirate radio via Radio

Alice in Bologna, Italy – a station linking education with political organization while promoting avenues of change and practices of mobilization. In sum, the Collège international de philosophie and pirate radio stations became means by which Deleuze and Guattari could combat the *nouveaux philosophes* and their patrons in the French corporate media. The way forward for us, accordingly, is to continue Deleuze and Guattari's battle against anti-intellectualism in its many forms – initiating lines of flight that transcend stifling post-neoliberal logics, while disseminating democratized forms of knowledge for the benefit of the public.

Forms of politico-economic autarky

The fourth guidepost that Deleuze and Guattari have left for us regards some new and promising forms of political economy that could potentially find applications in the wake of neoliberalism's slow death. In the case of Guattari's experiences in Brazil, the development of progressive and post-neoliberal forms of autarky was not just a speculative exercise. In Paris in the 1970s, Guattari served as the psychoanalyst of Suely Rolnik, then a student at Deleuze's university (Centre universitaire expérimental de Vincennes), who had earlier been imprisoned by authorities from the Brazilian dictatorship and fled into exile in France. Subsequently, Rolnik visited La Borde, the heterodox psychiatric clinic in the Loire Valley where Guattari worked, and participated in Deleuze's famous philosophy seminars at Vincennes.

Upon Rolnik's return to Brazil in 1979, her experiences and friendships with Deleuze and Guattari gave her powerful inspiration in the form of 'micropolitics' (Rolnik and Guattari 1986) – that is, the linkages between politics, culture and psychoanalysis that had coalesced in the wake of May '68. With help from Guattari, Rolnik disseminated Deleuzo-Guattarian thought and practice into a country that was slowly emerging from twenty years of military rule. More importantly, she established a series of mental health institutes in Brazil based on the ideas of 'schizoanalysis', a unique take on psychotherapy first formulated by Deleuze and Guattari in *Anti-Oedipus* (1972). As described by Dosse (2010, 484), these 'schizoanalytic' clinics played an essential role in the struggles within Brazil's psychiatric and psychoanalytic fields, even before the eventual demise of the dictatorship in 1985.

To analyse other post-neoliberal experiments in political economy that bear traces of Deleuze and Guattari, we stay in South America. The Andean indigenous idea of *Buen Vivir* (Spanish for 'good living' or 'living well') – translated as *sumac kawsay* in Quechua and *suma qaman* in Aymara – calls for socio-economic development that is ecologically balanced, egalitarian in orientation and culturally sensitive to the rights of all those in today's plurinational states (Grugel and Riggirozzi 2019, 6–7). Codified into the constitutions of Ecuador in 2008 and Bolivia in 2009, *Buen Vivir* has led to far-reaching changes in the political economies of these countries, particularly in the areas of cultural recognition and income redistribution. More difficult for these governments has been the adjudication of competing land-tenure claims among indigenous communities, particularly in light of intensifying natural resource extraction (in the form of oil, natural gas and agricultural commodities). Thus, as has been documented by Postero (2017) and Riofrancos (2020), the Bolivian and Ecuadorian governments have largely succeeded in extending material and cultural rights to historically marginalized populations, at the same time that they have been dragging their feet in giving political and economic self-determination to these countries' increasingly vocal and organized indigenous groups.

Indigenous issues such as these preoccupied Deleuze and Guattari starting in the 1970s, in both a political and conceptual sense. The celebrated third section of *Anti-Oedipus* (1972), entitled 'Savages, Barbarians, Civilized Men', is an anthropological survey of pre-capitalist forms of what the pair call 'desiring-production' – which was based in part on their conversations with ethnologist Pierre Clastres (1934–1975), whose studies of the Guayaki people of eastern Paraguay Deleuze and Guattari greatly admired (Collins, forthcoming). In a more conceptual register, indigenous peoples (such as the Guayakis and Palestinians, as noted previously) became inspirations for three of Deleuze and Guattari's most prominent ideas in *A Thousand Plateaus* (1980): 'nomads' who achieve 'lines of flight', or autarkic modes of 'minor' living and political engagement that exist outside the purview of hegemonic nation-states. The militant indigenous movements of today, as a result, channel the legacy of Deleuze and Guattari in their ongoing attempts to think beyond colonial and capitalist modes of living – from Bolivia and Ecuador to Palestine and elsewhere in the world.

A second example of post-neoliberal political experimentation in a Deleuzo-Guattarian vein takes us back to Brazil, a country that Guattari visited seven times in the last fifteen years of his life. In São Paulo in 1982, Guattari interviewed the then-trade unionist Luiz Inácio Lula da Silva, who detailed for him the progressive 'micropolitics' of the recently formed Workers' Party. This political effort would bear fruit twenty-one years later, when now-president Lula and his government passed legislation creating the *Bolsa Família* (Portuguese for 'Family Allowance') – a popular system of cash transfers to working-class and -poor Brazilians, who in response agreed to vaccinate their children and send them to school. The programme, which far-right president Jair Bolsonaro regrettably terminated in 2021, was not without its critics – including Saad-Filho (2015), who questioned the emancipatory potential of cash transfers, as well as their ability to improve health and economic outcomes among targeted populations. These misgivings notwithstanding, *Bolsa Família* has long been considered a leading factor in the reduction of poverty in Brazil during Lula's presidency, which fell an impressive 27.7 per cent in his first term (Brandão Junior and Aragão 2020). For this reason, it has served as a model for similar programmes in Mexico, South Africa and other countries.

Confronting Big Tech

The final guidepost left for us by Deleuze and Guattari is a set of revelatory, almost clairvoyant, analyses regarding post-neoliberal capitalism's current articulation with technologies of surveillance and control. In his celebrated essay 'Postscript on the Societies of Control' (1990), Deleuze examines the shift that he perceives from the 'disciplinary societies' of the modern era – theorized so brilliantly by Foucault – to the 'control societies' of our post-neoliberal world of today. An example of this shift can be seen in the realm of detention; penitentiaries, those awful creations of the nineteenth century, enclose their convicts via walls, bars and fences. To quote Brusseau: 'this is discipline in its starkest form: place [as] social imposition' (2020, 3). Deleuze then contrasts prisons as physical creations with that ur-technology of the contemporary carceral state: the ankle bracelet (1992, 7).

How did we so squarely arrive at the control societies that Deleuze anticipated over thirty years ago? In this regard, we can trace an arc from the neoliberalism of the early 1990s into the post-neoliberal present. The current dominance of the 'Big Tech' firms Amazon, Meta (née Facebook), Alphabet (née Google), Apple and Microsoft – which are 'are owned and governed as corporations, and yet [have] achieved a status as social infrastructure that goes well beyond the typical providers of a commercial service' (Davies and Gane 2021, 20) – is in large part due to the success of neoliberal critiques of antitrust law, which made regulators from the 1980s onwards far more amenable to monopolies and oligopolies, especially in the field of information technology. This ascendency was supercharged during the Covid-19 pandemic, as Big Tech's platforms sustained (as well as reconfigured) nearly all aspects of social and economic life during the lockdown periods of 2020–22.

In his 'Postscript', Deleuze provided two warnings that we would be wise to heed as Big Tech continues to tighten its grip under the conditions of post-neoliberalism. The first is how Big Tech's platforms never cease parceling us into the consumers of ever-more segmented markets for goods and services. In control societies, Deleuze laments that individuals have become 'dividuals' – that is, those persons who turn up in 'masses, samples, data, markets, [and] "*banks*"' (1992, 5; italics in the original). Brusseau reflects on his dividuality in the post-neoliberal control society of today:

> *I* do not want a four-wheel drive Land Rover; instead, the fifty-year-old male, married, with incompletely attained professional aspirations wants that powerful vehicle. And, it is not *me* who wants to visit [New York's] Whitney Museum on Saturday; it is the person whose name appears on three lists: Land Rover owners, Manhattan residents, Amazon Alexa users. The Whitney marketing department – with the help of big data operators like LiveRamp – has found that when those three slices of *dividuality* come together, the offering of a discounted membership likely receives an affirmative response. (2020, 14–15; italics in the original)

The potent linkage between dividuality and the likelihood that said dividuals will undertake a certain task points to the second clairvoyant warning in Deleuze's 'Postscript': in control societies, 'marketing has become the center or the "soul" of the corporation' (1992, 6). As such, the 'joys of marketing' (1992, 7), to use Deleuze's ironic formulation, entail not only the mobilization of desire among consumers, but also the uncanny ability to *predict* exactly when they will act to realize said desire. Indeed, the computers that Deleuze foresees '[tracking] each person's position' (1992, 7) can easily segue to predicting their future 'trajectories of consumption'. Brusseau highlights the near-limitless demand of companies for the predictive analytics sold by Big Tech firms:

> A vacationer who scuba dives off the Florida coast is targeted by online ads for a trip to Cozumel in Mexico. After the Cozumel dive, he is lured by a discounted flight to Australia's Great Barrier Reef. Then, while waiting in the Sydney airport for the flight back home, an intriguing article about cave diving crosses his Facebook feed. The advertising of trajectories converts experiences into the desire for another, further down the continuous line. (2020, 15)

Thus, already in the early 1990s, Deleuze had pinpointed what is now a centre of struggle in our post-neoliberal 'societies of control': those 'codes that mark access to [personal] information' (1992, 5). Even though he is unsettled by the mutations of capitalism taking place before him, Deleuze curiously does not pronounce today's control societies to be either more nefarious or benign than the disciplinary societies that they replaced. On this note, and with an eye to the future, Deleuze asserts that 'there is no need to fear or hope, but only to look for new weapons' (1992, 4). But what these are, he frustratingly does not say – which is not the only instance from Deleuze's career when he gives us guideposts with which to proceed even as the actual trail is ill defined.

Conclusion

Post-neoliberalism's emergence constitutes a challenge for today's society in the same way that the rise of neoliberalism confronted Deleuze and Guattari's generation, a shift that necessitated that the pair modify their thinking and political engagement. In this chapter, we have shown how Deleuze and Guattari responded to the conjuncture created by neoliberalism in the 1970s and 1980s – first in *Anti-Oedipus* (1972), then *A Thousand Plateaus* (1980) and finally in 'Postscript on the Societies of Control' (1990), as well as in other op-eds and interviews. In these interventions, Deleuze and Guattari acted in solidarity with oppressed peoples, condemned the predatory actions of nation-states, waged combat against pseudo-intellectuals, formulated progressive forms of political economy and warned us about the burgeoning 'societies of control'. As such, we believe that reflecting on how Deleuze and Guattari navigated the central interregnum of their lives provides us with an opportunity to sharpen our political and conceptual tools for future struggles in the post-neoliberal era.

In engaging in this thought experiment, we find ourselves agreeing with the long-time Deleuze critic Peter Hallward (see 2006), who – in a 2009 debate – nonetheless acknowledged the promising political orientation to be found in the pair's texts: 'if you aim to use Deleuze politically then this is the best way to do it: to think about what kind of resources he and Guattari give us for understanding how political composition works, how capitalism works, how political organisations might become more supple and inventive, and so on' (Alliez et al. 2009, 153). While the world has been transformed significantly since Deleuze and Guattari's untimely deaths in the 1990s, the models of engagement they left for us demonstrate that our challenges today oblige us to counter with new concepts, political responses and forms of critique. As Deleuze himself cautions in the 'Postscript', it is up to us 'to discover what [we are] being made to serve'

(1992, 7) in these post-neoliberal times. Let us hope, in this regard, that post-neoliberal repression against minorities, state violence, conspiracy theories and ever-more dystopian systems of exploitation and surveillance amount to the burrows of a molehill and not the coils of a serpent.

Notes

1 A curious historical irony is that Deleuze's untimely November 1995 suicide took place during a series of militant strikes and protests that rivaled May '68 in their scope and intensity. France's main trade unions called this 'convergence of struggles' (*convergence des luttes*) in response to the neoliberal Plan Juppé, which sought to raise France's retirement age and reduce its budget deficits via cuts to social spending.

2 Schleusener (2020, 39–40) notes that, while Deleuze himself never used the term 'neoliberalism', he is obviously referring to some of its more nefarious economic and social consequences in 'Postscript on the Societies of Control' (1990) and other works.

3 Weeks defines the Deluezo-Guattarian axiomatic as 'something akin to the global politico-economic order'. He continues, 'to use Deleuze and Guattari's parlance, we could say that an assemblage of diverse axioms – that is, specific politico-economic formations – constitutes the global axiomatic' (2019a, 101).

4 It is worth noting that many of these strongmen began their political careers as neoliberals, perhaps best seen in the trajectories of Putin and Erdoğan.

5 In his text *Barbarism with a Human Face* (1977), Levy attacked Deleuze and Guattari's *Anti-Oedipus* (1972) for being – according to him – 'a plea for amoral individualism (and the pursuit of gratification), and as such an enabling condition for fascism' (cited in Collins 2022).

6 Radio and other media constituted a state monopoly in France until Mitterrand liberalized them beginning in the mid-1980s.

References

Alliez, Éric, Claire Colebrook, Peter Hallward, Nicholas Thoburn and Jeremy Gilbert (2009), 'A Deleuzian Politics? A Roundtable Discussion', *New Formations*, 68: 143–87.

Aradau, Claudia and Lucrezia Canzutti (2022), 'Asylum, Borders, and the Politics of Violence: From Suspicion to Cruelty', *Global Studies Quarterly*, 2 (2): 1–11.

Brandão Junior, Nilson and Marianna Aragão (2020), 'Miséria no Brasil cai 27,7% no 1º mandato de Lula', *O Estado de S. Paulo*, 7 September. https://economia.estadao.com .br/noticias/geral,miseria-no-brasil-cai-27-7-no-1-mandato-de-lula,54881 (accessed 10 July 2022).

Brusseau, James (2020), 'Deleuze's "Postscript on the Societies of Control": Updated for Big Data and Predictive Analytics', *Theoria*, 67 (3): 1–25.

Canessa, Andrew (2014), 'Conflict, Claim and Contradiction in the New "Indigenous" State of Bolivia', *Critique of Anthropology*, 34 (2): 153–73.

Collins, Jacob (2022), 'Bernard-Henri Lévy Is the Leading Intellectual of French Anti-socialism', *Jacobin*, 29 June. https://jacobin.com/2022/06/bernard-henri-levy-french-anti-socialism-new-philosophy (accessed 19 September 2022).

Collins, Jacob (forthcoming), 'The Return of the Savage in 1970s French Political Thought', *Yale French Studies*, 143.

Davies, William and Nicholas Gane (2021), 'Post-Neoliberalism? An Introduction', *Theory, Culture & Society*, 38 (6): 3–28.

Deleuze, Gilles ([1977] 2006), 'On the New Philosophers (Plus a More General Problem)', in David Lapoujade (ed.), *Two Regimes of Madness*, 139–47, New York: Semiotext(e).

Deleuze, Gilles ([1983] 1988), 'The Grandeur of Yasser Arafat', trans. Timothy S. Murphy, *Discourse*, 20 (3): 30–3.

Deleuze, Gilles ([1990] 1992), 'Postscript on the Societies of Control', *October*, 59: 3–7.

Deleuze, Gilles and Daniel Defert ([1973] 2004), 'H.M.'s Letters', in David Lapoujade (ed.), *Desert Islands and Other Texts 1953–1974*, 244–6, New York: Semiotext(e).

Deleuze, Gilles and Félix Guattari ([1977] 2006), 'Europe the Wrong Way', in David Lapoujade (ed.), *Two Regimes of Madness*, 148–50, New York: Semiotext(e).

Deleuze, Gilles and Félix Guattari ([1980] 1987), *A Thousand Plateaus: Capitalism and Schizophrenia, Vol. II*, trans. Brian Massumi, Minneapolis: University of Minnesota Press.

Deleuze, Gilles and Félix Guattari ([1991] 1994), *What Is Philosophy?*, trans. Hugh Tomlinson and Graham Burchell III, New York: Columbia University Press.

Deleuze, Gilles and Elias Sandbar ([1982] 2006), 'The Indians of Palestine', in David Lapoujade (ed.), *Two Regimes of Madness*, 194–200, New York: Semiotext(e).

Di Leo, Jeffrey R. (2006), 'Public Intellectuals, Inc.', *symplokē*, 14 (1): 183–96.

Dosse, François (2010), *Gilles Deleuze and Félix Guattari: Intersecting Lives*, trans. Deborah Glassman, New York: Columbia University Press.

Farías, Mónica (2018), 'Contesting Exclusion: Solidarity Spaces and Changing Political Subjectivities in Buenos Aires', *Geoforum*, 217: 316–25.

Foucault, Michel and Gilles Deleuze ([1973] 1977), 'Intellectuals and Power', in Donald F. Bouchard (ed.), *Language, Counter-Memory, and Practice: Selected Interviews*, 205–16, Ithaca: Cornell University Press.

Grugel, Jean and Pia Riggirozzi (2023), 'Facing the Future: The Legacies of Post-Neoliberalism in Latin America', *Development and Change*, 54 (2): e1–e17.

Hallward, Peter (2006), *Out of This World: Deleuze and the Philosophy of Creation*, London: Verso.

Harcourt, Bernard E. (2021), "'Let Those Who Have an Experience of Prison Speak": The Critique & Praxis of the Prisons Information Group (1970–1980)', *Foucault Studies*, 31: 64–9.

Hayek, Friedrich (1948), *Individualism and Economic Order*, Chicago: University of Chicago Press.

Jameson, Fredric (1984), 'Postmodernism, or the Cultural Logic of Late Capitalism', *New Left Review*, 146: 53–92.

Macdonald, Laura and Arne Ruckert (2009), 'Post-Neoliberalism in the Americas: An Introduction', in Laura Macdonald and Arne Ruckert (eds), *Post-Neoliberalism in the Americas*, 1–18, London: Palgrave MacMillan.

Martin, Keir (2018), 'Post-Neoliberalism?', in Harald Wydra and Bjørn Thomassen (eds), *Handbook of Political Anthropology*, 205–17, Cheltenham: Edward Elgar Publishing Ltd.

Medien, Kathryn (2019), 'Palestine in Deleuze', *Theory, Culture & Society*, 36 (5): 49–70.

Negt, Oskar (1982), 'Reflections on France's "Nouveaux Philosophes" and the Crisis of Marxism', trans. Jamie O. Daniel, *Substance*, 11/12: 56–67.

Patton, Paul (2010), 'Activism, Philosophy and Actuality in Deleuze and Foucault', *Deleuze Studies*, 4: 84–103.

Pérez, Domingo and Sebastián Osorio (2021), 'Anti-Neoliberal Revolt and General Strike in Chile 2019', in Dario Azzellini (ed.), *If Not Us, Who? Global Workers against Authoritarianism, Fascism, and Dictatorships*, 48–54, Geneva: Rosa-Luxemburg-Stiftung.

Portelli, Alessandro (1985), 'Oral Testimony, the Law and the Making of History: The "April 7" Murder Trial', *History Workshop Journal*, 20 (1): 5–35.

Posner, Richard A. (2009), *A Failure of Capitalism: The Crisis of '08 and the Descent into Depression*, Cambridge: Harvard University Press.

Postero, Nancy (2017), *The Indigenous State: Race, Politics, and Performance in Plurinational Bolivia*, Oakland: University of California Press.

Reader, Keith (1987), *Intellectuals and the Left in France Since 1968*, New York: St. Martin's Press.

Riofrancos, Thea (2020), *Resource Radicals: From Petro-Nationalism to Post-Extractivism in Ecuador*, Durham: Duke University Press.

Rolnik, Suely and Félix Guattari (1986), *Micropolítica: Cartografias do Desejo*, Petrópolis: Vozes.

Saad-Filho, Alfredo (2015), 'Social Policy for Neoliberalism: The Bolsa Família Programme in Brazil', *Development and Change*, 46 (6): 1227–52.

Schleusener, Simon (2020), 'Deleuze and Neoliberalism', *Coils of the Serpent*, 6: 39–54.

Sobering, Katherine (2021), 'Working for Justice in Argentina', *Contexts*, 20 (1): 52–7.

Stiglitz, Joseph (2016), *The Euro: How a Common Currency Threatens the Future of Europe*, New York: W. W. Norton and Company.

Tooze, Adam (2018), *Crashed: How a Decade of Financial Crises Changed the World*, New York: Viking.

Weeks, Samuel (2019a), 'A Politics of Peripheries: Deleuze and Guattari as Dependency Theorists', *Deleuze and Guattari Studies*, 13 (1): 79–103.

Weeks, Samuel (2019b), 'Portugal in Ruins: From "Europe" to Crisis and Austerity', *Review of Radical Political Economics*, 51 (2): 246–64.

4

Postcapitalist Surplus Value

Humans, Machines, Information

Claudio Celis Bueno

Two vignettes

Let us begin with two vignettes. Vignette number one: the development of information technologies reaches a speed and scale in which capitalist relations of production, despite their flexibility and malleability, are no longer able to adapt. The logic of scarcity that regulates the price system clashes with the non-scarce character of information and pushes society towards a non-market, postcapitalist economy. In this new economy, automation and collaboration undermine the hierarchies of the market economy and open the door to a world of abundance. Vignette number two: the development of information technologies creates a new mode of production and hence a new form of class antagonism. Instead of the capital-labour conflict that defines capitalism, this new mode of production is characterized by the conflict between those who produce information but do not own the means to capture and process it and those who own the means to capture and process this information (and hence to benefit from it). In the first vignette, capitalism is replaced by a postcapitalist world of abundance and cooperation. In the second one, capitalism is replaced by an even more asymmetric social order, a type of 'techno-feudalism' in which a few monopolies reinstate new forms of social domination that circumvent some of the core antagonisms that had regulated social life in modernity (i.e. state vs market, public vs private, capital vs labour, etc.). The first vignette is presented in Paul Mason's *Postcapitalism* (2015). The second one, less optimistic, in McKenzie Wark's *Capital Is Dead* (2019).

Despite depicting opposite outcomes, both books conceive information technologies as a quasi-autonomous force capable of disrupting the existing mechanisms of social reproduction. In both cases, information technologies appear to defy the logic of scarcity that defines the market economy and to replace human labour as the moving force behind social production. Overall, both books pursue a conceptual provocation aimed at triggering urgent political discussions regarding the relation between information and (post)capitalism today. At the same time, however, both books fail to properly develop a consistent concept of information and to engage in a convincing examination of the relation between machines and value. This chapter would like to present a third vignette, one informed by Gilbert Simondon's concept of information and Gilles Deleuze and Félix Guattari's concept of machinic surplus value. This third vignette retains the provocative character of the first two. At the same time, however, it does not claim a sharp shift from capitalism to postcapitalism. Instead, this third vignette calls for a different definition of capitalism in which both human and non-human agents appear as potential sources of surplus value, a postanthropocentric twist from which to analyse the relationship between information technologies and value in the current mode(s) of production.

Information and (post)capitalism

In recent years, the question regarding the relationship between capitalism and information has been widely examined (e.g. Srnicek 2017; Zuboff 2019; Beller 2018; Celis Bueno 2017; Pasquinelli 2015; Fumagalli et al. 2018). Nick Srnicek (2017, 6), for example, has coined the term 'platform capitalism' in order to show how digital platforms have emerged as a new business model in contemporary capitalism 'capable of extracting and controlling immense amounts of data'. In this context, data is understood as the 'new oil', a 'raw material to be extracted, refined and used in a variety of ways' (Srnicek 2017, 40). Similarly, Shoshana Zuboff (2019) has explored how corporations and governments are using information in order to predict and shape individual behaviour, a phenomenon that she calls 'surveillance capitalism'. In both cases, information appears as a new source of economic value. In both cases, information technologies are put at the service of capital, intensifying and broadening its control not only over (human) labour but over all aspects of social (and natural) life. In contrast, Paul Mason (2015) and McKenzie Wark (2019) offer an alternative story: information technologies do not fully serve the purposes of capital; they may have contributed to the expansion of capitalism in the last 50–60 years, but they are now reaching a point of development that begins to clash with the relations of production required by capitalism in order to reproduce itself.

Paul Mason (2015, 9) defines capitalism as an open system capable of adapting to new historical, social and technical conditions. With the emergence of information technologies in the last few decades, however, this open and adaptable system appears to be reaching its own limits. This is so mainly because information technologies are qualitatively different from all previous technologies (Mason 2015, 9). Information technologies, Mason argues, are (a) reducing 'the need for work, blurr[ing] the edges between work and free time, and loosen[ing] the relationship between work and wages' (2015, 10); (b) 'corroding the market's ability to form prices correctly [. . .] because markets are based on scarcity while information is abundant' (2015, 10); and (c) giving rise to new forms of 'collaborative production: goods, services and organizations are appearing that no longer respond to the dictates of the market and the managerial hierarchy' (2015, 10). Based on these three claims, Mason argues that the emerging 'information economy might not be compatible with a market economy' (2015, 32) and that information technologies are robbing 'market forces of their ability to create dynamism' while at the same time 'creating the conditions for a postcapitalist economy' (2015, 35). Because of this, contemporary 'info-capitalism' has been forced to respond with a radical monopolization and centralization of production:

> If information corrodes value, then corporations are responding with three types of survival strategy: the creation of monopolies on information and the vigorous defence of intellectual property; the 'skating to the edge of chaos' approach, trying to live within the gap between expanded supply and falling prices; and the attempt to capture and exploit socially produced information such as consumer data, or by imposing contracts on programmers that say the company owns code they write in their free time. (Mason 2015, 115)

The centrality of information within the production process, Mason concludes, is creating an intensification of the contradictions of capitalism 'between the possibility of free, abundant socially produced goods, and a system of monopolies, banks and governments struggling to maintain control over power and information' (2015, 116).[1] Referring directly to this conclusion, McKenzie Wark (2019, 14) has argued that, in contrast to the stagnation of current Marxist critical theory,

> Paul Mason has risked the concept of postcapitalism, which has the merit of raising the stakes, even if it does not venture a language for an emerging mode of

production. [. . .] Through a fresh reading of Marxist political economy, Mason offers a way of thinking how capitalism may have mutated. [. . .] It is a stimulating read and implies two further projects: coming up with a renewed language for describing the present situation and identifying what in the received language about capitalism impedes forward movement in thought and action.

Unlike Mason, however, Wark (2019) is less optimistic. She does not see the tendency of the current mode of production as a straight line towards a world of abundance and collective production. She does indeed argue that information technologies are causing a transition towards a postcapitalist mode of production. But this new mode of production is not necessarily going to get rid of power asymmetries or economic inequalities. Therefore, new tools are required in order to properly understand the new social hierarchies that are being formed. To do so, Wark argues, critical theory needs to move beyond current Marxist thought, which insists on applying old categories to new phenomena. What is needed, instead, is to risk new concepts and new modes of thinking to fully grasp this new mode of production in its current formation. Wark (2019, 14) hence ventures a 'thought experiment' according to which information technologies are creating a postcapitalist mode of production no longer defined by the capital–labour antagonism but by a new class struggle, that between 'hackers' and 'vectorialists'.[2] Following a similar argument to that of Mason, Wark (2019, 13) contends that the main problem of contemporary capitalism is 'how to maintain forms of class inequality, oppression, domination, and exploitation, based on something that in principle is now ridiculously abundant'. Wark's thesis is that this contradiction can only be resolved through the emergence of a new mode of production:

> This is not capitalism anymore; it is something worse. The dominant ruling class of our time no longer maintains its rule through the ownership of the means of production as capitalists do. Nor through the ownership of land as landlords do. The dominant ruling class of our time owns and controls information. (2019, 14)

In this new mode of production, the asymmetry of information (and not the asymmetry of the 'material' means of production) becomes the main form of social control (Wark 2019, 11). The hacker class, the 'info-prole', produces information but does not own the means to realize its 'value'. Hence, the hacker class does not 'benefit from its predictive power', although it often suffers 'the downside' of those predictions (Wark 2019, 12). The vectorialist class, concurrently, derives its power from owning and controlling the vectors of information (Wark 2019, 21). These vectors include 'the capacity to transmit, store, and process information', that is, 'the material means for assembling so-called big data and realizing its predictive potential' (Wark 2019, 22). Put differently, the vectorialist class ensures its hierarchical position through the ownership and control of patents, 'which preserve monopolies on these technologies', of the 'brands and celebrities that galvanize attention' and of 'the logistics and supply chains that keep information in its proprietary stacks' (Wark 2019, 22).

One may argue that Wark ignores how most of the planet is still governed by the capital–labour conflict and that her analysis may, if anything, apply only to the realm of high-tech industries. Anticipating this critique, Wark offers two counterarguments. First, she argues that the rise of information technologies is in fact altering the whole chain of production and supply at a planetary level, from agriculture and mining to high-tech industries.[3] This does not mean, however, that there are no longer geographical, social, economic or technical asymmetries created by capitalism. It only entails that these asymmetries are now dependent on something else than the labour–capital relation. Second, Wark (2019, 22) introduces the idea of a coexistence of modes of production and class relations. In the contemporary world, she claims, 'there is still a landlord class that owns the land under our feet and a capitalist class that owns the factories' (2019, 11). At the same time, however, another kind of ruling class is emerging, 'one that owns neither of those things but instead owns the vector along which information is gathered and used' (Wark 2019, 12). Hence, in the contemporary world, these three modes of production 'co-exist and interact' (Wark 2019, 22). This means that the vectorialist–hacker struggle does not 'describe the totality', but a 'tendency' within the current modes of production (Wark 2019, 22).[4]

Information and value

It could be argued that in their attempts to examine the relation between information technologies and postcapitalism, neither Mason nor Wark offer a consistent definition of the notion of information or a convincing analysis of its relationship to the concept of value. Both authors claim that information technologies are pushing our current market economy towards a postcapitalist mode of production. Still, they only offer vague definitions of what this moving force, this 'thing' driving such radical transformations, really is. On many occasions, both authors tend to equate information with digital technologies and some of their current applications, such as digital platforms, big data, data extractivism, algorithms or even artificial intelligence. This lack of specificity appears as a significant shortcoming in these two books, in particular if we consider the centrality that they grant to the concept of information when analysing the relation between technology and (post)capitalism.

In the case of Mason, the concept of information is informed by Paul Romer (1990, 72) and is defined as 'the instructions that we follow for combining raw materials'. As such, information can be disentangled from the limitations of material processes of production and reproduced infinitely. Information appears then as a 'blueprint or recipe for making something either in the physical world or in the digital world' (Mason 2015, 98). Technological progress, furthermore, is here understood as the constant improvement of information (according to both Mason and Romer, raw materials hardly evolve, whereas new instructions for what to do with them is what defines technological revolutions). The current information revolution is then defined by the massification of these instructions at a scale in which the production of new goods tends to a 'zero marginal cost' (Mason 2015, 98).[5]

Similarly, Wark claims that 'information is a strange thing' (2019, 13) characterized by 'strange ontological properties': 'it is no longer scarce, it is infinitely replicable, cheap to store, and cheap to transmit' (2019, 50). Going a step further than Mason, Wark (2019, 86) attempts to provide a definition of information based on the relation between repetition and novelty, between difference and sameness. Like in Claude Shannon's theory (1948), Wark defines information as the amount of novelty (difference) that can be identified within a repetition (sameness). This relation between novelty and repetition, furthermore, is what supposedly allows those with the right tools to predict future behaviours (of the market, consumers, populations, 'natural' phenomena, etc.) and hence to establish an asymmetric power relation between those who produce that information and those who benefit from it (Wark 2019, 23). This new 'ruling class', Wark (2019, 63) adds, 'does not appropriate a quantity of surplus value so much as exploit an asymmetry of information'. This asymmetry is determined by the fact that one class ('hackers') produces the information (the novelty out of repetition) but does not own the means to 'store, transmit and process' it, in other words, the tools to extrapolate a vector in such a way that it can be acted upon.[6] Furthermore, the dominant class is no longer the capitalist class since the main 'substance' being exploited in this asymmetric relation is no longer surplus human labour. This also entails that the main aim of the new dominant class is not to accumulate capital (understood as objectified human labour), but to accumulate a 'surplus of information', that is, a surplus of difference within the repetition of sameness (2019, 19). In this new context, Wark concludes,

> Commodification now means not the appearance of a world of things but the appearance of a world of information about things, including information about every possible future state of those things that can be extrapolated from a quantitative modelling of information extracted from the flux of the state of things, more or less in real time. (2019, 23)

For both authors, but particularly evident in the case of Mason, the opposition between information and scarcity risks falling into an idealist division between the material and the immaterial. The fact that information allows for a world of abundance appears to render it as some form of immaterial substance, that is, as something that remains outside of the constraints of the material world. The material world is scarce, finite, entropic. Apparently, the immaterial realm of information depicted by Mason and Wark is not. The problem is that information is not immaterial.[7] It requires very concrete infrastructures that are exposed to the same constraints as the production of any other 'material' thing. The promised abundance of information clashes then with its very concrete material requirements. If we are to better grasp the relationship between information and (post)capitalism, a more precise (and less idealist) notion of information is thus required.

What is more, the limits of the concept of information in Mason and Wark bring into light the complex question regarding the notion of value. In Marxist terms, value refers to a measure of (abstract) human labour, that is, human labour measured in abstract, chronological time.[8] When Mason and Wark refer to the process of 'extracting value from information', they are often referring to 'use value' (i.e. to its potential to produce useful things in the physical or digital world), and not to its 'value' (understood as a social relation grounded on the quantification of abstract human labour). Put differently, Mason's account of information as the recipe or blueprint to produce things and Wark's definition of information as the production of difference within sameness both refer to a process of valorization of its concrete, practical features (use value), and not to a social relation measured in terms of abstract (human) labour time.

It could be argued that, precisely because Mason and Wark are referring to postcapitalist relations of production, Marx's concept of value (meant to explain capitalist society) becomes redundant. Put differently, one could say that Mason and Wark use the concept of value no longer to refer to the exploitation of human labour under capitalism but to the application of information in the production processes of postcapitalist societies. But in doing so, both Mason and Wark simplify Marx's analysis of the twofold character of human labour (abstract and concrete) into a single-sided definition of value as a measure of productivity.

In the case of Mason, one could respond that since information technologies give rise to a non-hierarchical and non-competitive society characterized by abundance and collaboration, value no longer exists as a social relation and is fully replaced by information as a new measure of productivity. In fact, Mason's postcapitalism can be read as a techno-enthusiastic version of communism, a social order in which the 'value form' no longer dominates or shapes social relations. Here the misunderstanding regarding value could just be solved by clarifying that 'value' is a strictly capitalist social relation and replacing it with notions such as 'productivity', 'efficiency' or 'utility' when referring to the social relation that will be established with information in a postcapitalist world – just like Marx (1973, 705) distinguished between 'value' and 'wealth' when analysing modern industry in the *Grundrisse*. But Mason does not opt for this. Instead, he insists on resorting to the concept of value in order to explain 'the transition from capitalism to a non-market economy' (Mason 2015, 32). And not just that, he even claims that in doing so he is offering the 'correct' interpretation of Marx's labour theory of value.[9]

In the case of Wark, the relation between information and value can be read as twofold. On the one hand, Wark follows Mason's understanding of the 'value' of information as 'productivity'. Hence, like Mason, she confuses 'value' with 'use value' when acknowledging the revolutionary power of information for shattering the 'value form' which defines the capitalist mode of production and its market economy (Wark 2019, 13; Mason 2015, 119). At the same time, however, Wark is concerned with the issue of how information technologies are establishing new forms of power asymmetries. The theoretical problem that she is trying to address is how can 'forms of class inequality, oppression, domination, and exploitation' be based 'on something that in principle is now ridiculously abundant' (Wark 2019, 13). This means that Wark's argument still requires a conceptual apparatus capable of explaining the reproduction of asymmetric social relations between those who produce information and those who own the means to capture it, process it and act upon it. In Mason's optimistic scenario this is not necessary, since postcapitalist social reproduction is guided purely by the productivity, abundance and collaboration made possible by information technologies (what Marx would call 'wealth'). But Wark's analysis of the new forms of class antagonism does require a conceptual framework capable of explaining the reproduction of asymmetric social relations, while at the same time she cannot resource to the Marxist analysis of the 'value form' precisely because she wants to emphasize that these asymmetric social relations are no longer based on the appropriation of human labour (but on the appropriation of a 'surplus of information'). This is where we find the main shortcoming of Wark's 'thought experiment': the absence of a conceptual apparatus capable of replacing the function that the analysis of the 'value form' had in Marx's thought, that is, a conceptual apparatus capable of accounting for the reproduction of asymmetric power relations. If the 'value form' is no longer the dominant mechanism regulating contemporary social reproduction, then how is social domination enforced?[10] Marxists would claim at this point that in fact 'value' continues to be the main mechanism of social reproduction, hence proving that capitalism is still very much alive (Caffentzis 2013; Morozov 2022). But if we want to remain with Wark and instead ask to what extent are information technologies transforming the mechanisms of social reproduction, a new conceptual apparatus is thus needed. Paraphrasing Wark herself, in order to strengthen her thought experiment what is needed is 'a new language' capable of replacing Marx's analysis of the 'value form' with a conceptual apparatus capable of examining social reproduction not on the basis of labour, but on that of information. And this new language, this new conceptual apparatus, needs a novel and more solid definition of both information and surplus value. It is at this point that Simondon's concept of information and Deleuze and Guattari's concept of machinic surplus value can offer a significant contribution.

Simondon's concept of information

Gilbert Simondon's philosophy is overall an attempt to redefine the concept of individuation.[11] In the Introduction to his 1958 doctoral thesis, Simondon (2020, 1) argues that Western metaphysics have only been able to define being by either focusing on already 'constituted and given individuals' or by searching for their 'principle of individuation'. In doing so, Western thought has failed to understand being as a 'process of individuation', that is, as an 'operation' (Simondon 2020, 3). This is so mainly because metaphysics had only known one notion of equilibrium, 'stable equilibrium' (2020, 5). This notion of stability implicitly presupposes that being is that which remains 'in a state of stable equilibrium' (2020, 5). From this perspective, becoming is conceived as the 'other' of being, its 'outside', that which needs to be excluded in order for individuation to take place. As Simondon (2020, 5) puts it,

> stable equilibrium is achieved in a system when all possible transformations have occurred and no propulsive force remains; all potentials have been

actualized, and systems that have succumbed to their lowest energetic levels cannot transform again.

In order to understand individuation as an operation, Simondon argues, we need a new concept of stability, that of 'metastability' (2020, 5). Metastability refers to the amount of potential energy of a system that remains in a state of 'relative unity' but which can become the source of future transformations of that system. Metastability 'describes systems macroscopically stable but internally characterised by an uneven distribution of potentials and hosting processes that make that stability only apparent' (Bardin and Ferrari 2022, 256). In this sense, metastable systems 'enjoy a stability far from equilibrium in which the aleatory encounter with a minimal quantity of energy or information can trigger a brusque alteration of equilibrium, and lead to the invention of new structures and hence to a new metastable state' (Bardin and Ferrari 2022, 256). From this perspective, the process of individuation does not simply entail the passage from becoming to being (from chaos to order; from movement to stable equilibrium; from operation to structure) but rather the constant resolution of energetic disparities and the consequent invention of new metastable structures. Put differently, the concept of metastability allows us to account for a type of operation of individuation in which the emerging structure does not exhaust the total amount of potential energy of a system. Instead, each operation of individuation maintains a certain degree of metastability, that is, a certain amount of 'energetic disparity' that allows for future transformations.

According to Simondon, in order to assume the point of view of individuation as ontogenesis, 'the notion of form must be replaced with that of information' (2020, 16). Unlike the notion of form (historically linked to the idea of stable equilibrium), the concept of information refers to an operation of transformation within a metastable system. This also entails, Simondon warns us, avoiding a 'technological theory of information' that reduces information to 'signals, or supports, or vehicles of information' (2020, 16). Pascal Chabot (2013, 79) suggests that in order to grasp Simondon's concept of information, a distinction must be established between syntactical, semantic and pragmatic approaches (2013, 79). The syntactical approach focuses on 'how information is to be coded, the channels of transmission, the physical capacities of information systems, and issues of redundancy and noise' (Chabot 2013, 79). In the semantic approach, instead, 'the primary concern is the meaning of the symbols that constitute a message' (Chabot 2013, 79). Simondon's original definition of information is neither syntactical nor semantic, but rather pragmatic. This means that

Simondon is mainly interested in how information affects 'the behaviours of transmitter and receiver' (Chabot 2013, 80). As Chabot (2013, 80) puts it, Simondon conceives information 'as an operation'. This means that the function of information is to cause a 'mutation', to trigger 'change'. It is in this sense that 'information becomes the factor that sets in motion the process of individuation' (Chabot 2013, 80).

Simondon further develops his concept of information in a conference given in 1962 titled *L'amplification dans les processus d'information* (2010). In this conference, Simondon argues that information should not be thought of as a 'thing' [*chose*], but rather as the operation of a 'thing' which reaches a metastable system and produces a transformation in this system (2010, 159). Information, therefore, cannot be defined beyond this act of transformative operation (and its reception). The function of information is to modify a local reality (to trigger a change in the energetic state of a metastable system) based on an incidental signal (Simondon 2010, 159). Likewise, a receiver of information is virtually any reality that does not possess entirely in itself the determination of its own process of becoming [*devenir*] (Simondon 2010, 159). In other words, every metastable system is a potential receiver of information, that is, a potential receiver of an incidental signal capable of triggering an operation in it (i.e. the emergence of a new structure). This means that a very weak signal (information) can in reality create a large energetic transformation (operation). This is so because the triggering information (incidental signal) only needs to alter the conditions of metastability in a system, which then utilizes its own metastable energy as the source of the energetic transformation. It is for this reason that Simondon defines every operation of information as an operation of 'amplification' (2010).

Neither in his 1958 doctoral thesis nor in the 1962 conference does Simondon use the concept of information in relation to information technologies. In both cases, the concept of information is used to describe a more fundamental operation of individuation that applies to all of the different domains of being (i.e. physical, vital, psychic, social and technical). Moreover, Simondon (2020) is quite explicit about the fact that he wants to differentiate his concept of information from Shannon's mathematical theory of information (1948) as well as from Wiener's (1948) cybernetic theory.[12] In spite of this, the concept of information as an operation of amplification offers a productive framework from which to analyse the current debates on the relation between information technologies and (post)capitalism.

As examined above, both Mason and Wark understand information technologies as a driving force that sends the logic of scarcity proper of capitalism into crisis. For Mason, the consequence of this is a postcapitalist world of abundance and collaboration. For Wark, instead, information technologies create a new mode of production in which new social hierarchies emerge. Despite describing opposite outcomes, both Mason and Wark define information as an immaterial 'thing' that opens the realm of production to endless abundance, a realm of production no longer constrained by the (entropic) limits of the material world. In this sense, Simondon's theory of information functions as an antidote to the idealism of immateriality that characterizes both Mason's and Wark's interpretation of the political and economic effects of information technologies. Information for Simondon is not an immaterial thing. It is an incidental signal (a weak source of energy) that triggers an operation of amplification. For Simondon (2010), this concept of information as an operation of amplification applies to an endless range of phenomena such as processes of crystallization, the spread of a fire in a forest, the triggering of a social revolt, the functioning of a microprocessor, and so on. In all these cases, information appears as a material thing that triggers material transformations. In this sense, Simondon's concept of information allows addressing the productivity of information technologies not through the lenses of immateriality and abundance, but rather through the concepts of operation and amplification. Furthermore, as we will see in the next section, the concepts of operation and amplification allow for a different understanding of the notion of surplus value, one that accounts for both human and non-human entities.

Machinic surplus value

In *Anti-Oedipus*, Deleuze and Guattari (1983, 232) introduce the concept of 'machinic surplus value'. At the heart of this concept, they tell us, lies the fundamental Marxist problem of how can capitalism maintain human labour 'as the basis for capitalist production', while at the same time 'recognizing that machines too "work" or produce value, that they have always worked, and that they work more and more in proportion to man, who thus ceases to be a constituent part of the production process, in order to become adjacent to this process' (1983, 232). In Marx's critique of political economy (1976), the concepts of labour and value are intrinsically linked to an anthropocentric world view: only humans labour and hence only humans produce surplus value. In fact, according to Marx (1991), the 'tendency of the falling rate of profit' that defines capitalist production (and its limit) results from the fact that only the human component in the production of commodities is capable of generating surplus value. As this human component is gradually replaced by machines, the total amount of surplus value in relation to the total amount of commodities decreases. From an anthropocentric perspective, it could be argued then that the gradual implementation of information technologies in the production process does not produce value but rather accelerates the tendency of the rate of profit to fall (Ramtin 1991; Caffentzis 2013).

Deleuze and Guattari (1983) challenge Marx's anthropocentric perspective and call for a redefinition of the notion of surplus value. The Marxist definition of surplus value, they claim, 'must be modified in terms of the machinic surplus value of constant capital, which distinguishes itself from the human surplus value of variable capital' (Deleuze and Guattari 1983, 239). In other words, Deleuze and Guattari argue that surplus value does not emanate only from the domain of variable capital (human labour) but also from that of constant capital (machines). In contemporary capitalism, they add, social reproduction is ensured through a threefold process:

> (1) the one that extracts human surplus value on the basis of the differential relation between decoded flows of labour and production [. . .]; (2) the one that extracts machinic surplus value, on the basis of an axiomatic of the flows of scientific and technical code [. . .]; (3) and the one that absorbs or realizes these two forms of surplus value of flux by guaranteeing the emission of both, and by constantly injecting anti-production into the producing apparatus. (Deleuze and Guattari 1983, 239)

There are at least two conceptual issues at stake here. First, the concept of machinic surplus value entails challenging the anthropocentric distinction between nature, culture and technology that informs Marx's own account of labour and value. All three domains, Deleuze and Guattari (1983, 32–3) argue, operate through machinic processes that connect, disconnect and amplify different flows of desire. There is only one kind of production, they tell us, 'the production of the real' (Deleuze and Guattari 1983, 32). Natural, organic, technical and social processes can all be understood through the concept of machine, that is, as processes of amplification through connection and disjunction (Bryant 2014). These machines only differ in terms of the regimes under which they are 'put to work'. This means that to a certain extent, at a more fundamental level, all forms of surplus value are already machinic. When analysing the capitalist social machine, however, Deleuze and Guattari retain Marx's distinction between variable capital (human labour) and constant capital (machines). But unlike Marx, they claim that constant capital can also produce surplus value. This 'machinic surplus value' no longer refers to the surplus produced by human labour measured in abstract time, but to surplus understood as the amplification of flows of energy through machinic connections and disjunctions (in Simondon's terms, machinic surplus value refers to any operation of information that triggers a process of amplification in a metastable system). From this perspective, human surplus value appears as a specific form of machinic surplus value which, under certain social, technical and historical conditions, became a highly efficient mechanism to amplify and organize flows of desire. At the same time, as Marx notes in the *Grundrisse*, with the development of constant capital, human labour becomes less and less central to the production process (1973, 704–5). This means that human surplus value gradually becomes secondary in relation to technology and science as primary forces of production. In this context, the social production, amplification and organization of flows of desire begins to depend less on human labour and more on technical and scientific processes. Like the concept of information in Simondon, Deleuze and Guattari's concept of machinic surplus value does not refer exclusively to the current context of post-industrial capitalism, but rather refers to a more fundamental (ontogenetical) process of individuation, a process that can be described as the amplification of flows by means of connection and disjunction. In this sense, machinic surplus value does not refer only to surplus value produced by technical machines. At the same time, however, Deleuze and Guattari introduce the concept of machinic surplus specifically when discussing the relation between human labour and technical machines. On the one hand, one might argue that they do so in order to highlight how the same 'machines' can be understood differently depending on the regime that puts them to work. On the other hand, it could be said that they do so in order to emphasize the singularity of their own critique of capitalism as an immanent system and to show how this critique departs from that of traditional Marxism.

This brings us to the second conceptual issue, Deleuze and Guattari's definition of capitalism. In *Anti-Oedipus*, Deleuze and Guattari define capitalism as a specific social formation characterized by the decoding of social flows. As such, capitalism appears as the outside of all other social formations in which social reproduction is grounded on the territorialization of flows, that is, social formations that ensure their stability through fixed codes. Capitalism emerges from the encounter of two decoded flows, the decoded flow of money and the decoded flow of abstract labour (Deleuze and Guattari 1983, 33). In this respect, capitalism is a unique social formation that operates by decoding the fixed codes of non-capitalist societies. At the same time, in order to ensure its own reproduction, capitalism puts forth a series of processes of reterritorialization that prevent the decoded flows from undermining itself: what capitalism deterritorializes with one hand must be continually reterritorialized with the other (Deleuze and Guattari 1983, 259). Capitalist reterritorialization is different from traditional forms of territorialization. Reterritorialization is not based on the repression and exclusion of decoded flows but on the imposition of abstract and universal axioms, that is, mechanisms that privatize the decoded flows of money and the decoded flows of labour. These axioms do not re-establish concrete and fixed codes. They rather operate as conditions of possibility for the decoded flows to be circulated, exchanged, consumed and most importantly, accumulated. Private property, the 'oedipal family' and individualized desire are all examples of mechanisms of reterritorialization that ensure that the decoded flows of capital will not undermine its own conditions of possibility, that is, its capacity to reproduce itself.

Let us return to Deleuze and Guattari's account of social reproduction under capitalism. According to them, this reproduction takes place through three specific mechanisms: the extraction of human surplus value, the extraction of machinic surplus value and the absorption or realization of these two forms of surplus value in the form of anti-production. The first two refer to mechanisms of deterritorialization (i.e. both human and machinic surplus value are understood as specific 'machines' that amplify decoded flows). The third refers to the mechanisms of reterritorialization which ensure the reproduction of capitalist relations of production, that is, which ensure the conditions of possibility for decoded flows to be accumulated. As Deleuze and Guattari sum it up, these three mechanisms of capitalist reproduction refer to the

> twofold movement of decoding or deterritorializing flows on the one hand, and their violent and artificial reterritorialization on the other. The more the capitalist machine deterritorializes, decoding and axiomatizing flows in order to extract surplus value from them, the more its ancillary apparatuses, such as government bureaucracies and the forces of law and order, do their utmost to reterritorialize, absorbing in the process a larger and larger share of surplus value. (1983, 34)

Deleuze and Guattari's definition of capitalism as an immanent system is strongly informed by Marx's own definition of capitalism (Holland 1999). At the same time, however, Deleuze and Guattari depart from the anthropocentric conceptualization of capitalism according to which only humans labour and hence only humans produce surplus value. Deleuze and Guattari thus provide a postanthropocentric analysis of capitalism as a social machine that has the unique ability to reproduce itself not based on fixed codes, but through the reterritorialization of decoded flows. These decoded flows can have a human component (human surplus value) and a non-human one (machinic surplus value). In a given social, historical and technical context, human labour appeared as the prevalent machine for producing, amplifying, organizing and accumulating decoded flows of energy. In this context, humans operated as information machines responsible for the key energetic transformations that regulated the capitalist social machine. With the development of the technological forces, however, other non-human machines are gradually becoming the primary forces responsible for the amplification and organization of these flows. In this context, machinic surplus value becomes a key aspect of social reproduction.

Conclusion: A third vignette

From a Marxist perspective, the concept of postcapitalist surplus value is nothing but an oxymoron. Value, for Marx, is the form that social relations take under capitalism. Hence, the overcoming of capitalism would also entail the end of value as a social relation. Vice versa, the end of the law of value would, in theory, mean that we are no longer under capitalist social relations. Why speak of postcapitalist surplus value then? As an oxymoron, it stresses the need to shift from an anthropocentric definition of capitalism based on the struggle between labour and capital towards a postanthropocentric definition of capitalism based on the twofold movement of deterritorialization and reterritorialization. If the concept of capitalism is grounded on the anthropocentric account of human labour, then postcapitalist surplus value does indeed appear as an oxymoron. If capitalism is instead defined as a mechanism of social reproduction grounded on the movements of deterritorialization and reterritorialization, then human surplus value and machinic surplus value can be seen as two complementary dimensions of social reproduction. Deleuze and Guattari's immanent analysis of capitalism offers a postanthropocentric framework capable of analysing the current role of information technologies as an apparatus of social reproduction. Furthermore, their threefold distinction between human surplus value, machinic surplus value and anti-production allows for an examination of current asymmetric and hierarchical relations. On the one hand, humans and machines amplify flows of desire, pushing forward the deterritorializing movement of capitalism. On the other, mechanisms of anti-production reterritorialize these flows in order to ensure the realization of surplus value and hence the reproduction of asymmetric power relations. As such, this threefold distinction offers a postanthropocentric alternative to the 'value form' that can complement and strengthen Wark's 'thought experiment', offering a 'new language' to explore how information technologies operate as apparatuses of social reproduction.

A third vignette can thus be sketched. The current development of information technologies does not entail the overcoming of capitalism (Mason) or the emergence of a new mode of production (Wark). The current development of information technologies rather calls for a postanthropocentric definition of surplus value capable of explaining the novel mechanisms of social reproduction. In a context in which human and non-human elements are more and more intertwined in the amplification and reproduction of asymmetric relations (of power, of resources, of agency, of uncertainty, etc.), Marx's analysis of the 'value form' becomes insufficient as a conceptual apparatus capable of explaining these asymmetries. This may not entail the end of capitalism, but it seems to unveil the limits of an anthropocentric definition of surplus value. In light of this, Simondon's concept of information and Deleuze and Guattari's notion of machinic surplus value can become valuable conceptual tools to further advance a critique of contemporary capitalism and its complex relation to technology.

Notes

1 Similar conclusions to those of Mason can be found in the work of Srnicek and Williams (2015) and Bastani (2019).

2 Wark had already developed the idea of a hacker class in *A Hacker Manifesto* (2004). The concept of 'vectorialists', on the other hand, is informed by Paul Virilio's (2009) work.

3 This is a similar argument to that put forth by Hardt and Negri (2000, 281) in relation to what they called the 'informatisation of production'.

4 Ryan Nolan (2021) highlights how this idea of the coexistence of modes of production and class relations offers an alternative to thinking about class as a fixed and reified category. According to him, one of the merits of Wark's provocation is to challenge essentialist and totalizing ways of thinking about class relations today, identifying the multiplicity and complexity that define economic and power asymmetries.

5 Regarding the relation between information technologies and the concept of 'zero marginal cost', see also Rifkin (2014).

6 As Wark (2019, 22) puts it, 'one thing that is distinctive about an information political economy is the way it instrumentalizes difference rather than sameness. The farmer and worker produce units of commodities that are equivalent within their kind. What I call the hacker class has to produce difference out of sameness. It has to make information that has enough novelty to be recognizable as intellectual property, a problem that landed property or commercial property does not have. By hacker class I mean everyone who produces new information out of old information, and not just people who code for a living'.

7 For an overview of the different materialist responses to the immateriality of information, see Casemajor (2015).

8 For a detailed presentation of the concept of value in Marxist thought, see Pitts (2021) and Postone (1993). For an analysis of the relationship between value and information in contemporary capitalism, see Hardt and Negri (2000).

9 See Chapter 6 of Mason's *Postcapitalism* (2015, 118–37). For a critique of Mason's (mis)interpretation of Marx's concept of value, see Pitts (2017) and Fuchs (2016).

10 Some authors have introduced the concept of 'techno-feudalism' to explain the reproduction of social asymmetries in the current context of datafication (see Durand 2020). For a critique of this concept, see Morozov (2022).

11 For a general introduction to Simondon's philosophy of individuation, see Combes (2013).

12 For a more detailed discussion of these differences, see Bardin and Ferrari (2022).

References

Bardin, Andrea and Marco Ferrari (2022), 'Governing Progress: From Cybernetic Homeostasis to Simondon's Politics of Metastability', *The Sociological Review Monographs*, 70 (2): 248–63.

Bastani, Aaron (2019), *Fully Automated Luxury Communism: A Manifesto*, London: Verso.

Beller, Jonathan (2018), *The Message Is Murder: Substrates of Computational Capital*, London: Pluto Press.

Bryant, Levi (2014), *Onto-Cartography: An Ontology of Machines and Media*, Edinburgh: Edinburgh University Press.

Caffentzis, Georges (2013), *In Letters of Blood and Fire: Work, Machines, and the Crisis of Capitalism*, New York: PM Press.

Casemajor, Nathalie (2015), 'Digital Materialisms: Frameworks for Digital Media Studies', *Westminster Papers in Culture and Communication*, 10 (1): 4–17.

Celis Bueno, Claudio (2017), *The Attention Economy: Labour, Time, and Power in Cognitive Capitalism*, London: Rowman & Littlefield.

Chabot, Pascal (2013), *The Philosophy of Simondon*, London and New York: Bloomsbury Academic.

Combes, Muriel (2013), *Gilbert Simondon and the Philosophy of the Transindividual*, Cambridge, MA: The MIT Press.

Deleuze, Gilles and Félix Guattari (1983), *Anti-Oedipus*, New York and London: Continuum.

Durand, Cédric (2020), *Techno-féodalisme*, Paris: Éditions La Découverte.

Fuchs, Christian (2016), 'Henryk Grossmann 2.0: A Critique of Paul Mason's Book "PostCapitalism: A Guide to Our Future"', *TripleC: Communication, Capitalism & Critique*, 14 (1): 232–43.

Fumagalli, Andrea, Stefano Lucarelli, Elena Musolino and Giulia Rocchi (2018), 'Digital Labour in the Platform Economy: The Case of Facebook', *Sustainability*, 10 (1757): 1–16.

Hardt, M. and A. Negri (2000), *Empire*, New York: Harvard University Press.

Holland, Eugene (1999), *Deleuze and Guattari's Anti-Oedipus: Introduction to Schizoanalysis*, New York: Routledge.

Marx, Karl (1973), *Grundrisse: Foundations of the Critique of Political Economy*, New York and London: Random House; Penguin.

Marx, Karl (1976), *Capital: A Critique of Political Economy*, vol. 1, New York and London; Harmondsworth: Penguin; New Left Review.

Marx, Karl (1991), *Capital: A Critique of Political Economy, Volume Three*, vol. 3, London and New York; Harmondsworth: Penguin; New Left Review.

Mason, Paul (2015), *PostCapitalism*, London: Penguin.

Morozov, Evgeny (2022), 'Critique of Techno-Feudal Reason', *New Left Review*, 133–4: 89–126.

Nolan, Ryan (2021), 'The Contemporaneity of Class Relations', *The Sociological Review (Online)*. https://doi.org/10.51428/tsr.jvcp4645

Pasquinelli, Matteo (2015), 'Italian Operaismo and the Information Machine', *Theory, Culture & Society*, 32: 49–68.

Pitts, Frederick Harry (2017), 'Beyond the Fragment: Postoperaismo, Postcapitalism and Marx's "Notes on Machines", 45 Years On', *Economy and Society*, 46 (3–4): 324–45.

Pitts, Frederick Harry (2021), *Value*, Cambridge and London: Polity Press.

Postone, Moishe (1993), *Time, Labor, and Social Domination: A Reinterpretation of Marx's Critical Theory*, Cambridge: Cambridge University Press.

Ramtin, R. (1991), *Capitalism and Automation*, London: Pluto Press.

Rifkin, Jeremy (2014), *The Zero Marginal Cost Society*, New York: Palgrave Macmillan.

Romer, Paul (1990), 'Endogenous Technological Change', *Journal of Political Economy*, 98 (5): 71–102.

Shannon, Claude (1948), 'A Mathematical Theory of Communication', *The Bell System Technical Journal*, 27: 379–423.

Simondon, Gilbert (2010), 'L'amplification Dans Les Processus d'information', in *Communication et Information InCours et Conférences*, 159–76, Paris: Editions de la Transparence.

Simondon, Gilbert (2020), *Individuation in Light of Notions of Form and Information*, Minneapolis and London: University of Minnesota Press.

Srnicek, Nick (2017), *Platform Capitalism*, Cambridge: Polity Press.

Srnicek, Nick and Alex Williams (2015), *Inventing the Future: Postcapitalism and a World Without Work*, London: Verso.

Virilio, Paul (2009), *Aesthetics of Disappearance*, Los Angeles: Semiotext(e).

Wark, McKenzie (2004), *A Hacker Manifesto*, Cambridge, MA: Harvard University Press.

Wark, McKenzie (2019), *Capital Is Dead: Is This Something Worse?* London: Verso.

Wiener, Norbert (1948), *Cybernetics, or Control and Communication in the Animal and the Machine*, Cambridge, MA: The MIT Press.

Zuboff, Shoshana (2019), *The Age of Surveillance Capitalism*, New York: PublicAffairs.

5

A Critique of the Post-Neoliberal Techno-Utopia of Transhumanism Drawing on Deleuze and Guattari's Philosophy

Francisco J. Alcalá[1]

Introduction

Transhumanism is an international cultural and intellectual movement that aims to transform the human condition through techno-scientific development directed towards the enhancement of physical, psychological and intellectual capacities (Bostrom 2005; Diéguez 2017, 2021). In the search for a precedent in philosophy, Friedrich Nietzsche is often singled out by his idea of the 'overman', which seems to anticipate those that animate the contemporary debate (Ansell-Pearson 1997; Tuncel 2017). However, Nietzsche does not yet pose the question of the overman in biological or techno-scientific terms: his philosophy is limited to the refinement of the human being through humanistic or cultural techniques (García-Granero 2020).

Moreover, transhumanism is a techno-utopia that makes ideological use of the future to justify a certain status quo in the present. And this status quo is not only that of neoliberalism but also that of so-called post-neoliberalism (see Davies and Gane 2021; Davies 2014), according to which transhumanism increases the inequalities associated with the former by replacing its commitment to competition with the naturalization of social inequalities at even a genetic level (Harari 2017). So, on the one hand, transhumanism can be qualified as neoliberal insofar as it makes the promised idyllic future into another consumer good for the satisfaction of individual aspirations rather than a collective aspiration based on a communitarian ideal (see Dardot and Laval 2014). Thus, although it explicitly assumes an emancipatory discourse, ascribing to liberal democracy and defining transhumanist enhancement as a human right whose guarantor should be the state (Bostrom 2011; The Transhumanist Declaration, in More and Vita-More 2013, 54–5; Hottois 2017), its actual development is closer to leading to the 'genetic supermarket' according to a strictly neoliberal logic (Nozick 1974, 315). On the other hand, this logic leads beyond neoliberalism, given the biological status that social inequalities would attain in the likely scenario of unequal access to these technologies, as well as the monopoly of them by powerful corporations asserting their interests to the detriment of states – which is already a reality (Linares 2020, 102; Diéguez 2021, 95).

In this chapter, I intend to develop a critical study of transhumanism based on the philosophy of Gilles Deleuze and Félix Guattari. I start from two hypotheses: (i) this philosophy updates Nietzsche's in the technological aspect since it raises the question of overman concerning the recourse to technology as a technique of enhancement that characterizes the transhumanist movement (Deleuze 1988, 131); (ii) the Deleuzo-Guattarian concept of assemblage is useful to criticize the assumptions, biases and interests present in transhumanism, given the intertwining of the social field with technology that this approach implies.

The assemblage theory distinguishes two dimensions in any social phenomenon. On the one hand, the material and expressive components that constitute the phenomenon under study and their possible interactions (in the case of transhumanism: the alliance of the human body with new technologies, the corresponding scientific discourse and the ideological discourse of the movement). On the other hand, the processes in which these components are complicated stabilize or destabilize the identity of the phenomenon over time (as when scientific discourse comes into conflict with the ideological discourse of transhumanism). Furthermore, the assemblage also establishes a priority of the social field over technology: social assemblages 'select' the technologies that go with them (Deleuze and Guattari 2004, 398). Therefore, the concept of assemblage makes it possible to show that the presuppositions, biases and interests of social phenomena are also present in the technological changes they promote. In short, the assemblage method will allow us to undertake the study and critique of transhumanism as a complex social phenomenon and to attend to the intertwining of the social field with technology. Hence, Deleuze and Guattari's philosophy provides a sound philosophical framework for transhumanism and, at the same time, offers an elaborate posthumanist conception of anthropology that provides conceptual elements to address its critique and is in tune with the current philosophy of science (see Samuels 2012, Ramsey 2013).

In accordance with the above, this chapter has the following objectives: (i) to elucidate the outlines of a rethinking of philosophical anthropology that responds to the transhumanist challenge, and (ii) to carry out a critique of the cultural assumptions and the socio-political biases and interests present in transhumanism, drawing on Deleuze and Guattari's concept of assemblage.

Anthropology in the era of transhumanism

The human being as 'unlimited finity'

In the search for a precedent for the current transhumanist movement in the field of philosophy, Friedrich Nietzsche is often mentioned, some of whose ideas seem to anticipate those that animate the contemporary debate, to the point that there are already monographs dedicated to the detailed study of this relationship (Ansell-Pearson 1997; Tuncel 2017). In this context, the Nietzschean concept of 'overman' (*Übermensch*) is particularly relevant; it has been the subject of multiple interpretations, many of which contribute to confusion, since they identify it with two equally hyperbolic extremes, either by excess or by default. The overman is neither the disappearance of the human species as we know it – an empirical fact – nor a simple modification of our conventional understanding of the human being, that is, an alteration of their concept – an epistemological change. What is at stake in the Nietzschean overman is, on the contrary, a whole event; that is, an imperceptible redistribution, in the transcendental realm, of those instances that determine our way of perceiving, understanding and relating to empirical reality.

In *The Gay Science* (2008, 119–20), Nietzsche linked the overman with the death of God and dedicated a famous passage to 'The "humanity" of the future' (190–1) – note the quotation marks. He established then as the most relevant feature of the human being of the time the 'sense for history' that they had managed to develop, which resembled more a reception of all past feelings than a new one. Thus, this feeling belongs to 'who is able to feel the history of man altogether as his own history', who undertakes an obligation: 'To finally take all this in one soul and compress it into one feeling – this would surely have to produce a happiness unknown to humanity so far: a divine happiness. . . . This divine feeling would then be called – humanity' (190–1). The lapidary statements in *Thus Spoke Zarathustra* (2006, 7) complete this small genealogy: 'Mankind is a rope fastened between animal and overman – a rope over an abyss.'

According to the above, can Nietzsche be considered a precursor of contemporary transhumanism, which advocates transcending the human through technology? It is clear that, in the texts cited, the philosopher alludes to the cultural progress of humanity, based on this 'sense for history'. It is, therefore, the capacity to assimilate the entire heritage of culture that the human being acquires in the absence of divine coercion that, according to Nietzsche, will eventually give rise to the overman through cultural enhancement. Hence the historical sense alludes to experimentation with the history of human beings as the 'personal' history of today's humans, who manage to refine themselves culturally in this way. In short, it is a matter of seeing in history a catharsis similar to the one Aristotle saw in Greek tragedy: an enhancement of one's passions through the more or less innocuous experimentation of others' passions. Thus, Nietzsche still poses the overman in cultural rather than biological or scientific-technical terms. His philosophy only brings into play a refinement of the human through humanistic or cultural techniques and, in particular, the historical sense that allows compressing in a feeling, mediator as it is in his thought between vital impulses and values, the cultural learning carried out by humans in pursuit of self-transcendence. However, it is undeniable that this cultural change also has something natural about it since humans are reconciled with their nature, from which nihilistic culture had separated them. Thus, in *Twilight of the Idols* (2005, 174), Nietzsche contrasts 'anti-natural morality' with 'naturalism in morality' as the only 'healthy morality' insofar as it is in harmony with life. Following the above, we must conclude, with Diego Sánchez Meca (2016, 52): 'Nietzsche thinks . . . in an evolution from the "last man" to the *Übermensch*, although not in a Darwinian sense but gravitating on a conception of life as creativity'.[2] In short, the techniques with which Nietzsche proposes to transcend the human being after the death of God are still humanistic or cultural, even if, through them, one can reconcile humans with their true nature, alienated in the culture in force.

Having established the scope of Nietzsche's proposal, we can turn to Deleuze to clarify the actuality of the overman concerning the recourse to technology as a technique of enhancement that characterizes the transhumanist movement. Deleuze interprets Nietzsche as the thinker of the death of Man, whose form comes only with the decline of the God-form so that this new form entails the assumption of its finitude and contains, consequently, the germ of its end. In *The Order of Things* (1994), Foucault had already noted the contingency of this 'recent invention' that is Man, which is thereby subject to disappearance. Therefore, in the framework of Deleuze's philosophy, we must understand the

Man-form as an assemblage, that is, as the product of the flows of desire in the historical stratum of knowledge, which give rise to a new reality that is not empirical but transcendental, or the condition of possibility of our relation to experience. So what is at stake in the change of form is an event in the sense we described it at the beginning.

On his own account, Deleuze (1988, 131–2) interprets the overman as the form that derives from the new relationship of forces that characterizes the present epoch. To determine the nature of the forces that create the overman, he briefly reviews those that constituted the characteristic forms of previous epochs. In the seventeenth century, the human being entered into a relationship with forces of elevation to infinity, and the result was not the Man-form but the God-form. Accordingly, the sciences of the time were general, this generality indicating an order of infinity: there was no biology, political economy, philology or linguistics, but only natural history, analysis of wealth and general grammar. The Baroque operation is, therefore, the 'unfold' as a function of infinite development. In the nineteenth century, humans came into contact with the forces of finitude, and a new type of science emerged: Life, Work and Language gave rise to biology, political economy and linguistics. Everywhere, the comparative-finite replaced the general-infinite characteristic of the seventeenth century. Thus, the human being folded into this new dimension of finitude, and thought was dominated by 'the fold' as an operative function, generating the Man-form. From the twentieth century onwards, on the other hand, the forces with which the human being comes into relationship correspond to an 'unlimited finity' as a combinatorial object, which originates the operative function of the time: the 'superfold' or 'folding of the fold', which inaugurates a form hitherto unprecedented in the world. This new form that humans take in the age of technology is that of the 'overman' or the human finitude raised to infinity by combining forces following the new model. Therefore, through the concept of 'superfold', Deleuze intends to address the symbioses and synergies that humans establish with other realities, from bacteria to technology, which raise their possibilities potentially to infinity but only as an object of combinatorics.

> It would no longer involve raising to infinity or finitude but an unlimited finity, thereby evoking every situation of force in which a finite number of components yields a practically unlimited diversity of combinations. It would be neither the fold nor the unfold that would constitute the active mechanism, but something like the Superfold, as borne out by the foldings proper to the chains of the genetic code, and the potential of silicon in third-generation machines, as well as by the

contours of a sentence in modern literature. . . . And is this unlimited finity or superfold not what Nietzsche had already designated with the name of eternal return? (Deleuze 1988, 131)

Cultural posthumanism and transhumanism: Two opposing anthropologies

This little-explored aspect of Deleuze's thought has acquired a renewed relevance with the rise of transhumanism in recent decades, not because it coincides with the anthropology proposed by transhumanists but for the reason that it allows us to undertake their critique without falling into the essentialism regarding human nature that is characteristic of a large part of the so-called bioconservatives, giving a solvent account of the human condition in the contemporary world. As Gilbert Hottois has rightly pointed out (2014, 76), in part, the success of the transhumanist movement is because 'humanism is based on an implicit and partially obsolete image of humans. The principal cause of this obsolescence is the development of modern science, techno-scientific r&d and theoretical (conceptual, paradigmatic) and technological revolutions'. So that, 'well understood, moderate transhumanism works for updating the image of humans and their place in the universe' (77). However, as I will try to show in this section, the secularization of the religious world view of human misery and the radical commitment to the individual freedom of first-world humans that transhumanism presents – uncritical both of the social and ecological implications of the enhancements it promotes and of the anti-naturalist, anthropocentric, neoliberal and post-neoliberal anthropological conception it entails – prevent us from endorsing Hottois's commendable optimism about the possibilities this cultural movement offers for rethinking anthropology in our time.

Following the above, we can affirm that Deleuze's philosophy belongs strictly to posthumanism, which refers to the philosophical current that has criticized the excesses of the humanist ideal inherited from modernity since the end of the last century. However, the term has often been used to designate the more radical currents of transhumanism, which promote the abandonment of human nature bordering on science fiction – either by abandoning the biological support of our minds or the extinction of the human species in favour of a superior lineage created by it through genetic engineering or artificial intelligence (Broncano 2020, 45–6, 52–3; Moravec 1988; Kurzweil 2005). To establish a clear distinction between the two uses of the word, I propose to describe them, respectively, as 'cultural posthumanism' and 'scientific posthumanism' – here I essentially follow Antonio Diéguez (2017, 42), who draws the same distinction, although he uses the noun transhumanism to qualify the two phenomena.

It can therefore be said that cultural posthumanism takes over from the anti-humanism that characterized a large part of the philosophies of the second half of the twentieth century, from which it differs mainly in the importance that the technological influence acquires in its critical approaches to the human condition and the growing prominence of the feminist, ecologist and decolonial critique of traditional humanism. Inescapable landmarks in this respect are Donna Haraway's *A Cyborg Manifesto* (1985) and Rossi Braidotti's *The Posthuman* (2013). Nevertheless, what is certain is that Deleuze's contributions anticipate the denunciation of the alleged universalism of human nature as an instrument of domination contained in both texts, as well as the unavoidable importance of symbiosis with other living beings and synergy with technology in future approaches to the human, placing him halfway between the anti-humanism characteristic of his time and the budding posthumanism. Cultural posthumanism consequently assumes a naturalistic position that does not aspire to modify the human condition biologically through technology, nor does it confirm the definitive failure of culture as a civilizing mechanism, but only pursues a deepening of the traditional humanist ideal in the sense of the emancipation of human beings, non-human animals and the planet earth.

But let us return to the contrast between the cultural posthumanism to which Deleuzean thought belongs and transhumanism. The anthropology that underlies each movement is radically at odds with the other, to the extent that cultural posthumanism can be said to constitute a new form of critical humanism or 'posthumanist humanism' (Hottois 2014, 35; Linares 2020, 71), whereas transhumanism presents manifestly anti-humanist anthropological assumptions (Linares 2020, 63; Broncano 2020, 53, 58–9). Let us consider the reasons for these assertions.

Transhumanists themselves often claim that this school of thought has its roots in the Renaissance and, above all, modern humanism (Bostrom 2011; Sandberg and Diéguez 2015), which is an intellectual and cultural movement in which the Renaissance's desire for integral enhancement of the human being and the attempt to achieve it through the emerging empirical science and critical reason converged. However, the truth is that the image of the human that transhumanism projects, both in anthropology and in history, really has little to do with an intellectual and cultural movement such as humanism, which optimistically emphasizes the plastic and perfectible nature of human beings.

Hence, we can define humanism as a philosophical conception that values human nature and capacities, inviting us to develop the potential they contain as a result of a cultural and evolutionary process. In other words, humanism welcomes from the outset the natural and cultural evolution that has shaped human beings and assumes with pleasure this starting point for the proposed further enhancement programme. That is why, as Linares points out (2020, 63), 'humanism cannot imply . . . the denial or the attempt to overcome the ontological foundations and evolutionary roots of our natural origin'. In this sense, humanism assumes a naturalistic approach that transhumanism rejects outright, assuming an anti-naturalistic perspective under the premise, more ideological than scientific, that indefinite material progress is possible and desirable, also when it concerns human nature. It thus describes the evolutionary characteristics of the human species as imperfect or deficient and promotes their radical modification through technology. In Fernando Broncano's words (2020, 50), transhumanism 'differs from humanist perfectionism in that it considers the human condition to be radically flawed and to find salvation only in technical redemption'. As I have shown in other work (Alcalá 2022b), this attempt to redeem the anthropological ideal is made at the expense of the human being, which is why Diéguez (2021, 83) is right when he defines it as a 'surrender of our species'.

It is no coincidence that Renaissance humanism emerged as a counter to the Christian world view, which denigrated the finite and imperfect condition of the human being in favour of their non-earthly redemption, ultimately disdaining the body opposed to the soul or spirit. Thus, discourses such as that of Giannozzo Manetti (*De dignitate et excellentia hominis*, 1452) or Pico della Mirandola (*Oratio de dignitate hominis*, 1486) founded the humanist anthropology of the Renaissance, which emphasized the plasticity and autopoietic character of human nature through the humanities, sciences and technology, but without going so far as to propose the overcoming of this nature through the latter. In contrast to the Renaissance, modernity wants to realize a moral ideal of humanity by these same cultural and scientific-technical means, as evidenced in Francis Bacon's *New Atlantis* (1627), which posits the possibility of organizing life in society according to scientific criteria. Likewise, as Hottois (2014, 26–7) points out, the principal antecedent of the meliorative theses of transhumanism is Nicolas de Condorcet (*Tableau historique des progrès de l'esprit humain*, 1793), who invokes the indefinite perfection of the human species through the life sciences and, in particular, medicine. In any case, there is a discontinuity between the proposals of both Renaissance and modern humanism and the transhumanist programme based on the radical optimism and consequent attachment to human nature espoused by the former. More recently, this is evident in the case of evolutionary biologist Julian Huxley, who coined the word 'transhumanism' in 1957 in a sense more akin to the Renaissance and modern humanist ideal than today's transhumanism: 'The human being remains human but transcends itself, realizing new possibilities of and for human nature' (cited by Hottois 2014, 30).

The particularities described concerning the transhumanist movement configure a new anthropology which, although it has the advantage of definitively establishing the renunciation of essentialism in the debate about human nature (Hottois 2014, 76–7; 2017, 486), implies, on the other hand, that human beings are by nature sick or deficient, reaching a curious harmony with religious discourses that disdain the corporeal or the biological in favour of the spirit. In this sense, indeed, transhumanist programmes generally promote the enhancement of the human body through the application of various technologies, from prostheses to genetic engineering, but only as provisional measures while waiting for the definitive abandonment of the body, understood as mere biological support for our minds, which is proposed by scientific posthumanism to be feasible (Diéguez 2021, 89).

Finally, this negative evaluation of the human biological condition in its current state and of the humanist tradition that has cultivated it for centuries determines the markedly anti-humanist character of transhumanism, that is, its express will to go beyond this condition by employing technology in a way unprecedented in the past. As Anders Sandberg openly states, 'being human is probably not the best possible state of existence' (Sandberg and Diéguez 2015, 376). The following statements by Max More are also eloquent in this respect:

> 'Transhuman' emphasizes the way transhumanism goes well beyond humanism in both means and ends. Humanism tends to rely exclusively on educational and cultural refinement to improve human nature whereas transhumanists want to apply technology to overcome limits imposed by our biological and genetic heritage. (More and Vita-More 2013, 4)

From the above, it follows that transhumanism shapes its anthropological proposal in a polarized and exclusionary way. In my opinion, this is not so much an epistemological position as a strategic one, whose aim is, on the one hand, the ideological seduction of a large part of the population and, on the other, the unqualified relegation of critical voices to the categories of 'bioconservatives' and 'technophobes' who are against progress. As Diéguez (2021, 77) has rightly shown, the category of bioconservatives lacks any theoretical consistency, given the variety of positions it encompasses, from religious orthodoxies to ecosocialists, many of which are well informed and sensible. To conclude this section, I will describe the main inconsistencies I believe transhumanism presents concerning human beings and their relationship with technology:

1. It commits the mistake of taking the well-being and aspirations of the current human individual – or, at most, those of a hypothetical posthuman individual who is thought of in the image and likeness of the former – as a criterion for decisions regarding transhumanist development, which openly aims to transcend this form of existence (see Sandberg and Diéguez 2015, 376). In this way, transhumanism begs the question (*petitio principii*) and neglects the variability of human life projects according to culture and history.

2. Accordingly, transhumanism assumes a purely neoliberal perspective which, on the one hand, does not problematize the social consequences of the individual enhancements promoted (see article 8 of 'The Transhumanist Declaration', in More and Vita-More 2013, 55) and, on the other hand, universalizes the aspirations of the current first-world individual and wrongly imposes them on future generations and different cultures. Thus, 'it is located in the ethical-political spectrum of a libertarian pragmatism (which mythicizes individual freedom, a typical dogma in the richest and most developed countries)' (Linares 2020, 69).

3. Transhumanism presents a paradoxical biologistic anti-naturalism that, on the one hand, aims to detach human beings from their evolutionary origin and, on the other hand, proposes that we humans take control of our evolution by generally biological means such as genetic engineering. This position is based on the belief that the limitations and deficits that burden human beings are due to Darwinian evolution, which transhumanists understand in the manner of Robert Nozick (1974, 314) as a 'modest deity' that can be overcome by technical means. Transhumanism also assumes the definitive failure of the techniques of cultural enhancement that characterize the programme of humanism so that, in order to continue the process of civilization, the human being must escape the randomness imposed on them by nature to take control of their evolution. The latter is not only a human right but even a moral imperative (see 'The Transhumanist Declaration', article 8 of the 2012 version, in More and Vita-More 2013, 55; and articles 4 and 5 of the 1998 version, in World Transhumanist Association 1998). Therefore, according to the transhumanists, the 'tragedy

of culture' that Georg Simmel (1968) warned us about, defining it as the fact that cultural objects cease to promote the intellectual and moral enhancement of human individuals, is the culture itself.

4. In line with the above, transhumanism espouses the claim to provide an exclusively technical solution to problems of a social, political and cultural nature, contrary to two of the main findings of the twentieth-century philosophy of technology: the intertwining of the social with the technological and the essential inability of technology to provide a substantive life project on its own. On the one hand, it is inevitable to ask whether the transhumanist pretension of developing the possibilities contained in the human through technoscience might pave the way for the emergence of new forms of domination, reproducing or even increasing the inequalities endemic to our societies. In this sense, Deleuze and Guattari (2004, 398) asserted that societies 'select' the techniques that characterize them so that technology cannot be expected to disrupt the status quo but rather to reproduce it. Langdon Winner also warned us about this intertwining of the technological and the social in a now-classic book (1986) when he pointed out that technology inevitably brings with it values. Consequently, technologies with transhumanist pretensions will probably carry over the democratic, humanitarian and ecological defects of the societies in which they emerged. As I have pointed out in another work (Alcalá 2022a), the uneven distribution of Covid-19 vaccines, which has even overshadowed this undoubted techno-scientific success, is an example of that interweaving between society and technology. On the other hand, transhumanist ideology neglects the inability of technology to provide by itself a substantive project of life, which is rather what determines the configuration of technology in every age and culture (Ortega y Gasset 1964), and even to relate in an appropriate or 'human' way to other living beings and nature, not reducing them to mere resources to be disposed of at will (Heidegger 1977).

5. Finally, transhumanism falls into the incoherence of appealing to technological determinism as an argument in favour of implementing the enhancements it promotes (see article 5 of 'The Transhumanist Declaration', World Transhumanist Association 1998) and, at the same time, suggesting the possibility of controlling the unwanted effects of technology's action on human nature and our societies (see 'The Transhumanist Declaration', article 4 of the 2012 version, in More and Vita-More 2013, 54).

In the following section, we will see how this anthropology does not imply a utopian project for the human species in the humanist sense, but only an ideological masking of the irreversible course that our societies and our relationship with the planet are taking, orientated in the end to safeguarding the interests of a minority and, in the meantime, to making as much money as possible.

From *Mundus* to *Exit*: A critique of transhumanist post-neoliberal techno-utopia

In an influential book, Pierre Dardot and Christian Laval (2014) have defined neoliberalism as a global logic with a normative character, in both meanings of the first adjective: on the one hand, it is a reason on a worldwide scale and, on the other, it shapes a world view that involves all dimensions of human existence, far transcending the realm of economics with which it is usually identified. Thus, the ideology of accepting the free market as the natural state of society, which would spontaneously tend towards abundance and welfare and would advise against state intervention, has inspired the economic policies promoted globally since the times of the governments of Ronald Reagan and Margaret Thatcher. What these authors note, however, is the materialization of neoliberalism in a practical reason for the world that shows a resilience far more obstinate than that of the ideology that inspires it and even than the measures it promotes in the political sphere. In short, the discrediting of the neoliberal ideology of laissez-faire economics since the 2008 crisis does not seem to have affected the global hegemony of neoliberalism.

Returning to the previous argument, we can affirm that transhumanism, like technology, does not promote a radical discontinuity concerning the status quo of our societies but rather develops in harmony with the powers that govern them, whether tacitly or explicitly. As I said in the introduction, transhumanism can be qualified as neoliberal insofar as it makes the promise of overcoming the limitations that follow from the biological condition of human beings a commodity for the satisfaction of individual aspirations, continuously projected into the ever-near future and carefully anticipated, in the meantime, in a series of products already available today. Hence, at first sight, transhumanism also seems to obey the neoliberal logic that shapes the contemporary world. This first commitment already contradicts the utopian character of the movement and thereby its claimed continuity with the humanist project: as Hottois (2014, 29–30) perceptively warns, the real interlocutor of transhumanism is not the human species and its conditions of existence, that is, a collective subject that aspires to an improvement in the status quo for future generations. Transhumanism, on the other hand, speaks to the individual and, more specifically, to the individual of the present: it promises a radical improvement of individual living conditions without demanding any renunciation or sacrifice. Therefore, rather than questioning the status quo, transhumanism reproduces it ad infinitum on the condition that it improves the individuals who must submit to it. Thus, unlike the messages of collective hope contained in traditional utopias, the transhumanist pseudo-utopia starts from a submission to the political and cultural framework, turning discontent or insubordination towards the biological and ultimately earthly condition of the human individual.

But it is possible to see in transhumanism a new trend in our societies, marked by a radicalization of the neoliberal ethos that leads beyond neoliberalism and its commitment to free market competition. Without wishing to fall into psychologism, I propose to express the psychological aspects of this transition in psychoanalytical terms: it seems as if a certain kind of neoliberal individual ceases to recognize the sovereignty of the reality principle and aspires to an unrestricted pleasure principle. Then, the subjection of their expectations to any constraint beyond their control becomes unbearable, whether this is the finitude that belongs to the biological condition of human beings or, in social terms, the free competition in which it is possible to lose even when at an advantage. This is a mutation of the neoliberal ethos that leads, in our societies, beyond neoliberalism, as William Davies and Nicholas Gane (2021, 23) perceptively observe, noticing 'a shift from a neoliberal order defined by a commitment to competition and governmental enforcement of rules of the game to a different type of order in which winning at all costs becomes the primary objective' (see also Davies 2014). So if '"neoliberalism" implies the use of state powers to expand and enforce market mechanisms and competition in society' (Davies and Gane 2021, 22), then the authoritarian tendencies of governments and the anti-democratic power exercised in the shadows by many multinational corporations seem to suggest the existence of goals that go beyond the logic of the market in our societies.

In this sense, Bruno Latour notes a similar shift in the attitude of many of the world's elites, who, instead of aspiring to lead the world as in the past, now seek to protect themselves from it, renouncing any collective project in favour of an individualistic retreat:

A single historical situation: it is as though a significant segment of the ruling classes (known today rather too loosely as 'the elites') had concluded that the earth no longer had room enough for them and for everyone else. Consequently, they decided that it was pointless to act as though history were going to continue to move toward a common horizon, toward a world in which all humans could prosper equally. From the 1980s on, the ruling classes stopped purporting to lead and began instead to shelter themselves from the world. (Latour 2018, 1–2)

This characterization of elites disregarding world affairs to focus on their strictly individual interests is in line with both the post-neoliberal shift in our societies and the spirit of the transhumanist movement and the technological changes it promotes. Moreover, this definitively confirms the rupture of transhumanism with the humanist project that its promoters often invoke as an antecedent since the tacit renunciation of any shared horizon while publicly maintaining the opposite places this cultural and intellectual movement closer to the ideological masking of the failure of the modern project than to any utopia. Surprisingly, Latour (2018, 30) ends up being too generous with transhumanism, defining it as a 'neo-hyper-modernism' that still aspires to a global project and is foreign to the post-neoliberal drift of our societies. Thus, he places transhumanism in the wake of the project of modern humanism, the planet Mundus model that still aspires to a shared destiny for humanity, neglecting its actual adherence to the planet Exit model, which aims only for an escape from the looming global catastrophe for a select few (Latour and Chakrabarty 2020).

Therefore, the transhumanist discourse and the technological changes that transhumanism promotes reveal the post-neoliberal drift of a movement aimed at materializing social inequalities in the biological configuration of our bodies and intellectual capacities. Yuval Noah Harari puts it eloquently:

The great human projects of the twentieth century – overcoming famine, plague and war – aimed to safeguard a universal norm of abundance, health and peace for all people without exception. The new projects of the twenty-first century – gaining immortality, bliss and divinity – also hope to serve the whole of humankind. However, because these projects aim at surpassing rather than safeguarding the norm, they may well result in the creation of a new superhuman caste that will abandon its liberal roots and treat normal humans no better than nineteenth-century Europeans treated Africans. (Harari 2017)

While Harari identifies this drift as a potential risk of transhumanism, seduced as he is by many of its promises, I believe it is its true nature, which becomes evident in the technological changes it promotes, in the light of the intertwining of the social and technology that the Deleuzo-Guattarian concept of assemblage shows. In my opinion, the ideological function of transhumanism is to contribute to the masking of the collapse of the modern collective project denounced by Latour. It is an elitist techno-utopia driven by the logic of every man for himself, devoid of any message of hope for humanity, not even the modest and naturally unjust hope that comes from free competition in the face of a state reduced to a neutral arbiter, far removed from its role as guarantor of rights. Consequently, transhumanism is a corrupt utopia.

Conclusion

In this chapter, I have tried to criticize transhumanism based on the philosophies of Deleuze and Deleuze and Guattari. With this aim, I began the first section by clarifying the limits of the Nietzschean proposal concerning the overman to explain the framework of a strong influence of technology on the humans' configuration in which transhumanism is situated. I then set out the outlines of Deleuze's anthropology of the 'unlimited finity' based on the concept of overfold, showing how it fits in with the synergy between the human and technology described by contemporary approaches within the context of cultural posthumanism. Finally, I contrasted cultural posthumanism and transhumanism from an anthropological point of view, characterizing the former as a 'posthumanist humanism' that does not aim to undermine the biological foundations of our species but to deepen the humanist ideal in the sense of emancipation and describing the latter as an anti-naturalist and individualist anthropology that secularizes the disdain for the human body characteristic of some religions. In the second section, I have tried to trace the implications for world view and history that follow from transhumanist anthropology, characterizing the movement as a post-neoliberal techno-utopia that seeks to mask the failure of the modern project of a shared global horizon to safeguard the interests of elites whose privileges are intended to be naturalized in the very biological condition of humanity, divided by the limited scope of new enhancement technologies.

From the above, I conclude that, except for its more cautious and moderate versions, transhumanism is a profoundly regressive movement from an anthropological and political point of view, which opposes the ideal of collective well-being and equity that still drives the thought and action of cultural posthumanism.

Notes

1 Francisco J. Alcalá holds a PhD in Philosophy from the University of Granada and is a postdoctoral researcher at the University of Valencia (CIAPOS programme, funded by Conselleria d'Innovació, Universitats, Ciència i Societat Digital, and European Social Fund). Email: fjalcalar@gmail.com
2 These and the other translations of non-English texts I quote are my own.

References

Alcalá, Francisco J. (2022a), 'Pensar el acontecimiento de la COVID-19: acerca del impacto sociocultural de la primera enfermedad posverdadera', in Ana Gallego Cuiñas and José A. Pérez Tapias (eds), *Pensamiento, Pandemia y Big Data*, 69–88, Berlin: De Gruyter.

Alcalá, Francisco J. (2022b), 'Plegar el pliegue. Una aproximación al desafío transhumanista en clave de Neobarroco', *Hipogrifo*, 10 (2): 17–33.

Ansell-Pearson, Keith (1997), *Viroid Life: Perspectives on Nietzsche and the Transhuman Condition*, London: Routledge.

Bostrom, Nick (2005), 'A History of Transhumanist Thought', *Journal of Evolution and Technology*, 14 (1): 1–25.

Braidotti, Rosi (2013), *The Posthuman*, Cambridge: Polity Press.

Broncano, Fernando (2020), 'El humanismo en la época del posthumanismo', in Jorge E. Linares Salgado and Edgar Tafoya Ledesma (eds), *Transhumanismo y tecnologías de mejoramiento humano*, 44–61, Ciudad de México: UNAM.

Dardot, Pierre and Laval, Christian (2014 [2009]), *The New Way of the World: On Neoliberal Society*, trans. Gregory Elliott, New York: Verso.

Davies, William (2014), *The Limits of Neoliberalism*, London: Sage.

Davies, William and Nicholas Gane (2021), 'Post-Neoliberalism? An Introduction', *Theory, Culture & Society*, 38 (6): 3–28.

Deleuze, Gilles (1988 [1986]), *Foucault*, trans. Seán Hand, Minneapolis: University of Minessota Press.

Deleuze, Gilles and Félix Guattari (2004 [1980]), *A Thousand Plateaus: Capitalism and Schizophrenia*, trans. Brian Massumi, Minneapolis: University of Minnesota Press.

Diéguez, Antonio (2017), *Transhumanismo. La búsqueda tecnológica del mejoramiento humano*, Barcelona: Herder.

Diéguez, Antonio (2021), *Cuerpos inadecuados. El desafío transhumanista a la filosofía*, Barcelona: Herder.

Foucault, Michel (1994 [1966]), *The Order of Things. An Archaeology of the Human Sciences*, trans. Alan Sheridan, New York: Vintage Books.

Gane, Nicholas (2020), 'Competition: A Critical History of a Concept', *Theory, Culture & Society*, 37 (2): 31–59.

García-Granero, Marina (2020), '¿Un transhumanismo nietzscheano?', *Logos. Anales del Seminario de Metafísica*, 53: 33–54.

Harari, Yuval Noah (2017), *Homo Deus. A Brief History of Tomorrow*, New York: Random House International.

Haraway, Donna J. (1991 [1985]) 'A Cyborg Manifesto: Science, Technology and Socialist-Feminism in the Late Twentieth Century', in Donna J. Haraway (ed.), *Simians, Cyborgs, and Women. The Reinvention of Nature*, 149–81, New York: Routledge.

Heidegger, Martin (1977 [1953]), *The Question Concerning Technology and Other Essays*, trans. William Lovitt, New York and London: Garland Publishing.

Hottois, Gilbert (2014), *Le transhumanisme est-il un humanisme?*, Bruxelles: Académie Royale de Belgique.

Hottois, Gilbert (2017), *Philosophie et idéologies trans/posthumanistes*, Paris: Vrin.

Kurzweil, Ray (2005), *The Singularity is Near. When Humans Trascend Biology*, New York: Viking.

Latour, Bruno (2018 [2017]), *Down to Earth. Politics in the New Climatic Regime*, trans. Catherine Porter, Cambridge: Polity Press.

Latour, Bruno and Dipesh Chakrabarty (2020), 'Conflicts of Planetary Proportions – A Conversation', *Journal of the Philosophy of History*, 14 (3): 1–36.

Linares Salgado, Jorge E. (2020), 'El transhumanismo no es un humanismo', in Jorge E. Linares Salgado and Edgar Tafoya Ledesma, *Transhumanismo y tecnologías de mejoramiento humano*, 63–121, Ciudad de México: UNAM.

Moravec, Hans (1988), *Mind Children: The Future of Robot and Human Intelligence*, Cambridge, MA: Harvard University Press.

More, Max and Natasha Vita-More, eds (2013), *The Transhumanist Reader*, Chichester: John Wiley & Sons.

Nietzsche, Friedrich (2005 [1888]), *The Anti-Christ, Ecce Homo, Twilight of the Idols*, trans. Judith Norman, Cambridge: Cambridge University Press.

Nietzsche, Friedrich (2006 [1892]), *Thus Spoke Zarathustra*, trans. Adrian del Caro, Cambridge: Cambridge University Press.

Nietzsche, Friedrich (2008 [1882]), *The Gay Science*, trans. Josefine Nauckhoff and Adrian del Caro, Cambridge: Cambridge University Press.

Nozick, Robert (1974), *Anarchy, State, and Utopia*, Oxford: Blackwell.

Ortega y Gasset, José (1964 [1939]), 'La meditación de la técnica', in *Obras completas tomo V (1933–1941)*, 317–75, Madrid: Revista de Occidente.

Ramsey, Grant (2013), 'Human Nature in a Post-essentialist World', *Philosophy of Science*, 80 (5): 983–93.

Samuels, Richard (2012), 'Science and Human Nature', *Royal Institute of Philosophy Supplement*, 70: 1–28.

Sánchez Meca, Diego (2016), 'Introducción al volumen IV. El pensamiento del último Nietzsche', in Friedrich Nietzsche, *Obras Completas. Volumen IV*, trans. Jaime

Aspiunza, Manuel Barrios Casares, Kilian Lavernia, Joan B. Llinares, Alejandro Martín Navarro and Diego Sánchez Meca, 17–58, Madrid: Tecnos.

Sandberg, Anders and Antonio Diéguez (2015), 'Una mirada al futuro de la tecnología y del ser humano. Entrevista con Anders Sandberg', *Contrastes*, 20 (2): 373–90.

Simmel, Georg (1968 [1911]), 'On the Concept and the Tragedy of Culture', in *The Conflict in Modern Culture and Other Essays*, trans. K. Peter Etzkorn, Columbia: Teacher College Press.

Tuncel, Yunus, ed. (2017), *Nietzsche and Transhumanism*, Newcastle: Cambridge Scholars Publishing.

Winner, Langdon (1986), *The Whale and the Reactor. A Search for Limits in an Age of High Technology*, Chicago: The University of Chicago Press.

World Transhumanist Association (1998), 'The Transhumanist Declaration'. https://itp .uni-frankfurt.de/~gros/Mind2010/transhumanDeclaration.pdf (accessed 7 March 2023).

6

Analog and Digital Power

Jens Schröter

Introduction

In the following, I want to discuss the role of the difference between analog and digital in Deleuze's paper 'Postscript on the Societies of Control'. I want to follow the idea that certain, let's say, institutions are analog and some are digital and ask what that could mean, because the usage of such terms is quite unusual (more on this below). Finally, I want to relate this discussion to wider political notions, especially 'neo-liberalism' and the alleged transformation to 'post-neoliberalism' (Davies and Gane 2021). I will start with two longer quotes on the problem and discuss them in the course of this chapter, adding context and trying to find out what it could mean that not only technologies, but also institutions might be analog or digital.

Starting point: Two quotes

I want to start my discussion with two longer quotes, in which the problem is sketched. Deleuze writes in his 'Postscript':

> The different internments or spaces of enclosure through which the individual passes are independent variables: each time one is supposed to start from zero, and although a common language for all these places exists, it is *analogical*. On the other hand, the different control mechanisms are inseparable variations, forming a system of variable geometry the language of which is *numerical* (which doesn't necessarily mean binary). Enclosures are *molds*, distinct castings, but controls are a *modulation*, like a self-deforming cast that will continuously change from one moment to the other, or like a sieve whose mesh will transmute from point to point. (1992, 4)

The second quote is from a very interesting paper, in which Mark G. E. Kelly criticizes Deleuze's conception of the control society in recourse to Michel Foucault. He argues in detail that Foucault already had a conception of control and that therefore the allegedly new conception of Deleuze is deeply indebted to Foucault. Moreover, he criticizes Deleuze's conception – I think correctly most of the time – for many implausible implications and also empirical errors. I do not want to go into this debate deeply and just turn to the passages where the question of analog and digital is present. Kelly criticizes the passage of Deleuze quoted above:

> Deleuze alleges that we have moved from analogue to digital institutions (analogique-numérique in French, though translators of the 'Postscript' get this wrong: the earlier is slavishly literal, giving us 'analogical'-'numerical'; the more recent translation renders numérique as 'digital', but oddly counterposes it to 'analogical'). While clearly several technologies have made this shift, I don't understand what this could refer to in terms of power, and am reminded of Sokal and Bricmont's assessment of Deleuze's use of technical vocabulary. (2015, 158)[1]

These are only two quotes – but they can be starting points for a discussion of the question of whether the dichotomy analog/digital can be meaningfully applied to wider fields than just, for example, media technologies.

On terminology

First of all, as Kelly correctly remarks in his quote, we have to say some words on the question of terminology. Deleuze (1990, 112) uses the notions 'analogique' and 'numérique' and adds to the last notion: 'ce qui ne veut pas dire nécessairement binaire' in the French original of his essay on the societies of control. 'Analogique' and 'numérique' translate to English as 'analog' (and indeed, as Kelly correctly observes, not as 'analogical'[2]) and 'digital', which is confirmed by Deleuze's remark that it does not necessarily mean 'binary' – because the much-discussed binary-digital code of computer technologies is just one form of a digital code. This is already a hint that the question of whether institutions are analog or digital is not reducible to the question of whether a given institution uses computers or not.

History and meaning of analog/digital

Before we proceed, it seems helpful to define analog and digital and have a look into the history of this dichotomy. It has indeed become one central distinction of media historiography (see Schröter 2020a). The transition from analog to digital media, mostly meaning the transition from photographic and analog-electronic images and analog-electronic/mechanical sound media to their digital successors, is often understood as an important caesura. It appears as a rupture, the significance of which can only be compared to the emergence of the analog media in the nineteenth century, that of the printing press or even that of writing. Nevertheless, it is understood, accentuated and weighted very differently in various theoretical frameworks (symbol- and system theory or media archaeology, etc.) – not to mention the question of when exactly the 'digital era' had begun: Is the introduction of the number zero – coming from what is India today, via the Arabs to the West in the twelfth century – or Leibniz's binary calculus of the seventeenth century to be mentioned as precursors? Or are Fourier analysis, Boole's logic, Babbage's *Difference Engine* (not built in his time), the telegraphs of the nineteenth century the actual forerunners? Or is the invention of the flip-flop in 1919 and/or the development of both analog and digital computers – soon based on semiconductor technology – in the middle of the twentieth century the condition for the rupture? Or must the diffusion of 'digital new media' into the most diverse discursive practices up to everyday life on the threshold of the twentieth to twenty-first centuries be named as the starting point for the upheaval from analog to digital? Or did the dichotomy already exist from the very beginning of writing or language, insofar as these (in contrast to images, for instance) are based on discrete sign repertoires – a thought that, however, could probably only be formulated in the late twentieth century (Goodman 1968, 159–64; I will come back to this in a moment)? Moreover, there are voices that generally warn against overestimating the 'digital revolution' and underline continuities in use, in the transported semantics and forms or in the regulating institutional structures: the family, the state, capitalism and so on still exist and do not seem to be fundamentally overcome by the change from analog to digital technologies – today there are notions like 'digital capitalism' (Staab 2019). On the one hand this shows a continuity, that capitalism is still with us. On the other hand, there is a transformation: capitalism is now digital. This specification of contemporary platform capitalism as digital is a hint that there can be – contrary to Kelly's critique – meaningful uses of 'digital' to designate institutions.

Apart from the question of the genealogy of analog and digital codes and although the terms analog and digital have a long and meaningful history independently of each other, the emergence of the *distinction* analog/digital can be dated relatively precisely. Apparently, it first appeared (in a technical sense) in a patent specification in 1938. Based on his experiences with the first American digital computer ENIAC (MacCartney 1999), Douglas R. Hartree (1946, 500) wrote in *Nature* of on 12 October 1946: 'I have found it convenient to distinguish the two classes by the terms "instruments" and "machines" respectively; the American usage is "analogue" and "digital" machines.'[3] Interestingly, the ENIAC was operating decimally rather than binary. The later establishment of the binary principle was mainly due to the simplicity of its implementation (switch on/off), which held out the prospect of the imminent feasibility of programmable, electronic-digital computers around 1945. And it prevailed, although mathematically ternary systems – based on 0, 1 and −1 – can be, in principle, much more efficient (a remarkable example of such an experiment was the SETUN[4] developed around 1958 in the USSR). It took several years before 'digital media' appeared to the general public: in 1982, the *Compact Disc* appeared as the first digital new medium on the market with a huge amount of marketing. During this time, there was a lot of talk about AAD, ADD and DDD – the question of whether recording, mixing and finally storing music production was analog or digital. The distinction became, via the 'new media', public knowledge.

According to the apparent *common sense*, this (and other developments) marks the beginning of the 'digital age' – and that's why Deleuze's paper from 1989 can already refer to the then already quite well-known difference between analog and digital.[5] But, of course, such a simple model is relatively problematic: *First*, analog media continue to exist in niches (such as analog records in the DJ scene and they have actually been having a certain comeback in the last years). Conversely, analog, (proto-)digital and hybrid media coexisted side by side in the nineteenth century already – for example, the clearly digital Morse telegraph. *Second*, digital media must remain *aesthetically* analog on the surface (and if necessary sample and/or simulate analog media), because human senses normally only process continuous signals first of all. *Third*, digital media are necessarily based on ultimately analog electronics.

After these short historical remarks, I now want to turn to the question of the definition of the terms: at one of the birthplaces of the dichotomy, the Macy conferences on what was from 1946 onwards to become known as 'cybernetics', it was by no means clear what *exactly* the difference analog/digital implies or connotes – beyond the somewhat vague contrast of continuous vs discrete (see Schröter 2020a). But in 1968, long before the spread of digital media such as CDs, Nelson Goodman formulated a symbol-theoretical conceptualization of the distinction in his book *Languages of Art*. This sign-theoretical formulation describes signs regarding the rules of their identification: Are all traits potentially constitutive for the sign? Such a symbol scheme would be analog. For example: every little shade of green might be relevant in an image. There is no criterion where to draw a line between two shades; there could always be a third, it is continuous. A digital symbol scheme has a differentiated and disjunctive repertoire, like the alphabet: the German alphabet defines twenty-six basic characters to which every written mark must be related. As Deleuze puts it – 'numerique' does not necessarily mean binary, although the repertoire of today's digital computers is defined by two 'letters': 0 and 1. A given mark must be clearly identifiable as either 'A' or 'B' (or 'C' and so forth), that is its disjunctive character, and between the two characters 'A' or 'B', there is no third one (differentiated character). If a given sign can be related to a repertoire, certain traits can be excluded as contingent (a green 'A' is as good as a black one). This distinction between analog and digital would then correspond to the distinction between image and text,[6] however it is also more widely applicable, since it allows the differentiation of continuous and discrete schemes. All of Goodman's arguments show that the difference between analog and digital, although its explicit formulation seems to begin with computing after 1945, is much older and fundamental for every civilization: images are analog, writing and money are digital and so on. Moreover, analog and digital operations always already coexisted: 'All natural systems of communication employ both analog and digital communication at some level in the system' (Wilden 1972, 155).

If we now try to describe ordinary surroundings with the analog/digital distinction, we find many examples: a ramp is analog, because it continuously changes height, while a staircase is digital, because it has a clear countable number of discrete staircase steps (although it seems to make no sense to say that a staircase accords to a disjunct and differentiated repertoire). Does this mean that analog institutions are more barrier free than digital ones? Is not a simple light switch an example of binary-digital, since it has two discrete states, on or off, while a dimmer is analog, allowing a continuum between the brightest light and darkness? Is not a door binary-digital too (open and closed) or is it analog, since it can be a little opened up to being wide open? But when we ask if the door is locked or not, this seems to be a clearly digital situation, since a door cannot be a 'little locked'. This example is not as farfetched as it may seem at first. Lacan (1988, 307–9) meditated lengthily on the door, its seemingly binary character of being either open or shut and related this explicitly to the binary code of computing.

All these questions regarding the analog and/or digital character of ordinary things seem outlandish, but we will see where our question leads us, especially if these descriptions as analog or digital add anything to our understanding of the phenomena at hand. But at least Deleuze (1990, 112; 1992; 4) obviously thinks that this makes sense, otherwise he would not have introduced it right at the beginning of his famous essay under the heading of 'logic'.

Moulding and modulation

Another notion has to be discussed, namely 'modulation'. Let us repeat the quote from Deleuze: 'Enclosures are *molds*, distinct castings, but controls are a *modulation*, like a self-deforming cast that will continuously change from one moment to the other, or like a sieve whose mesh will transmute from point to point' (1992, 4). Yuk Hui (2015) has discussed the notion and its genealogy in some detail; these points are important: First, Hui underlines that the change from moulds and moulding to modulation can be reformulated as the shift 'from a form imposing-mode to a self-regulating mode' (74). This is the usual sense that is given to Deleuze's description of the control society in comparison to Foucauldian disciplinary society: while the latter encloses the people in institutions like school, prison and so on, where they are (sometimes violently) pressed into a mould and formed, so to speak (75), control society is more about soft surveillance, observing and adapting to people's behaviour, so that the people in turn adapt. The spaces are modulated and so is the behaviour. Second, Hui insists that 'modulation is not necessarily digital, but can also be present in analogical forms' (79). Self-regulation has not necessarily something to do with the difference of analog and digital.[7] Does this mean that also moulds and moulding can be present in digital forms?[8] Then we would have a 2*2 matrix: mould/moulding and modulation, both in analog and digital forms (and perhaps hybrids).

The situation gets even more complicated, since Hui also argues, with Simondon, who was an important source on 'modulation' for Deleuze, that 'analogue is the background to the digital' (78),[9] here using 'analogue' instead of 'analogical'. Third, 'in reality, modulation and moulding co-exist' (79). That leads to the question if the relation between disciplinary society and societies of control – if this difference is valid at all, which is doubted by Kelly (2015) – is one of succession or if they coexist as different 'modes', as Hui puts it, in the same society and/or if they coexist perhaps on earth, in different societies.[10] The clear correlation of analog with the disciplinary society and moulding contrasting digital with society of control and modulation seems to have vanished. Or at least the picture is more complex.

This is underlined by the following statement: 'Perhaps it is money that expresses the distinction between the two societies best, since discipline always referred back to minted money that locks gold in as numerical standard, while control relates to floating rates of exchange, modulated according to a rate established by a set of standard currencies' (Deleuze 1992, 5, see Schröter 2020b). Confusingly in this – according to Deleuze – 'best expression' of the difference of the two forms of society, 'numerical' is connected to 'minted money' (moulding) that 'locks gold in as a standard' (also: moulding) and is associated with disciplinary society while 'control' relates to 'floating rates of exchange', which is seemingly, because of its floating character, analog.[11]

Kelly's (2015, 158/159) critique of the quote of Deleuze in the second section of this chapter is similar: '[I]t is actually discipline in his schema that is digital and control that is analogue, since it is the former that involves discrete units, whereas the latter is continuous and without boundaries.' Insofar disciplinary society is marked by discrete separated enclosures (school, prison, etc.) through which the subject passes,[12] it is not only discretized, but gives an important role to the allegedly, at least according to Lacan, digital door. The locked door is a necessary component of enclosure.

Some remarks on the digital in sociology

However, the picture becomes even more complex when we recognize some recent theoretical writings in sociology. Staab (2019) was already mentioned, who introduced the notion of 'digital capitalism'. His argument is basically centred around the reorganization of the global economy through the introduction of digital technologies and locates the decisive shift in the power of Big Tech companies (Amazon) in constructing proprietary markets. Here 'digital power' is – to cut a long story short – the power to produce a new enclosure, this time by producing enclosed markets: Amazon is not a company acting on a market, but it *is* a market (that absorbs more and more other markets). Obviously, on the one hand, this description does not match well with Deleuze's suggestion that the age of enclosures is over in control society. On the other hand, Deleuze's (1992, 6) argument, that the 'family, the school, the army, the factory are no longer the distinct analogical spaces that converge towards an owner – state or private power – but coded figures – deformable and transformable – of a single corporation that now has only stockholders', could be read as a description of Amazon, since this company, to an ever greater extent, provides material and even infrastructure for all the named institutions. Interestingly, Staab explicitly underlines that the construction of proprietary markets is a step away from the former hegemonic neoliberal regime (Staab 2019, ch. 1, the whole chapter is called 'After Neoliberalism', my translation). Here we have a first hint on how to connect the question of (post-)neoliberalism to the question of analog and digital power. I will come back to that soon.

But there is an even more radical position from sociology, namely Nassehis (2019) theory of 'digital society'. Nassehi argues that the reason why 'digitization', meaning the relentless expansion of digital technologies, was so successful or at least unavoidable is that *society is always already digital*. 'Digitization is directly related to the social structure' (18; my translation). The thesis is 'that digitization has met with so little resistance because modern society itself has always been digital' (Passoth and Rammert 2020, 315). But there seem to be two different arguments intertwined: First, since he works from the perspective of Luhmannian systems theory (Luhmann 2012; 2013)[13] he argues that every social subsystem is always already organized around a binary central difference, for example the scientific system has the central difference true/false, while in the economic system it is payment/no payment (see Nassehi 2019, 150–4). 'From this approach digitization only repeats what the differentiation of modern society into binary-coded functional systems already has done' (Baecker 2019, my translation). Second, statistics become central to modern societies.[14] Statistics discover patterns in the population. And now all of us, by ourselves, by leaving traces in social media and other digital media, take over the work of quantifying ourselves and producing statistic patterns. 'With digitization society has revealed what statistics and empirical social research have long known for a long time' (Baecker 2019, my translation). It seems to me that these two ways of arguing are different (and not necessarily related to each other), but in both cases it is about a kind of primordial societal digitality that is the precondition for digital technologies and not the other way round.[15] 'Insofar as modern society counts and relates what it counts to each other, it has always been digital' (Baecker 2019, my translation). But this last argument should make us wonder. When we speak about the fact that society 'counts', why only speak about statistics? Should the capitalist form of society not be the first and foremost example for counting, accounting and quantifying in society? Is that not a blind spot, typical for Luhmannian-inspired social theory, forgetting the obvious fact that the pattern production of data companies is mainly performed to generate sensational profits. To be sure: Nassehi discusses, since it is simply unavoidable, 'digital capitalism' and several approaches that try to describe this phenomenon. He mentions the 'colonization of the world through numbers' (2019, 298), feared by some – but it is never mentioned that capitalism was long before the emergence of digital technologies exactly that kind of colonization.[16] Early computing machines, like the abacus, were mainly used in calculating money and an invention like double-entry bookkeeping was a central technique of counting (Chiapello 2007). Beniger (1986), Agar (2003) and recently Beller (2021) have analysed in detail how economic and political regimes of quantification – capitalism – resulted in digital computing. And as was argued above (with Goodman 1968): language is a digital code itself, therefore society was always dominated by digital codes – therefore even the title of Nassehis (2019) book can be criticized. Does it really make sense to say that we are entering a digital society now?

Continuation and discretization

A preliminary result of the discussion so far is first, that Kelly's critique of Deleuze – 'Deleuze alleges that we have moved from analogue to digital institutions. [. . .] I don't understand what this could refer to in terms of power' (2015, 158) – is insofar unfounded since there are institutions and other relevant entities like the door, language, money, statistics and so on that can be described as digital and exercise power in one way or another. But second, the situation seems complex, if not confused. On the one hand we have very local, concrete phenomena like the door and on the other hand 'society as such' that can be described as digital. How are these phenomena related? And moreover: Does this situation not suggest that describing these phenomena as digital is not very helpful? And what about the analog part of the discussion? It should become clear that the popular talk of 'digitization', vaguely meaning the wide introduction of computing technologies and its alleged consequences, is not correctly understood when societies[17] before the introduction of computing are described as being 'analog' and without any digitality at all.[18] I cannot answer these questions here; there would be a lot more research necessary to reach comparative studies of digitization.[19]

I want to insist here that analog and digital have to be seen, first and foremost, as processes or operations and not mainly as static entities. This is already true in comparatively simple technologies such as CD players. They transform the digital data on the disc into analog sounds that can be heard (and before the analog sound waves of the music were turned into digital data to store them on the disc). Analog is becoming-analog and digital is becoming-digital (see Deleuze/Guattari 1987, 232–309). There is a multitude of heterogeneous practices that produce and stabilize the analog/digital distinction in various fields in the first place. *Operations of discretization* can be seen as processes of cutting and dividing, analysing, measuring and counting, that is, transforming given continua into discrete and possibly countable sets of elements. *Operations of continuation*, on the other hand, comprise processes of connecting, gluing together, homogenizing, smoothing, synthesizing, reconstructing continuous signals, that is, the transformations of sets of discrete elements into continua. Operations of continuation and discretization occur in complex and even historically changing constellations. At given points in time, accumulations of such procedures lead to historical shifts on a larger scale; shifts that can be described as 'digitization' (and the respective construction of a corresponding 'analog'). A working hypothesis can be that one can probably also observe phases of 'analogization' (and the construction of a corresponding 'digital'). It is also to be expected that operations of discretization and continuation have different functions in different cultural contexts.

The opposition of discretization/continuation reminds of the difference of striated and smooth spaces (Deleuze and Guattari 1987, 474–500). Seen in that way, we can observe that political shifts, like that described as a mutation from neoliberalism to post-neoliberalism, be it in the form of proprietary markets (Staab 2019) or an increasing borderization – 'forms of nationalism and protectionism that refocus attention on territory and borders as the objects and limits of sovereign power' (Davies and Gane 2021, 13) – are operations of discretization that cut into the flows and enclose fields. In that sense, to construct proprietary markets or to reconstruct a certain sovereignty by enclosing borders are operations of digitization that striate space. In both cases, the door as a fundamental digital operation plays a central role. In the case of proprietary markets on a platform, it is the *access* that can be seen as a door operation. In the case of borders, this is even more obvious – since either one can pass the border or not. In these two cases, it becomes clear that the different levels can be systematically connected. These operations are always also operations of moulding and modulation. If borders play a heightened role in post-neoliberalism, this means that the modulation of your status is dependent on the crossing of the digital border, while you are moulded in being a citizen of a certain state.

Analog and Digital Power

Power can be described as a set of operations that either produces separations (by discretizing for example space by borders) that cut flows, or it produces continuations for wanted flows of energy, people, information or whatever. Both can happen at the same time at different levels. These operations work on the level of the local (the door) up to the level of the global (borders) or the societal (e.g. discretizing the continuum of needs by money). Therefore, Deleuze's hint in his 'Postscript' pointed to an important feature of power: the power to separate (digital) and to connect (analog) are basic operations whose configurations can be seen as a general scheme to describe different historical constellations. However, this is a research programme that is just beginning to emerge right now.

Notes

1 He alludes to Alan Sokal's and Jean Bricmont's (1998, 154–68) devastating critique of Deleuze and Guttaris's philosophy regarding their use of natural-scientific terminology. Unfortunately, they are mostly right – but 'analog' and 'digital' in the work of Deleuze are not terms that are criticized by them. We will see that the use of 'analog' and 'digital' to designate certain institutions can be meaningful.

2 Although Deleuze also writes (1992, 6): 'The family, the school, the army, the factory are no longer the distinct analogical spaces that converge towards an owner – state or private power – but coded figures – deformable and transformable – of a single corporation that now has only stockholders.' In this quote, 'analogical' seems to be actually more correct than 'analog', because Deleuze seemingly wants to say that the different spaces are *similar* to each other and not 'analog' in any technical sense, although an analog relation between two signals (as compared to a digital one) has obviously something to do with the similarity of the signals (we disregard here the question if it is really true that the family, the school, etc. are in some sense transformations of the same corporation today). This ambiguity will stay with us; I will come back to that.

3 The analog computers developed in the 1930s – such as Vannevar Bush's particularly important *Differential Analyser* – were apparently not yet *called* 'analog computers' at that time, as seen in Bush (1931). At that time, the term 'computer' was still reserved for (mostly female) calculating people.

4 See Malinovskiy and Brusentsov (2001). Various reasons prevented the further development of ternary computers in the USSR, which switched to the IBM standard in 1972 at the latest. Only when the so-called Moore's Law comes to an

104   *Deleuze, Guattari and the Schizoanalysis of Post-Neoliberalism*

end and further miniaturization of the established architecture will no longer be possible, could such computer concepts – besides others like quantum computing – get a chance again.

5 There are other passages in Deleuze where he uses the distinction analog/digital. In the *Postscript* itself, he mentions the 'numerical language of control' (1992, 5), which again seems to suggest that control societies are 'more' digital than disciplinary societies. In other books by Deleuze, we can also find allusions to the analog/digital distinction and its relation to media; see Deleuze (1989, 265), where Deleuze discusses in passing and rather enigmatically the 'numerical image'.

6 Consequently, a term such as 'digital images' – based, for example, on images consisting of pixels – would be simply absurd in the context of this concept: 'In other words, nondotted pictures belong to as many digital schemes as do dotted pictures' (Goodman and Elgin 1988, 128). For Goodman, '[. . .] no symbol by itself is digital, and none by itself is analog' (Goodman and Elgin 1988, 127). Image and text are even interchangeable when the schema changes: Is 'oo' the presence of two specimens of the fifteenth letter of the alphabet (digital) or a picture of eyes (analog)?

7 Think of a thermostat forming a self-regulating system with a heater – it does not matter whether the thermostat is analog or digital.

8 See the following quote from *Cinema 2* by Deleuze (1989, 27): 'The similar and the digital, resemblance and code, at least have in common the fact that they are moulds, one by perceptible form, the other by intelligible structure: that is why they can so easily have links with each other. [. . .] But modulation is completely different; it is a putting into variation of the mould, a transformation of the mould at each moment of the operation.' See also Harper and Savat (2016). Apart from the fact that 'analogical' is here replaced by the 'similar', it is somewhat irritating that the 'digital' is itself seen as a 'mould [. . .] by intelligible structure'. Obviously, the digital is here not associated with modulation – the last term seems to designate a mobilization of moulds; Hui (2015) argues in the same direction.

9 This argument is in accordance with a remark made in the section on the history of the analog/digital-distinction, namely that every digital technology is ultimately based on analog electronics.

10 I made this suggestion in Schröter (2020b), where I argued that the societies of the Global North tend to be societies of control, while in the societies of the Global South you find examples closer to disciplinary societies.

11 The shift described here by Deleuze relates to the end of the Bretton Woods global economic regime around 1973 (see Schröter 2020b).

12 Kelly emphasizes, rightly in my mind, that Deleuze's argument is flawed anyway, since schools, prisons and so on obviously still exist in our so-called societies of control.

13 See Luhmann (2012, 55): 'In the terminology of informatics, we could say that structural couplings *digitize analog* relations. [. . .] Since the environment and the other systems within it always operate simultaneously with the given reference

system of observation, we are initially dealing only with analog (parallel) relations. The participating systems cannot extract any information, for this requires digitization. Structural couplings must therefore first convert analog into digital relations if they are to influence a system.'

14 I think it is very problematic that Nassehi does not quote studies like that of Beniger (1986) or Agar (2003) – obviously he and most of his sociological commentators do not know that his argument is not as 'original' (Passoth and Rammert 2020, 315) as they think. Beniger (1986) is also interesting in our discussion here, because he already postulated a 'control revolution' three years before Deleuze (1989) – and dated its origin back to the nineteenth century, which seems to come close to Kelly's argument (2015), identifying Deleuze's 'control society' with Focault's notion of 'disciplinary society', but only the other way round.

15 This would fit with an argument by Deleuze (1988, 39): 'In other words, the machines are social before being technical.' Interestingly, in this book on Foucault that appeared only a few years before his 'Postscript', he does not mention the difference between analogical or analog vs numerical and digital at all, and modulation is mentioned only a very few times (58, 103, 147).

16 Also in a very literal sense: the expansive accumulation of capital has subjected the whole world, turning, for example, black bodies in the Global South, into commodities to be exchanged against money.

17 One must be very careful not to be Eurocentric. While language and money as digital systems may be present in virtually all societies, other societies might operate in different ways. Eglash (1999, 192) warned: 'Social theorists from many different disciplines have used two mathematical concepts [. . .], recursion and the analog-digital dichotomy, in constructing their ideologies.'

18 After the Covid-19 pandemic and the diffusion of videoconferencing systems like Zoom, it became popular to call a meeting in person 'analog'. Nothing could be more wrong (the right dichotomy would be virtual/actual), although this itself is symptomatic of the false and way too narrow identification of digitality with binary computing technologies.

19 This is a topic we are intensely discussing at the University of Bonn. The following passages are based on discussions with Christoph Ernst, Kathrin Friedrich and Dominik Maeder.

References

Agar, Jon (2003), *The Government Machine. A Revolutionary History of the Computer*, Cambridge, MA: MIT Press.

Baecker, Dirk (2019), 'Auf dem Weg zu einer Theorie der digitalen Gesellschaft: Rezension zu "Muster – Theorie der digitalen Gesellschaft" von Armin Nassehi',

Soziopolis: Gesellschaft beobachten. https://nbn-resolving.org/urn:nbn:de:0168-ssoar
-81735-2 (accessed 6 February 2023).

Beller, Jonathan (2021), *The World Computer. Derivative Conditions of Racial Capitalism*, Durham: Duke University Press.

Beniger, James (1986), *The Control Revolution. Technological and Economic Origins of the Information Society*, Cambridge, MA: Harvard University Press.

Bush, Vannevar (1931), 'The Differential Analyzer: A New Machine for Solving Differential Equations', *Journal of the Franklin Institute*, 212 (4): 447–88.

Chiapello, Eve (2007), 'Accounting and the Birth of the Notion of Capitalism', *Critical Perspectives on Accounting*, 18 (3): 263–96.

Davies, William and Nicholas Gane (2021), 'Post-Neoliberalism? An Introduction', *Theory, Culture and Society*, 38 (6): 3–28.

Deleuze, Gilles (1988), *Foucault*, Minneapolis: University of Minnesota Press.

Deleuze, Gilles (1989), *Cinema 2. The Time-Image*, Minneapolis: University of Minnesota Press.

Deleuze, Gilles (1990), 'Les sociétés de contrôle', *L'autre journal*, 1: 111–14.

Deleuze, Gilles (1992), 'Postscript on the Societies of Control', *October*, 59: 3–7.

Deleuze, Gilles and Felix Guattari (1987), *A Thousand Plateaus. Capitalism and Schizophrenia 2*, trans. B. Massumi, Minneapolis: University of Minnesota Press.

Eglash, Ron (1999), *African Fractals. Modern Computing and Indigenous Design*, New Brunswick: Rutgers University Press.

Goodman, Nelson (1968), *Languages of Art: An Approach to a Theory of Symbols*, Indianapolis: Bobbs-Merrill.

Goodman, Nelson and Catherine Elgin (1988), *Reconceptions in Philosophy and other Arts and Sciences*, Indianapolis: Hackett Pub. Co.; London: Routledge.

Harper, Tauel and David Savat (2016), *Media after Deleuze*, London and New York: Bloomsbury.

Hartree, Douglas R. (1946), 'The ENIAC, an Electronic Computing Machine', *Nature*, 158: 500–6.

Hui, Yuk (2015), 'Modulation after Control', *New Formations*, 84–85: 74–91.

Kelly, Mark G. E. (2015), 'Discipline is Control: Foucault contra Deleuze', *New Formations*, 84–85: 148–62.

Lacan, Jacques (1988), *The Seminar of Jacques Lacan, Book II: The Ego in Freud's Theory and in the Technique of Psychoanalysis, 1954–1955*, New York: Norton.

Luhmann, Niklas (2012), *Theory of Society, Volume 1*, trans. R. Barrett, Stanford: Stanford University Press.

Luhmann, Niklas (2013), *Theory of Society, Volume 2*, trans. R. Barrett, Stanford: Stanford University Press.

MacCartney, Scott (1999), *Eniac: The Triumphs and Tragedies of the World's First Computer*, New York: Walker.

Malinovskiy, Boris N. and Nikolai P. Brusentsov (2001), 'Nikolai Petrovich Brusentsov and his Computer SETUN', in G. Trogemann, A. Y. Nitussov and W. Ernst (eds),

Computing in Russia. *The History of Computer Devices and Information Technology Revealed*, 104–7, Braunschweig: Vieweg.

Nassehi, Armin (2019), *Muster. Theorie der digitalen Gesellschaft*, München: Beck.

Passoth, Jan-Hendrik and Werner Rammert (2020), 'Digitale Technik entspricht digitaler Gesellschaft?', *Soziologische Revue*, 43 (3): 312–20.

Schröter, Jens (2020a), 'Analogue/Digital – Opposition or Continuum', Preprint, *MediArXiv*. https://mediarxiv.org/x7eq3/ and https://doi.org/10.33767/osf.io/x7eq3 (accessed 6 February 2023).

Schröter, Jens (2020b), 'Money, Technology and Capitalism in Deleuze's "Postscript"', *Coil of the Serpent*, 5: 66–76. https://coilsoftheserpent.org/2020/07/money-technology-and-capitalism-in-deleuzes-postscript/ (accessed 6 February 2023).

Sokal, Alan and Jean Bricmont (1998), *Fashionable Nonsense. Postmodern Intellectuals' Abuse of Science*, New York: Picador.

Staab, Philipp (2019), *Digitaler Kapitalismus. Markt und Herrschaft in der Ökonomie der Unknappheit*, Berlin: Suhrkamp.

Wilden, Anthony (1972), *System and Structure. Essays in Communication and Exchange*, New York: Tavistock.

7

Agroecology and *Zoë*

Beyond the *Bios* of Neoliberalism

Adrian Konik

Introduction

In 'Postscript on the Societies of Control', Deleuze advances that control societies began replacing disciplinary societies after World War II and intimates that through the *dividuality* they precipitate (1992, 5), the author function is becoming so multiplied, attenuated and rarefied that it can no longer serve as a viable site of minoritarian war machine construction. That is, because the ceaseless economic dividuation definitive of dividuality renders it akin to the schizophrenic 'body-without-organs' thematized in *The Logic of Sense* (1990, 88), Deleuze emphasized not the minoritarian possibilities of cyberspace, but rather its vulnerability to 'jamming . . . piracy and . . . viruses', while simultaneously looking beyond the internet's striated channels for 'new weapons' (1992, 4) – weapons which might comprise nomadic war machines in an era otherwise dominated by digitality. Deleuze's latter contention contrasted with the then nascent enthusiasm over digital connectivity, with the first electronic mail having been sent over twenty years earlier, and the concept/ term already established by 1992. But for Deleuze, proliferation of information against a hegemonic project does not necessarily entail opposition, unless such 'counter information' also entails 'an act of resistance', similar to artistic generation of new space(s) for thought and relationships (1998, 18) – which differs from desires simply following the established channels of the image of thought presented by email, as the communicative nexus of digital technology, neoliberal capitalist economics and liberal democratic dialogue. Deleuze's position has been critiqued in light of Web 2.0 – which he did not experience –

because emerging digital war machines have been identified within its growing dimensions of cyber interactivity/interface developments. However, while focus on them has tended to eclipse Deleuze's own trajectory towards the construction of future war machines in spaces *beyond* those of neoliberal cyber channels, renewed interest in this trajectory has resulted from recent developments in global food production.

To explore this, in what follows, first, Foucault's contentions concerning the author function will be considered, because of their important bearing on Deleuze's intimation that, through dividuality, multiplied, attenuated and rarefied variants thereof persist in control societies as mechanisms of domination. Correlatively, what will be considered is Deleuze's argument that such dividualizing dynamics operate in ways so inimical to political agency, that nomads today – in addition to disrupting digital flows by jamming and viruses – also need to look for new weapons beyond those of cyberspace. In this regard, focus will fall on how the vestiges of individual *corporeality, temporality, identity* and *geneses* are transmuting into virtual forms more assimilable into the majoritarian neoliberal-digital economy, but which simultaneously diminish the minoritarian possibilities of cyberspace. Second, the contrasting growth in the minoritarian possibilities of agricultural space, under the *Via Campesina* or peasant way, will be thematized as an important offline domain of minoritarian–majoritarian interface. And this is because, in order for societies of control to become a fait accompli – rather than a hegemonic project – the above processes of dividualization need to be extended over global food production. However, currently only around 30 per cent of global food requirements are met by corporate agribusiness, while the remaining 70 per cent is still produced the 'peasant way' (Bello 2022, 18). Third, within this majoritarian–minoritarian interface, agroecology will be advanced as an important war machine, with reference to Deleuze and Guattari's articulation of the concept via the three features of Franz Kafka's minor literature. As will be argued, agroecology *deterritorializes* majoritarian agricultural approaches by inflecting farming practices in minoritarian ways, and that out of the ensuing *political immediacy, collective assemblages of enunciation* are emerging – as socio-political forces increasingly capable of reshaping land ownership around the world. Moreover, what will also be thematized is how Deleuze and Guattari's concept of minoritarian becoming – although illustrated through Kafka's literature – has less to do with the author function than it has with the 'infinite life' of *zoë* (Kerényi 1976, xxxiv–xxxvi), so important to agroecology too.

Multiplication, attenuation and rarefaction of the 'author function' in societies of control

For Foucault, discursive production – particularly in modern society – is subject to controls/organizational schemas initiated to avoid its random proliferation, by channelling its generative force instead into orbit around certain constructs (1972, 216). Key to this is the principle of an author, underwritten by the (inadvertent) eighteenth-century concept of 'man' he explores in *The Order of Things*, and which – its ephemerality notwithstanding (Foucault 2003, 422) – went on to inform humanistic conceptions of the author as an existential ground for statements. Against this, Foucault contends that the 'author function' is less a site of discursive agency than a construct which makes 'positions for a subject' possible within a discourse (2002, 98, 122). And in 'What is an Author?' Foucault specifically focuses on how the figure of the author served the ends of control (1969, 115, 124). First, Foucault recalls that many mythical stories/folk tales previously circulated without concern for an author's identity, but that from the Middle Ages such identity became increasingly imperative to establish, in order to censure authors whenever their discourses were deemed morally transgressive (1969, 124–6). Second, Foucault indicates that, although such religious bias diminished in the nineteenth century through progressive secularization, it was replaced by an analogous disciplinary prejudice, as the 'author function' gained sufficient momentum to generate 'initiators of discursive practices', whose work provided criteria for the acceptance of *other* writings – as in the case of Marx and Freud (1969, 131–6).

That is, on the one hand, Foucault's subsequent genealogical trajectory partly traced the multiplication and attenuation of the author function under the emerging eighteenth-century disciplinary regime. This was when the 'political axis of individualization' was reversed, through replacement of the previously individualized sovereign with the anonymous bureaucracy of government, and the correlative individualization of each member of the previously anonymous masses (Foucault 1991, 192–3). But while the technology of the dossier involved collating evidence on every disciplinary subject's activities over time, to determine how each had hitherto *authored* their life, this multiplication of the author function was also accompanied by its attenuation, because such individualized authorial activity was evaluated against normative criteria derived from treatises on societal development *authored* by various initiators of discursive practices (Foucault 1991, 177–92). Indeed, both these inflections of the author function were 'correlative with the new techniques of power' (Foucault 1991, 160), exemplified in those disciplinary discursive practices predicated on the principle of individual rational autonomy – like those of Marx, as indicated above.

But on the other hand, in relation to the discourse(s) initiated by Freud, the author function, so multiplied and attenuated, also became subject to rarefaction. That is, the above principle of rational autonomy derived in part from the imperative, since the Middle Ages (via Aquinas and against the backdrop of Aristotle), to construct the author as a 'knowing subject' based on the rationality they were believed to share with God (Foucault 2005, 26). However, while construction of the author as a 'rational entity' could lead to their indictment for perceived transgression in their work, ambiguity derived from how certain registers always decouple the author from their work – for example, allegories employed by a 'fictional narrator' (Foucault 1969, 127–31). And in the nineteenth century, such anomalies were co-opted into discursive practices initiated by Freud and others, which worked to rarefy the author function in relation to the concept of sexuality as an inherently *latent* force. Historically, such conceptions contrasted with the principle of 'self-mastery' obtained through growing maturity of insight, which had pervaded the Classical era and the Roman/Hellenistic worlds through Platonic *epistrophē* and the first-/second-century CE 'cultures of the self', respectively; moreover, such conceptions were also in tension with the principle of 'self-decipherment' around which the subsequent confessional practices of Christian pastoral power became orientated (Foucault 2005, 209–23). Nevertheless, in the nineteenth century, the vestiges of such self-mastery and self-decipherment were further eclipsed, as 'decipherment *of* the subject' came to underpin the new therapeutic procedures of secularized/medicalized confession, which correlatively advanced individual *in*capacity to meaningfully descend into either 'the depths of oneself' (Foucault 2005, 85, 222) or 'the depths of the soul' (Foucault 1979, 143). Such decipherment *of* the subject was also increasingly legitimated by the medical procedures surrounding its implementation, which were inscribed in scientific terms, and connected to the new notion of sex as the perennially opaque origin of all psychological anomalies – which rendered interpretation of its latent intimations *by* a medical practitioner crucial, before more mature self-understanding could occur, and healing could take place (Foucault 1998, 65–7). Indeed, within this context, the ostensibly *increasing* mental (and physical) fragility of modern people was generally propagated (Foucault 1967, 171–2), which contributed both to the progressive 'infantilization' of the adults in question (Foucault and Deleuze 1972, 210), and to a proportional rarefaction of the author function such adults might assume.

However, Deleuze maintains that reference to 1950s/1960s society as 'disciplinary' is anachronistic, because the changes wrought by Keynesian economics during and after World War II had by then already birthed societies of control (1992, 3). In this regard, Keynesian orientation around trade regulation, public ownership of key assets and social spending (Klein 2008, 54–7) sought to maintain socio-economic stability by facilitating 'full employment' (Keynes 2018, 15, 222, 333, 339) – thereby empowering individuals to *author* their own life paths. However, such exponential multiplication of the author function was also coterminous with its progressive attenuation, because existential authorial capacity from the Great Acceleration onwards was also increasingly articulated *in terms of* other initiated discursive practices. These advanced the 'sovereignty' of the consumer and valorized their agency in the supermarket – despite the irony of such consumerism serving as compensation for experiences of subjugation and exploitation in the workplace (Princen 2005, 65, 75–6). Moreover, such attenuation of the author function thus multiplied, coincided once more with its rarefaction, as psychological research expanded after World War II. Indeed, a 'boom in psychotherapies' saw its refinement into an array of specializations, and its application within a multiplicity of domains beyond the university (McAdams 1997, 13). And this legitimated the latency of sexuality as an additional inscrutable authorial register, indissociable from rarefaction of the author function, as discussed.[1]

However, as mentioned earlier, Deleuze intimates that through the *dividuality* precipitated by societies of control (1992, 5), the author function is becoming so multiplied, attenuated and rarefied that it can no longer serve as a viable site of minoritarian war machine construction. Thus, instead of seeing catalytic minoritarian capacity in related majoritarian developments like email, Deleuze instead emphasized the vulnerability of online exchanges to sabotage and piracy, while simultaneously looking beyond cyberspace for 'new weapons' (1992, 4). And closer consideration of certain points he makes in 'Postscript on the Societies of Control' arguably indicates the extent to which Deleuze's concerns remain warranted.

First, Deleuze points to the new multiplication of the author function as a product of intensified marketing, which has even birthed the notion that 'corporations have a soul' (1992, 6). That is, given the emerging limitations of Keynesian capitalism after its preceding 'thirty golden years' (Labonté and Ruckert 2019, 94), the nascent 1970s neoliberal capitalism was obliged to expand globally. To such ends, the domestic protectionism of Keynesianism was deemed inhibitory of (in)dividuals' initiative to *author* their life paths in more enterprising ways (Powell 1971, 12–14). Instead, neoliberalism focused on a 'policy suite' that included increasing trade deregulation, privatization of state assets, and reduction in social spending (Cahill 2014, 15), to *initiate* discursive practices orientated around dissolving the erstwhile Keynesian social safety net, and correlatively precipitating more market-related authorial innovation. Of course, the initiators of such discourse were governments in association with corporations, and their collective interests were also thereafter served through ensuing neoliberal legislation that extended corporations' rights – even granting them de facto political agency. Indeed, for many, the 2010 US Supreme Court ruling to this effect made it possible for corporations to use their immense financial resources to determine the outcome of elections and to co-opt the allegiance of elected representatives (Clements 2012, 2).

Second, though, the above multiplication of the author function became indissociable from its attenuation, as the primary device of social control became 'the operation of markets' (Deleuze 1992, 6). That is, the above growth of corporate political power *beyond* that of voters reflects a far broader trend, whereby creative individual critical-constructive authorship is increasingly being drowned out by ranges of comparable corporate products/services, which are advertised moreover across multiple platforms, through high-end marketing beyond most entrepreneurs' means. Yet, even corporate authorship itself is ultimately subject to attenuation by the very dimensions of its economy. After all, the more a corporation establishes monopoly over a market, the more the requirements/infrastructure of this now-established market begin to factor into cost–benefit analyses by management, leading to 'responsible innovation' involving the rejection or indefinite shelving of innovations – no matter how good – when their introduction would not financially complement the status quo (Lukovics, Nagy and Buzás 2019, 138).

Third, the resultant multiplying and attenuating author function became subject to rarefaction. This no longer occurred principally through psychotherapeutic channels as during the Great Acceleration, partly because the 'individualistic self-empowerment' narrative of neoliberalism marginalized enduring psychotherapeutic relationships, in favour of 'facilitative counselling skills' focused instead on dealing practically with destabilizing issues as they arise (Wilson 2003, 3–4). But while such developments diminished emphasis on the latency of sexuality as an additional inscrutable authorial register, a myriad other virtual registers and personae were proliferating within an expanding cyberspace – all predicated on the increasing fragmentation of erstwhile individuality, through its endless *dividualization* within a virtual dimension of economic

Agroecology and Zoë 115

containment. That is, like the nineteenth-century medical processes related to the latency of sexuality, digital processes involve the commercial fragmentation of individuality, through the introduction of a newly imagined virtual realm, over which individuals then increasingly diffract themselves, in response to related interpellations. However, unlike in the nineteenth century where the latency of sexuality functioned as the primary virtual realm commodified in this way, in control society the virtual realm of cyberspace effectively comprises a multiplicity *of* commercial realms. Accordingly, while a nineteenth-century individual may have been haunted by the dark doppelgänger of the *Id*, as its protean desires struggled to manifest in ways inimical to decorum, *dividuals* are haunted by the protean desires *of* cyberspace, as these struggle to manifest in ways inimical to the formation of *in*dividuality. After all, the resultant *dividuality* is something required within a neoliberal-digital context, to translate the Keynesian remains of disciplinary individuality – its vestiges of *corporeality, temporality, identity* and *geneses* – into rarefied forms more easily digestible by the dominant economic system.

In this regard, first, Deleuze points to the rarefaction of disciplinary *corporeality*, by referring to how signatures are being replaced in control societies by a 'code' or 'password' (1992, 5), and the implications of this become clearer through reflection on personal banking. Within the disciplinary era, requirements for signatures tied bank accounts to the body and mind of the account holder. Thus, the *individuality* of a signature – its division being fraudulent – coupled the individual to the economy within 'an "ideological" representation of society' (Foucault 1991, 194), consisting of embodied beings engaged in commercial competition. Accordingly, as passwords replace such signatures, they proportionately reduce emphasis on a corporeal-economic identity and give rise to a virtual-economic identity. But the latter, while divisible among the trustworthy, is also vulnerable to hijacking either in part, through for example credit card theft, or in its entirety. And in the year of Deleuze's death, the concept of such complete hijacking of a virtual-economic identity was already commonplace enough to serve as the narrative basis for Irwin Winkler's 1995 blockbuster *The Net*. Arguably, though, such scenarios are the consequence of how the *dividuality* of a given code/password renders it neither a function of a person's 'civil status, nor . . . fictional', but rather – like the author function – something situated somewhere 'in the breach' (Foucault 1969, 123).

Second, for Deleuze, dividuality sees the regimented single *temporality* of disciplinary individuality rarefied into proliferating virtual slivers, located within the multiple temporalities of cyberspace, where corporate institutions are themselves now also 'metastable states' (1992, 5). Accordingly, obliged to respond virtually to corporate interpellations from different temporalities, dividuality entails an increasingly fragmentary constellation that 'orbit[s] . . . a continuous network' of economies (Deleuze 1992, 6) – alternately pulsing with capital flow, or fading into devaluation. But any imagined virtual constellation shimmering in hauntingly human form would be an abstraction, since each proliferating virtual fragment is effectively a portal through which digital-neoliberalism taps into the *time* of the (erstwhile in)dividual, leading to an increasingly schizophrenic existence *of* constant commodification. Indeed, Deleuze expressly links neoliberalism as a transmuting 'sieve' (1992, 4), to his concept of the schizophrenic body as a 'sieve', which instead of impenetrable surfaces has only surfaces that 'split open', leading to chaotic intertwining of otherwise disparate things (1990, 87). Correlatively, Deleuze's characterization of the schizophrenic body as a 'gaping depth' representing 'a fundamental involution' that draws everything into itself (1990, 87), would be an apt description of the maelstrom that *is* digital neoliberalism. However, what it draws into itself without cessation, through the above virtual portals of commodification, is the *time* of the (erstwhile in)dividual – time previously corralled within and ushered between actual disciplinary enclosures. That is, neoliberalism dividualizes this time by siphoning it through multiplicities of interfaces into its striated system of virtual containment, which is 'extensive, divisible, and molar' (Deleuze and Guattari 1987, 33, 238) enough to co-opt and channel such temporal flows as per global market whims.

Third, for Deleuze, an isomorphism exists between rarefaction of disciplinary *identity* into identifiable dividual desires for commodification, and the mutability of the market through which the 'serpent' of neoliberalism constantly sheds its skin (Deleuze 1992, 5, 7). At first glance, processes through which this rarefaction has been normalized *do* appear to multiply, rather than rarefy, the author function. As Turkle explains, following Web 2.0, earlier notions of a consistent identity were increasingly replaced by the concept of 'identity as multiplicity', where in each case different '[v]irtual personae' function 'as objects-to-think-with' (1995, 260). But to recall Foucault's earlier contention that the author function primarily *reveals* possible subject positions in a discourse, along with the fact that *authors* create personae, is to see how recourse to the virtual personae valorized by Turkle, in principle, allows the cyber system itself to assume the author function. Indeed, as an authorial system that increasingly determines the narratives (if not fates) of its now dividualized characters, it exemplifies its origins in the Greek term for steersman, *cybernetes* (κυβερνήτης), as is so poignantly reflected in the 'spectacle/performance paradigm', where passive consumption of media artefacts is accompanied by active DIY media production (Longhurst et al. 2017, 81). While the latter may reflect some consumer creativity, this nonetheless unfolds largely at the behest of 'horizontally integrated media conglomerates' that foster such DIY production and dissemination over multiple virtual platforms (Jenkins 2006, 136), precisely *because* of the viral marketing/research facilitated by such expressions. Thus, in the face of virtual personae and profiles proliferating online, as aesthetic inflections of corporate content are virtually shared, Deleuze could still maintain that such expressions derive their value *from* the dividual desires they render identifiable as targets for future marketing, rather than *as* markers of emerging individuality.

Indeed, fourth, Deleuze makes it clear that while disciplinary enclosures persist in control societies, their containment capacity has been usurped by 'debt' (1992, 6), which erodes the *geneses* of disciplinary individuality. Although debt has always accompanied capitalism, before World War II it was viewed mostly in pejorative terms and was thus generally entered into as a last resort, or at least with due trepidation (Jentzsch 2006, 81). After all, since disciplinary emphases on the 'progress of societies' and on the 'geneses of individuals' sought to 'economize' life (Foucault 1991, 160–2), debt was seen to evince the ethical failings of economic negligence or impulsiveness. However, subsequent Keynesian capitalism sought to de-stigmatize debt, via the popularization/ normalization of the instalment credit mechanism, such that by the mid-1950s, around two-thirds of American households had *some* form of debt (Katona 1964, 231). Moreover, thereafter, neoliberal influence saw credit card advertising rise from $16 million in 1972 to $876 million in 1999 (Hovland and Wolburg 2010, 34), and by mid-2022 household debt had increased to $16.15 trillion – $2 trillion higher than in 2019 (Federal Reserve Bank of New York 2022). In short, from within the sovereign consumer paradigm advanced since the Great Acceleration, the promotion of credit makes possible market freedom and empowerment. However, once exercised, this freedom renders the consumer captive of the market, disempowered in proportion to their debt, which can usually only be paid off by the person they might otherwise have become – through the rarefaction of their future possibilities for *geneses*, in the disciplinary sense.

Rarefaction of the remains of disciplinary *corporeality*, *temporality*, *identity* and *geneses* in societies of control, through the above processes of dividualization, is thus a function of the neoliberal-digital economy these societies share, and a means of its expansion. And this is presumably why Deleuze did not explore the possibility of *digital* war machines beyond those which simply break down neoliberal-digital organization, like piracy and viruses, as discussed earlier. After all, for Deleuze, any such minoritarian digital initiative imaginable in 1992 would *by default* be so thoroughly part of the cyber system, that any oppositional gesture it might make at the level of interface would struggle to be of consequence.

The limits of dividualization

In contrast to the above diminishing minoritarian possibilities of *cyber*space, the emerging minoritarian possibilities of *agricultural* space, under the auspices of the *Via Campesina* or peasant way, among others, indicate growing resistance to (what are often less conspicuous) patterns of augmenting majoritarianism. Such growing pressure follows logically from how, as mentioned, while control societies need to extend corporate dividualization processes over global food production in order to become hegemonic, currently only around 30 per cent of global food requirements are met by corporate agribusiness. The remainder is thus still produced through minoritarian small farmer means, which tend to be both 'more efficient' than expansive 'mechanized farms', and less dependent on 'synthetic chemical pesticides' and 'fertilizers'; moreover, through the latter, healthier foods are generally produced in ways that are also more sustainable (Montgomery 2007, 159). However, following corporations' astronomical gains during the Covid-19 pandemic (Robinson 2020, 6) – which Robert Kennedy argues was itself a 'coup d'état against . . . democracy' (2021) – corporations and associated elites began unprecedented purchases of agricultural land (Estes 2021; Mercola and Shiva 2021; Malkan 2022). Arguably, this land grab reflects the disturbing ease with which the minoritarian efficiency of small farms can be tentatively included by majoritarian bodies like the World Bank, as a legitimate 'debate and policy concern' (Courville and Patel 2006, 6–7), only for corporate-led land reform through 'privatization' without 'limits [on] landownership' (Borras 2006, 99, 102–3) to ensue. The justification for such majoritarian land reform is often that, given the need for *food security*, renewed agricultural 'efficiency' is today more imperative than the 'distributive justice' focus of the preceding decolonization era (Courville and Patel 2006, 6). And this is often based on correlative claims that the 'Green revolution', involving industrial-scale agriculture through technology such as 'hybrid seeds, chemical fertilizers and pesticides', is the only viable path (Rosset and Altieri 2017, 5). However, this entails orchestrated majoritarian manoeuvres geared towards dividualizing food production. This much emerges from Shiva's explanation that, despite being expensive, hybrid seeds do not yield more produce than organic seeds; moreover, they require growing 'use of hazardous chemicals' – from the chemical fertilizers they are designed to absorb, to the pesticides designed to kill everything except those plants genetically engineered to withstand their toxins (Shiva 2016, 97–101). Via such ecologically damaging practices, though, corporate monoculture yields can be processed in concentrated ways that affect market prices, even to the point of displacing questions of food safety whenever consumers cannot *afford* to ask them. The economically dividualizing majoritarian processes of the hybrid seed–chemical fertilizers–pesticide nexus are thus as apparent as its negative ecological effects are clear – from immediate loss of biodiversity, to chronic marginalization (into extinction) of organic alternatives resulting from millennia of creative evolution. Such ecological dangers, though, are often obscured through enthusiastic majoritarian coupling of 'biotechnology' with 'information technology', which is then collectively touted as the panacea for food scarcity (Shiva 2016, 97) under the optimistic banner of 'industrial digital agriculture' (Villa 2022).

Accordingly, strong parallels exist between the impasses facing small farming today and those identified by Deleuze and Guattari as the genetic site of Franz Kafka's minor literary war machine, since both contexts involve unthinking majoritarian desires steadily congealing into habit. But as these are considered in what follows, along with how such small farming – like minor literature – entails processes of 'deterritorialization', 'political immediacy' and 'collective assemblages of enunciation' (Deleuze and Guattari 2000, 18), from which a 'people to come' (Deleuze 2005, 215) stand to emerge, it must be remembered that the stakes are far higher today than in Kafka's time. Still at stake is the domain of creative cultural expression, but at stake too, now, is the continued freedom of life *itself* – the 'infinite life' of *zoë* (Kerényi 1976, xxxiv–xxxvi) – to evolve creatively at its own pace, in line with the kaleidoscopic genetic permutations it has carefully curated within the biosphere over the course of millennia.

The 'impasses' to which minor literature is a response (Deleuze and Guattari 2000, 16) are clearly mirrored in the three impossibilities facing small farming today: the impossibility of small farmers *not* producing good food (analogous to the 'impossibility' of Kafka *not* writing), the impossibility of these farmers producing good food *just* as well through majoritarian means, and the impossibility of them farming *without* majoritarian means because of increasing corporate-based economic pressure to do so. But faced with the schizophrenic will to entropy of control societies manifest in such majoritarian madness, an important minoritarian 'line of flight' (Deleuze and Guattari 1987, 9) today would be that of agroecology.

First, like minor literature, agroecology entails 'a high coefficient of deterritorialization' (Deleuze and Guattari 2000, 16), insofar as it inflects the dynamics of food production around 'local autonomy' and 'farmer-to-farmer networks'; in this way, its practices disseminate 'agroecological innovations and ideas' that comprise a 'food sovereignty strategy' for a 'new "agrarian revolution" worldwide' – one predicated on biodiversity, energy efficiency, social justice and sustainability (Altieri and Toledo 2011, 587, 607). Food sovereignty has admittedly 'become increasingly diffuse' as the concept has been appropriated by different 'interests' (Tilzey 2018, 4) within this broadening minoritarian spectrum. But historically, the concept emerged as a 'term' in the 1980s and as a 'project' antithetical to the 'corporate food regime' in the 1990s (McMichael 2016). Accordingly, food sovereignty refers to various 'alternative' modes of politico-economic organization emerging in response to repeated capitalist crises (Bello 2022, 18). In agroecology, specifically, food sovereignty does not simply entail reversion to traditional farming methods; rather, it involves recourse to both traditional insights and scientific analyses to create 'agroecosystems' minimally dependent on 'high agrochemical and energy inputs' – because natural synergies instead recycle 'nutrients' and facilitate soil enhancement to optimize 'interactions' (Altieri and Toledo 2011, 588). Thus, while the divide between traditional and modern farming was initiated by disciplinary power, societies of control are seeking to render this cultural memory chasm unbridgeable – on the premises of food security. But in response, agroecology is deterritorializing such designs through emphasis instead on food sovereignty, which establishes creative and critical-constructive connections with such agrarian cultural memory, to continually fine-tune those practices that, for centuries already, have proven quite capable of consistently producing good food.

Second, like minor literature, agroecological initiatives entail political immediacy, since they occur in a context fraught with pressure to assimilate into majoritarian modes of corporate agribusiness. Moreover, such majoritarian pressures are similarly understood as reflecting society-shaping desires, namely those manifest in the *cybernetes'* guiding hand, and those driving neoliberal capitalism – which together comprise the *bios* identified by Deleuze as societies of control. However, while in minor literature, the dynamism of Kafka's culturally decentreed and creatively contorted desires merely clashed with conservative majoritarian ways of channelling desires into cultural life, in societies of control, life itself must now increasingly compete with profit for priority. After all, if neoliberal-digital desires were to attain hegemonic sway over global agriculture, the progressive dividualization of life *out of* food would ensue, as its nutritional value is increasingly sacrificed to sustain the economic vitality of those corporations vying for monopoly over the sector. Yet, despite the cost to health and life of such a process, neither neoliberal nor digital desires have reason to diminish, because the dividualization of *all* time for commercial exploitation comprises the blind axiom that interlinks them. Thus, there is little by way of connecting intelligence that might instead ground their orientations *in time* – the time of *zoë* or infinite life – save for the dwindling rhizomes of minoritarian small farmer practices, which both neoliberal and digital desires are in the process of eradicating.

But third, like in minor literature, those agroecological desires that *do* survive the political immediacy of neoliberal-digital efforts towards their eradication, can prove intense enough to birth collective assemblages of enunciation. Deleuze and Guattari's example of Kafka's minor literature effectively articulates the related dynamics in subcultural terms, where the nomadic people to come constitute a relatively disparate group of displaced persons, who begin to emerge into existence as a tentatively coherent collective, through the processes of deterritorialization and the experiences of political immediacy, discussed above. And to the extent that they do not assimilate into the majoritarian mode, they can produce a 'collective assemblage of enunciation' – the tentative and often practical coherence of which Deleuze and Guattari juxtapose against the eloquent 'individuated enunciation' of a given master, whose work is reified within a hierarchical majoritarian tradition (2000, 17–18). Such collective enunciations are thus experimental articulations *by* an emerging people, precisely *as* they proceed to speak themselves into existence – in a process that is interminable, on account of the rhizomatic impulse informing both its operations and its conditions of possibility. In agroecological terms, though, this dynamic has manifested in forms of organization that, while cultural in a similar sense to minor literature, are also far more socio-politically provocative. For example, under the auspices of the Brazilian Landless Workers' Movement or MST (*Movimento dos Trabalhadores Rurais Sem Terra*), such collective assemblages of enunciation have extended into socio-political activism resulting in the successful redistribution of millions of hectares of land to hundreds of thousands of families for sustainable farming (Friends of the MST 2023). Here groups from the most disaffected social 'segments' in Brazil – the landless, the homeless, the unemployed and those with histories of substance abuse – are drawn together through activism and offered a temporary place in 'rural "camps"', involving temporary residence in shacks along highways, until a 'suitable estate' of vacant land is identified for occupation; after this, a rapid dawn invasion is followed by the immediate planting of crops and establishment of community infrastructure, while measures are simultaneously taken to resist aggressive eviction efforts (Rosset 2006, 223). And these measures are required because violence is often the response to the *right* of MST members to 'pre-emptively occupy land', when its vacancy qualifies it for expropriation (*ocupación previa*) – which remains MST's 'principal tactic' (Wilpert 2006, 256). Intriguingly salient, though, is both the success of these initiatives – as such occupied land tends to be farmed sustainably when majoritarian eviction strategies are resisted or defused – and the minoritarian means by which such success is being realized. Indeed, 'almost by accident' it emerged that an initial period in the rural camps was crucial to 'forging new people', especially among those from disadvantaged backgrounds, because through 'communally imposed' discipline and reciprocal caring practices, along with education and skills training, the communities learn 'to live cooperatively' in ways that lay the foundation for their future collective farming success (Rosset 2006, 223). And to get perspective on this success, one has only to recall that, to date, MST has initiated over '2500 land occupations', through which nearly 400,000 families have repurposed '7.5 million hectares' for sustainable farming (Friends of the MST 2023). This amounts to an enormous collective assemblage of enunciation, the socio-political significance of which can scarcely be missed, even if its minoritarian voice is at times muted by majoritarian agribusiness monologues.

Conclusion

For Deleuze, the striations of control society deriving from neoliberal-digital dividualization of time should inspire in us neither 'fear nor hope' despite their apparent ubiquitous power, for as in any such historical context, it only remains for us to find 'new weapons' (1992, 4). Although digital minoritarian initiatives leading to the formation of cyber variants of such weapons may be more possible today than Deleuze could have envisioned in his final years, this chapter nevertheless responded to Deleuze's above provocation by considering possible reasons for his pessimism over the diminishing minoritarian capacity of cyberspace, before considering the growing minoritarian possibilities of *agricultural* space, under the auspices of the *Via Campesina*, among others. And here, focus fell on the parallels between the impasses facing small farming today and those impossibilities which catalysed Kafka's minor literature, along with the ways in which minor agroecological practices entail *deterritorialization* of majoritarian corporate agribusiness models, leading to *political immediacy*, out of which *collective assemblages of enunciation* are emerging – with the Brazilian Landless Workers' Movement presented as a case in point. In the process, though, what also emerged was that Kafka's minor literature has less to do with the author function than with *time* – understood as the limitless creative life of *zoë* – immersive connection with which is also required for successful agroecological practice. However, given the suicidally myopic desires of neoliberalism and digitality, it remains to be seen whether such agroecological war machines can keep open a portal through which the time of *zoë* can continue to sustain life, or whether societies of control will dividualize this portal for profit, in ways that also destroy genetic aspects of it forever. But in response to the question which often arises from such dire prognostications, concerning what action might be undertaken to avoid the latter fate, we might remind ourselves once more, that there really is no need to hope or fear. And this is because it is already abundantly clear that the gentle act of growing good food is now the most beautifully dangerous of all weapons, since regardless of where it takes place, its processes actually connect us to – rather than virtually distance us from – that most precious of all things, the very *time* of life itself.

Note

1 Admittedly, from the 1970s, Foucault's and others' insights into the discursive construction of 'man' also contributed to a growing eschewal of discourses centred on the latency of sexuality, and a correlative gravitation towards a focus on how psychological distress can also be underwritten by biological and/or cultural variables – as in narrative therapy (McLaren 2002, 161).

References

Altieri, Miguel A. and Victor M. Toledo (2011), 'The Agroecological Revolution in Latin America: Rescuing Nature, Ensuring Food Sovereignty and Empowering Peasants', *Journal of Peasant Studies*, 38 (3): 587–612.

Bello, Walden (2022), 'Is the Global Value Chain Breaking Up? The "Perfect Storm" and the Crisis of Capitalist Agriculture', in Walden Bello (ed.), *The Global Food Crisis, This Time*, 2–26, Focus on the Global South.

Borras, Saturnino M. Jr (2006), 'The Underlying Assumptions, Theory, and Practice of Neoliberal Land Policies', in Peter Rosset, Raj Patel and Michael Courville (eds), *Promised Land: Competing Visions of Agrarian Reform*, 99–128, Oakland: Food First Books.

Cahill, Damien (2014), *The End of Laissez-Faire? On the Durability of Embedded Neoliberalism*, Cheltenham: Edward Elgar.

Clements, Jeffrey D. (2012), *Corporations are Not People: Why They Have More Rights Than You Do and What You Can Do About It*, San Francisco: Berrett-Koehler.

Courville, Michael and Raj Patel (2006), 'The Resurgence of Agrarian Reform in the Twenty-First Century', in Peter Rosset, Raj Patel and Michael Courville (eds), *Promised Land: Competing Visions of Agrarian Reform*, 3–22, Oakland: Food First Books.

Deleuze, Gilles (1990), *The Logic of Sense*, ed. Constantin V. Boundas, New York: Columbia University Press.

Deleuze, Gilles (1992), 'Postscript on the Societies of Control', *October*, 59 (Winter): 3–7.

Deleuze, Gilles (1998), 'Having an Idea in Cinema', in Eleanor Kaufman and Kevin J. Heller (eds), *Deleuze and Guattari: New Mappings in Politics, Philosophy, and Culture*, 14–19, Minneapolis: University of Minnesota Press.

Deleuze, Gilles (2005), *Cinema 1: The Movement-Image*, trans. Hugh Tomlinson and Barbara Habberjam, London: Continuum.

Deleuze, Gilles and Félix Guattari (1987), *A Thousand Plateaus: Capitalism and Schizophrenia*, trans. Brian Massumi, London: University of Minneapolis Press.

Deleuze, Gilles and Félix Guattari (2000), *Kafka: Toward a Minor Literature*, trans. Dana Polan, Minneapolis: University of Minnesota Press.

Estes, Nick (2021), 'Bill Gates is the Biggest Private Owner of Farmland in the United States. Why?' *The Guardian*, 5 April. https://www.theguardian.com/commentisfree /2021/apr/05/bill-gates-climate-crisis-farmland.

Federal Reserve Bank of New York (2022), 'Total Household Debt Surpasses $16 trillion in Q2 2022; Mortgage, Auto Loan, and Credit Card Balances Increase', *newyorkfed.org* , 2 August. https://www.newyorkfed.org/newsevents/news/research/2022/20220802.

Foucault, Michel (1967), *Madness and Civilization: A History of Insanity in the Age of Reason*, trans. Richard Howard, New York: Mentor.

Foucault, Michel (1969 [1977]), 'What is an Author?' in Donald Bouchard (ed.), *Language, Counter-memory, Practice: Selected Essays and Interviews by Michel Foucault*, 113–38, New York: Cornell University Press.

Foucault, Michel (1972), 'The Discourse on Language', in *The Archaeology of Knowledge and the Discourse on Language*, trans. Alan M. Sheridan Smith, 215–37, New York: Pantheon Books.

Foucault, Michel (1979 [1999]), 'Pastoral Power and Political Reason', in Jeremy R. Carrette (ed.), *Religion and Culture: Michel Foucault*, 135–52, New York: Routledge.

Foucault, Michel (1991), *Discipline and Punish: The Birth of the Prison*, trans. Alan Sheridan, London: Penguin Books.

Foucault, Michel (1998), *The Will to Knowledge: The History of Sexuality*, vol. 1, trans. Robert Hurley, London: Penguin.

Foucault, Michel (2002), *The Archaeology of Knowledge*, trans. Alan M. Sheridan Smith, London: Routledge.

Foucault, Michel (2003), *The Order of Things*, London: Routledge.

Foucault, Michel (2005), *The Hermeneutics of the Subject: Lectures at the Collège de France 1981–1982*, trans. Graham Burchell, New York: Palgrave Macmillan.

Foucault, Michel and Gilles Deleuze (1972 [1977]), 'Intellectuals and Power', in Donald Bouchard (ed.), *Language, Counter-memory, Practice: Selected Essays and Interviews by Michel Foucault*, 205–17, New York: Cornell University Press.

Friends of the MST (2023), 'What is the MST?' *mstbrazil.org*. https://www.mstbrazil.org/content/what-mst.

Hovland, Roxanne and Joyce M. Wolburg (2010), *Advertising, Society, and Consumer Culture*, New York: M.E. Sharpe.

Jenkins, Henry (2006), *Fans, Bloggers, and Gamers: Exploring Participatory Culture*, New York: New York University Press.

Jentzsch, Nicola (2006), *The Economics and Regulation of Financial Privacy: An International Comparison of Credit Reporting Systems*, New York: Physica-Verlag Heidelberg.

Katona, George (1964), *The Mass Consumption Society*, New York: McGraw Hill.

Kennedy, Robert F. (2021), *The Real Anthony Fauci: Bill Gates, Big Pharma, and the Global War on Democracy and Public Health*, New York: Skyhorse Publishing.

Kerényi, Carl (1976), *Dionysos: Archetypal Image of Indestructible Life*, trans. Ralph Manheim, London: Routledge & Kegan Paul.

Keynes, John M. (2018), *The General Theory of Employment, Interest, and Money*, New York: Palgrave Macmillan.

Klein, Naomi (2008), *The Shock Doctrine: The Rise of Disaster Capitalism*, London: Penguin.

Labonté, Ronald and Arne Ruckert (2019), *Health Equity in a Globalizing Era: Past Challenges, Future Prospects*, Oxford: Oxford University Press.

Longhurst, Brian, Greg Smith, Gaynor Bagnall, Garry Crawford and Miles Ogborn (2017), *Introducing Cultural Studies*, 3rd edn, London Routledge.

Lukovics, Miklós, Benedek Nagy and Norbert Buzás (2019), 'First Steps in Understanding the Economic Principles of Responsible Research and Innovation', in René von Schomberg and Jonathan Hankins (eds), *International Handbook on Responsible Innovation: A Global Resource*, 134–49, Cheltenham: Edward Elgar.

Malkan, Stacy (2022), 'Critiques of Gates Foundation Agricultural Interventions in Africa', *usrtk.org*, 8 September. https://usrtk.org/bill-gates/critiques-of-gates-foundation/.

McAdams, Dan P. (1997), 'A Conceptual History of Personality Psychology', in Robert Hogan, John Johnson and Stephen Briggs (eds), *Handbook of Personality Psychology*, 3–39, San Diego: Academic Press.

McLaren, Margaret A. (2002), *Feminism, Foucault, and Embodied Subjectivity*, Albany: SUNY Press.

McMichael, Philip (2016), 'Historicizing Food Sovereignty', in Marc Edelman, James C. Scott, Amita Baviskar, Saturnino M. Borras Jr, Deniz Kandiyoti, Eric Holt-Giménez, Tony Weis and Wendy Wolford (eds), *Critical Perspectives on Food Sovereignty: Global Agrarian Transformations*, vol. 2, 21–46, New York: Routledge.

Mercola, Joseph and Vandana Shiva (2021), 'Vandana Shiva: Bill Gates Empires "Must Be Dismantled"', *The Defender*, 29 March. https://childrenshealthdefense.org/defender/vandana-shiva-gates-empires-must-dismantle/.

Montgomery, David R. (2007), *Dirt: The Erosion of Civilization*, Berkeley: University of California Press.

Powell, Lewis F. (1971), 'Confidential Memorandum: Attack of American Free Enterprise System', memorandum to Eugene B. Sidnor Jr, Chairman, Education Committee, US Chamber of Commerce, 23 August. http://old.mediatransparency.org/story.php?storyID=21.

Princen, Thomas (2005), *The Logic of Sufficiency*, Cambridge, MA: The MIT Press.

Robinson, William I. (2020), 'Global Capitalism Post-Pandemic', *Race & Class*, 62 (2): 3–13.

Rosset, Peter (2006), 'Alternatives: Between the State Above and the Movement Below', in Peter Rosset, Raj Patel and Michael Courville (eds), *Promised Land: Competing Visions of Agrarian Reform*, 221–4, Oakland: Food First Books.

Rosset, Peter and Miguel A. Altieri (2017), *Agroecology: Science and Politics*, Nova Scotia: Fernwood Publishing.

Shiva, Vandana (2016), *Stolen Harvest: The Hijacking of the Global Food Supply*, Lexington: The University Press of Kentucky.

Tilzey, Mark (2018), *Political Ecology, Food Regimes, and Food Sovereignty: Crisis, Resistance, and Resilience*, Cham: Palgrave Macmillan.

Turkle, Sherry (1995), *Life on the Screen: Identity in the Age of the Internet*, New York: Simon & Schuster.

Villa, Verónica (2022), 'What Is the Industrial Digital Agriculture and Why Is That a Threat to Food Sovereignty?' *capiremov.org*, 14 December. https://capiremov.org/en/analysis/what-is-the-industrial-digital-agriculture-and-why-is-that-a-threat-to-food-sovereignty/?utm_source=substack&utm_medium=email.

Wilpert, Gregory (2006), 'Land for People Not for Profit in Venezuela', in Peter Rosset, Raj Patel and Michael Courville (eds), *Promised Land: Competing Visions of Agrarian Reform*, 249–64, Oakland: Food First Books.

Wilson, Jenifer E. (2003), *Time-Conscious Psychological Therapy*, London: Routledge.

8

A Radical Ecology to Believe in This World

Aline Wiame

'The modern fact is that we no longer believe in this world', Deleuze (1989, 171) states in a well-known passage from *The Time-Image*. While a lot has been written about this modern fact and its connection to both Deleuze's approach to modern cinema and his conception of thought,[1] I first want to take this statement at face value. What is striking with the identification of no longer believing in this world as a modern fact is that we can relate quite intuitively to this statement and, at the same time, we feel that we are aesthetically, politically and conceptually ill equipped to properly understand and assimilate it. Don't we recognize phenomena akin to no longer believing in this world when we are 'doomscrolling'[2] on our tactile screens, from images of wars and oppressions of popular uprisings to videos of megafires or deadly floodings? Aren't the states of bewilderment, of utter shock and the inhibition of action that ensues from the spectacularization of newsworthy disasters concrete manifestations of this lost connection to a world that could be invested by our desire? And yet, identifying utterances of modern disbelief in this world does not bring us any closer to practical tools to resist it.

In this chapter, I want to argue that Deleuze's diagnosis from the middle of the 1980s (*L'Image-Temps* was first published in French in 1985) not only retains its provocative power today but moreover gains new layers of meaning and affecting forces when confronted with the state of bewilderment brought forth by the (post)neoliberal media apparatus that reduces ecological destructions to spectacular images. But in order to better understand this diagnosis's relevance to our own era of disbelief and bewilderment, we need a proper term for it. The contemporary lexicon is rich, from Guattari's 'Integrated World Capitalism – IWC' (2000) to Massumi's 'ontopower' (2015). However, I choose to call our era by the triple name 'Anthropocene/Capitalocene/Plantationocene' suggested by Donna Haraway (2016, 100) for three main reasons. First, Haraway refuses to choose between the numerous '-cenes' that populate academic books and articles since the coining of the term 'Anthropocene' in the beginning of this century. Anthropocene ('Man' as the main actor of climate change), Capitalocene (capitalist exploitation as the main force driving climate change)[3] or Plantationocene (the logic of plantation and monoculture impoverishing human and other-than-human ways of inhabiting the earth, with the colonial origin of this logic being acknowledged) all form different aspects of the same stratum we are engulfed in; each of them taken individually is insufficient to understand the state of disbelief they collectively produce. Second, according to Haraway, the Anthropocene/Capitalocene/Plantationocene is not the critical name of an enemy too big to fail that we could only analyse and condemn; on the contrary, the three terms name an outrage by condensing reductionist stories of ongoing, massive processes of destruction that we should fight with other, regenerative stories (101–2). Consequently and finally, in Haraway's understanding, the name Anthropocene/Capitalocene/Plantationocene should engender rebellion rather than bewilderment; the (out)rage that comes with this triple name could lead us to act in such a way that we actively work to make it a 'boundary event' rather than a full geological epoch (100).

Connecting the true sense of rage and urgency Haraway brings to the battle with Deleuze's diagnosis about the modern state of disbelief in this world seems crucial to me if we want a mere chance of escaping stupor and disbelief towards a radical ecology. Haraway allows us to escape any temptation for a melancholic understanding of the 'loss' of belief in the world and urges us to transform this disbelief into a call to pragmatic action (a suggestion that is already present in *The Time-Image* but that needs to be thought anew). Deleuze, on his part, grounds the social, subjective and ecological emergencies of the Anthropocene/Capitalocene /Plantationocene into a genealogy of modern affects and assemblages of images and subjectivities. Combined, those two approaches sketch the traits of a radical ecology that encompasses what Guattari (2000, 28) calls the three registers of ecology – the environment, social relations and human subjectivity – as well as an ecology of images and the affects they carry or inhibit, since Deleuze's claim about our modern lack of belief in this world is deeply interwoven with a reflection about the effects and the fate of cinema. If a pragmatic activation is the opposite of the state of bewilderment, how do we activate this radical ecology to resist the incredulity manufactured by the (post)neoliberal, media apparatus? We are faced with three tasks. Firstly, we need to establish a genealogy of the modern discredit of belief in what can be called a society of clichés. Secondly, we have to better understand the political ecology in which images and affects can be (at least marginally) freed from the reign or occupation of clichés. Thirdly and finally, we can pragmatically activate this 'affective' political ecology in order to create a memory of the world as a super-ject able to break through the 'spectacular shields' (Pisters 2012, 276) of the Anthropocene/Capitalocene/Plan tationocene.

The reign of clichés and the modern unlearning of belief

In the context of the *Cinema* books, Deleuze equating the modern fact with us no longer believing in this world must be understood at the crossing of two inseparable phenomena: the assumption of inner and outer clichés as the trademark of Western(ized) societies, on the one hand, and modern philosophy's inability to encompass belief as a power of thought that cannot be limited to knowledge, on the other.

According to Deleuze (1986), the death of classical cinema in the aftermath of World War II is strongly correlated with the reign of clichés, 'both internally and externally, in people's heads and hearts as well as in the whole space' (212). Numerous factors, both internal and external to cinema, have contributed to this reign, such as the consequences of the war (and the necessity to hide from the atrocities it engendered), the end of the American dream while the American way of life was conquering the whole Western world, cinema becoming the dominant media across the masses with a 'quantitative mediocrity' in its industrial production of contents (Deleuze 1989, 164), the multiplication and accelerated diffusion of images (and then screens, one may add today) and so on. The list is not exhaustive, but one can easily get the gist of the argument: what happened to classical cinema was not limited to cinematographic aesthetics in any way and reached way beyond to standardize our ways of being at individual, social and soon planetary levels. In *The Movement-Image*, Deleuze (1986), following a 'Romantic' approach inspired by William Blake, sees the reign of clichés as the realization of a whole organization of misery (209). This misery can only be one and the same, whether external or internal, as the social imposition of misery by external factors only would soon be deemed intolerable. But, if the social, external organization of misery meets a powerful organization of 'internal', subjective, affective misery through the hegemony of mental clichés, we can adhere to misery from the inside, clichés shielding us from the intolerable. In *The Time-Image*, Deleuze (1989) leaves behind Blake's conspiracist undertones for a Bergsonian understanding of clichés that nevertheless leads to the same conclusion: clichés are sensory-motor images of things and events, that is, the reduction of things and events to what we are interested in perceiving 'by virtue of our economic interests, ideological beliefs and psychological demands' (20). Clichés, in other words, allow us not to see, hear and feel what is too unpleasant, too terrible or even too beautiful.

Something has happened to us, leading to the 'modern fact' that we no longer believe in this world (how could we, if the connection between our subjective and eco-social existences only relies on clichés?). And if cinema has played an undeniable part in this process, it is because it has inserted itself in a bigger assemblage, that Deleuze and Guattari would qualify as 'cosmic' in *A Thousand Plateaus* and that, I want to argue, is also an ecological disaster. The theme of clichés is already present in *A Thousand Plateaus*, although not under that name. In the 'Postulates of Linguistics' plateau, Deleuze and Guattari (1987) make clear that the generalized use of mass media for disseminating news and opinions can only produce redundancies, that is, I suggest, the repetition of clichés. Clichés function here as the false representation of what we are always already supposed and even commanded to feel, know and believe since they are *order-words*: 'Newspapers, news, proceed by redundancy, in that they tell us what we "must" think, retain, expect, etc.' (79). The use of mass media not to create individualized masses but to incessantly repeat the reign of clichés can be seen as a massive hijacking: mass media (such as cinema and the most part of contemporary artistic creation) have been reduced to means of destruction that substitute opinion and clichés for creation. The idea that today's means of creation are exactly identical to means of destruction is the 'cosmic' problem diagnosed towards the end of the 'Refrain' plateau (346). If artists use the same materials for their creation as mass media, the great people's organizations of the party or union type use for the fuzzification and the scrambling of 'all the terrestrial forces of the people' (345), how can artists resist this massive destruction of terrestrial forces and rather open up those forces to a cosmos where creation can still prevail beyond clichés and the redundancies of opinion? In the Anthropocene/Capitalocene/Plantationocene, the 'cosmic' problem diagnosed in *A Thousand Plateaus* clearly turns into an ecological disaster at both practical and theoretical levels. When means of creation – be they of the technological and mass media kind or related to thought as the creation of concepts and not opinions – are hijacked to become means of destruction, we lose a whole array of terrestrial forces, human and other-than-human, that have been structurally and vitally oppressed, silenced and made invisible by the powerful circulation of clichés. This ecological disaster, it is worth repeating, is all the more concerning as it occurs through the same means and materials that can be used to (try to) avert it. Despite all our goodwill, our concepts, our creations, our stories could very well feed the machines of fuzzification. The powerful organization of misery is strong enough to turn ideas, concepts and creations into clichés or spectacular shields if we let them become majoritarian representations in the mass media bewildering circuits. The massive and reductionist stories of the Anthropoce ne/Capitalocene/Plantationocene can fiercely reclaim any creative attempt if we are not careful enough to always confront creation with its pragmatic effects on singular, terrestrial forces in situated milieus[4] – in *this* world, that cannot be confused with a spectacular representation.

But how exactly can we relate to *this* world and not its representation or clichés? We may now have a first understanding of what no longer believing in this world means in the *Cinema* books and in the frame of a radical ecology: we cannot believe in this world because it has been reduced to lethal clichés only feeding spectacularizing machines. However, the puzzlement caused by the phrase 'The modern fact is that we no longer believe in this world' remains. As Deleuze (1989) underlines, we understand what believing in *other* worlds means: one can believe in religious or metaphysical other worlds, and the nineteenth century and the first half of the twentieth century have been rich with political utopias, from the soviet comrades' society to the American dream of a society of brothers. But once we feel 'not a need to believe in something else, but a need to believe in this world, of which fools are a part', we make 'fools laugh' (173) because we are all fools, all ill equipped to 'get' what believing in this world means and how to practically implement such a strange faith. And this modern inability to develop an immanent belief, I argue, is the other side of the ecological disaster that is the reign of clichés; we cannot fully comprehend our society of clichés without relating it to the modern unlearning of belief. In *The Time-Image*, Deleuze suggests as much when, shortly after his phrase about the modern fact, he calls for a double transformation of thought: at first, we have to replace the model of knowledge with belief (a movement already initiated in philosophy from Pascal to Nietzsche); then, we have to convert belief (in other worlds) into belief in this world, as it is (172). The fact that we are baffled by the mere idea of what believing in this world practically implies may actually be a good sign: through this bafflement, we begin to approach the powerlessness of thought, that is still thought but that is most definitely no longer in the realm of knowledge. In *The Time-Image*, Deleuze sees in Artaud a precursor who felt this powerlessness of thought (if we reduce thought to knowledge) but who also *lived* this powerlessness as a superior power of thought: a thought at last freed from its circumscription to knowledge that opens up to immanent belief as an act of connection, of love, of affective engagement with the world (170). As Marrati (2008) explains, 'What is at stake in cinema – and in our modern condition – is not "reality." We do not doubt exterior reality or the existence of the world: our skepticism is not cognitive. We lack neither knowledge nor certainty' (86). We fail at understanding what believing in this world means because it is not a matter of knowing; it is literally a matter of living, of existing. More precisely, as Deleuze and Guattari (1994) make clear in *What Is Philosophy?*, believing in this world does not engage a new kind of understanding but an 'empiricist conversion' that requires the invention of new modes of existence allowing us to still inhabit this world and connect with its forces of life (74–5). In Zourabichvili's terms, believing in this world means leaving behind the conception of thought as the knowledge of the truth of being towards the contraction of practical habits engaging events and creation (2012, 39–40).

I want once again to underline how strangely those formulas sound to our modern ears, and for a reason that can be traced back, according to Deleuze, to the roots of modern philosophy. In his 1984 Vincennes seminars, when he is writing *The Time-Image*, Deleuze establishes that modern philosophy has always fought with the status of belief. Hume, Deleuze (1984) says, is the first to erode the equation between thought and knowledge, since the empiricist thinker stated that every bit of our knowledge is constructed on the basis of the contraction of habits – that is, on the basis of belief. That kind of belief is immanent and does not require any mysticism: there is a belief at stake every time we affirm something that is not a given on the basis of what is given (the well-known example 'the sun will rise tomorrow, as it did every past days' comes to mind). But the coexistence of belief and knowledge in the elaboration of modern, philosophical thought will meet a strange faith once Kant works it out in the frame of the *Critique of Pure Reason*. In the preface to the second edition of his *Critique*, Kant ([1787] 1998) writes: 'I had to deny knowledge in order to make room for faith [*Glauben*]' (117), meaning that objects that are not given in sensible perception can only be thought in an act of faith (or belief, the two terms being synonymous here), unreachable through knowledge. However, Deleuze (1984) continues, if Kant opens a breach in the very foundations of modern thought, he immediately tries to seal it off as strongly as possible, since the main argument of the *Critique of pure reason* is that thought, if it wants to be rightly used, must limit itself to what can be *known*, that is the realm of the sensible. What remains outside of this realm – God, the soul, the world – is a matter of faith that thought should not approach. Kant, in other words, traps modern thought in a double bind: on the one hand, he clearly establishes the boundaries of the legitimate use of thought (sensible data that can be known); on the other, he suggests that everything that makes our sense of purpose and the very fabric of our lives requires an abolishment of knowledge for belief or faith. No wonder modern thought finds itself in a schizoid state that makes it unable to resist the rise of clichés: by depriving thought of the power of belief, Kant turns it into an exterminator of situated habits, events and practices – all the modes of thought and existence that cannot be reduced to knowledge and representation and that, for this very reason, would be able to fight clichés on their own ground and beyond.

In order to emphasize why this Kantian deprivation of thought plays a part in the ecological disaster diagnosed above, I suggest we connect Deleuze's short genealogy of the modern loss of belief to Bruno Latour's inquiries into what has characterized the anthropological group he devoted his life studying: the so-called Moderns. If Deleuze's and Latour's respective approaches differ in scopes, purposes and objects of study, their echoes are useful and creative in order to fight the bewilderment generated by the Anthropocene/Capitalocene /Plantationocene's conceptual and aesthetical shields. According to Latour (2013), the Moderns (a population with elastic borders made of Westerners as well as of all of the 'modernized' by will or, more often, by force) were those who believed they had to leave any kind of belief (seen as archaic credulity) behind them in favour of 'rational', objective, knowable facts. This movement from a phantasmic, archaic, credulous past to a bright, enlightened future of pure knowledge constitutes what Latour calls the 'Modernization front', similar to the Frontier of the American pioneers (8). Like the pioneering front, the Modernization front gave to those who followed it an exhilarating impulse towards an ideal of 'freedom' and emancipation from any kind of past attachments (seen as credulous amalgams of facts and values); like the pioneering front, the Modernization front was synonymous with massive destructions, for both the 'non-Moderns' and for the Moderns themselves. For the (human and other-than-human) non-Moderns, the disqualification of anything but 'rational' facts, supposed to stand alone without any social or subjective intermixing, meant the destruction of a whole array of diverse, situated, mixed practices that did not fit the reductionist grid of abstract 'Knowledge' – an ecological disaster by itself. But even for the Moderns, the Modernization front has become an exterminator: it was supposed to help the Moderns be at home everywhere on the Globe (why would any square metre on the planet escape the universality of objective knowledge?) but it made the earth uninhabitable. Who could seriously inhabit a world only made of 'objective facts', without the various values and institutions able to protect the numerous practices and modes of existence the Moderns hold dear, without being able to properly name, describe and defend them? Nobody lives in a world of mere facts unrelated to ways of being (biologically, politically, religiously, lawfully, artistically and so on). This is why I follow Latour's suit by using the past tense when writing about the Moderns: with the Anthropocene, the dualistic separation between facts and values, Science and Society, knowledge and belief that characterized the Modernization front comes to an end (Latour 2013, 9). If the stable ground of facts (geology, climate and everything the Moderns used to call 'nature' as opposed to 'culture') begins to tremble and react to 'human', social, cultural conducts, how could the Modern parenthesis not come to an end? But yet again, the former Moderns find themselves ill equipped to face this new challenge because of their schizoid relationship to belief: if the Moderns were those who believed they were done with belief by (de)populating the world with univocal, reductionist knowledge, how could they find an inhabitable world as it has been poisoned by the destructions of modernity? In *Down to Earth*, Latour (2018) goes as far as stating that the expression 'modern world' is an oxymoron: 'Either it is modern, but has no world under its feet, or else it is a true world, but will not be modernizable' (32). The choice the Moderns – and, truly, every being that has been affected by the poisonous Modernization front – face is clear: 'between modernizing and ecologizing, we have to choose' (Latour 2013, 8). Ecologizing, for Latour, means repopulating the world with the various modes of existence the Modernization front had silenced.

Although I am slightly twisting Latour's arguments in order to bring them closer to Deleuze's genealogy of the modern disbelief (Latour rather thinks that we should abandon the concept of belief altogether, as it has been polluted by modern dualisms (2013, 14)), the echoes between the two thinkers are striking: the modern understanding of thought as a reductionist conception of knowledge has led to the eradication of numerous modes of existence that cannot stand this reduction, thus making 'the world' an ecologically impoverished and uninhabitable place unable to accommodate the modes of existence making the very fabric of our lives. Naming the resistance to the 'modern fact' an ecologizing process is significant: modern thought has had life-and-death consequences on existential, metaphysical, aesthetic and political levels. Being able to believe in and to connect to a world worthy of our worries, care and affects – a world we have to reclaim after the modern unlearning of belief – is then a truly ecological emergency in the Anthropocene/Capitalocene/Plantationocene.

A cinematographic, political ecology: The resistance of affects

Characterizing the two faces of the modern fact – the reign of clichés and the unlearning of belief – as vectors of a massive, ecological disaster clearly carries political implications. For Deleuze, this strange kind of politics is connected to an assemblage in which cinema has a central position. In *The Time-Image*, the chapter 'Thought and cinema', in which the phrase about the modern fact is inserted, begins with the utopia that characterized classical cinema (Deleuze writes mostly about Eisenstein, but his point stands more generally for all of classical cinema, notably the American one): as a *mass* medium by essence, cinema was seen by its pioneers as a privileged tool for creating a coherent, singular people, for the individuation of the masses as a historical, political and aesthetic subject, rather than an object of representation (Deleuze 1989, 163). However, something happened to cinema or, rather, with the complicity of cinema, that made this utopia of a people already there, already constituted, just waiting for a (cinematographic) becoming conscious of the masses, a bad cliché (219–20). What happened is not only the quantitative mediocrity of cinematographic production – even though that counts for an art singularized by its massive outreach – but also the compromission of classical cinema with fascism, what Deleuze calls 'Hitler and Hollywood, Hollywood and Hitler' (164).[5] When used for propaganda purposes by filmmakers that are not inherently mediocre (Leni Riefenstahl was not mediocre, Deleuze claims [164]), cinema ceases to be an art individuating the masses and, on the contrary, subjugates – and bewilders – them. Even worse, Deleuze continues following Daney (1983) and Virilio (1989), what becomes clear in the compromission of classical cinema with fascism is that cinema was guilty as charged from the very beginning: it had always developed in connection to the logistics of war and state propaganda; it had always been working as a shield from the unbearable that was hidden behind images (the Nazi camps as the dark consequence of the handling of masses of humans that the camera's eye could operate) (Deleuze 1989, 164–5).

After World War II, in other words, (classical) cinema was dying from the quantitative mediocrity of its general production and from its compromission with fascism. If it had to come back from the dead, it would be on whole new bases – modern cinema, that has renounced any attempt at emancipating the masses by knowledge and becoming (self)conscious and that rather films our link to the world, the specific modes of existence able to make us believe in this world, unknowable as it is. What matters in the frame of a new reading of Deleuze's phrase about the modern fact in the face of the Anthropocene/Capitalocene/Plantationocene is less the technical ways by which modern cinema films our link to the world than the political assemblage Deleuze examines when dealing with those questions.

Here, we should first highlight that the death (or murder) of cinema is not a thing from the past, resolved once and for all when modern cinema invented itself on the ruins of classical cinema. Already in the 1980s, in the conclusion to *The Time-Image* as well as in his 'Letter to Serge Daney' (Deleuze 1995), Deleuze noticed that cinema could very well die a second time from its lack of reinvention and its progressive, social insignificance because of the competition of television and other media devices (video and digital images) aimed at propagating information and opinions – clichés and order-words – rather than creation (see, for instance, Deleuze 1995, 75). When Deleuze (1989) wrote about the frame of the screen now functioning as 'instrument panel, printing or computing table', the image being constantly 'cut into another image, being printed through a visible mesh, sliding over other images in an "incessant stream of messages", and the shot itself . . . less like an eye than an overloaded brain endlessly absorbing information' (267), how could we not think of our present condition, of the multiplication of spectacular shields and screens feeding us the univocal stories of the Anthropocene/Capitalocene/Plantationocene? The death of cinema, or at least its social insignificance, thus becomes a present threat that seems to actualize Deleuze's prediction according to which 'the modern world is that in which information replaces nature' (1989, 269). The political assemblage in which Deleuze thought the modern fact reinforces the diagnosis of an ecological disaster (information replacing nature, no less) but this time with an insistence on the potential complicity of cinema (when it stops creating) and, more broadly, of audiovisual production, in the devastations happening and forthcoming.

But if cinema can be complicit in the Anthropocene/Capitalocene/Plantatio nocene, it can also create weapons to resist it or, in Deleuze's phrasing, give us access to the 'subtle way out' of our state of disbelief (1989, 170). When writing about the potential second death of cinema and its rivalry with television, we should always keep in mind that Deleuze's thinking on these topics is informed by his intellectual dialogue with French film critic Serge Daney (and, conversely, that Daney's writings are informed by Deleuze's books). In an interview given in the beginning of the 1990s, Daney states that cinema, in the best-case scenario, can give us an inhabitable world worthy of our desire:

> I still think the world is wonderful as it is, and I think it is wonderful I have been able to inhabit it. It was this idea: we'll have this world, but we will finally inhabit

it. This is the essence of my love for movies [*cinéphilie*]: we will finally inhabit it. But we will inhabit the world and not society, never. From society, you can only expect terrible things. (Daney 2004; my translation)

By contrasting the world with society, Daney makes a direct reference to his other talks and writings where he associates cinema with the world, on the one hand, and television with society, on the other. Television, Daney argues, standardizes neoliberal individuals to better inscribe them in a 'global village' with no place for desire and creation (2015, 31) but plenty of room for technically perfect images, deprived of any intellectual or aesthetic function in favour of the repetition of clichés (1983, 19).

The fact that cinema resists social normativity because of its very imperfections that leave room for creation and desire can lead us to understanding the political 'subtle way out' of the reduction of the modern world to information and clichés. I want to argue that the radical ecology called for by Deleuze's statement about the modern fact and our present state of unbelief must be assembled at the level of desire and affects if it wants to reach a modicum of political efficacy. When looking for the political input of modern cinema in *The Time-Image*, most commentators turn to the pages Deleuze (1989) devoted to 'fabulation' at the end of chapter 8 (215–24). They have every reason to do so: not only is the section about fabulation entitled 'Cinema and politics' but, in addition, one can find a symmetry between the first section of chapter 7, about the death of classical cinema's utopia of individuating masses into a people already defined, and the last section of chapter 8, about the people that is missing as the new condition of filmic creation. However, I want to emphasize that Deleuze is always very clear about the political scale of cinematographic fabulation: it is, and it always has been, the matter of cinema of what was called, in the 1980s, the 'third world' – and what we should rather call, following Latour's suit, the forcibly modernized. If the people is also missing in the Western world and in Western cinema – we have seen that Western classical cinema has even been complicit in this loss of the people, – Deleuze carefully distinguishes the politics of Western cinema from the politics of fabulation. Deleuze writes: 'No doubt this truth [the people is missing] also applied to the West, but very few authors discovered it, because it was hidden by the mechanisms of power and the systems of majority. On the other hand, it was absolutely clear in the third world' (1989, 217). Fabulation then seems to be the exclusive political tool of the disfranchised of modern reason; the politics of Western cinema, the tools it can furnish to make the bewildering machines leak from the inside, must be sought for elsewhere. Deleuze gives us a clue, as he writes about the 'few authors' that discovered that the people is missing in the West too. Most specifically, Deleuze gives three names: the Straubs (Jean-Marie Straub and Danièle Huillet) and Alain Resnais (215).

Resnais's case is particularly interesting here. Deleuze immediately alludes to *La Guerre est finie* (*The war is over*, a 1966 film about an exiled resistant to Franco's Spain) after having mentioned Resnais as one of the few authors of the West taking into account the missing people, and one can think of several Resnais movies with direct political messages and undertones (*Night and Fog* about Nazi camps, *Muriel* about the Algerian war). However, just before turning to fabulation in cinema of the Third World, Deleuze devotes plenty of pages to Resnais's 'cerebral' cinematography, focusing on films that do not seem political at first sight – at least if one reduces politics to the realm of knowledge of modern, political philosophy. Deleuze especially deems *L'Amour à mort* (*Love unto death*, 1984) 'one of the most ambitious films in the history of cinema' (1989, 208). But *L'Amour à mort* has all the aspects of an intimist movie, following only a quartet of characters and more specifically focusing on a couple – the man dies at the beginning of the movie, then comes back to life, then dies again because he wants to go back to the country of the dead, and the dark ending of the movie suggests his partner will join him there, not because of a fascination for death, but as an act of love to be with him.[6] *Je t'aime, je t'aime* (1968), another movie by Resnais Deleuze writes profusely about, can also be seen as intimist despite some very short flashes of occupied Europe during World War II and a voluntarily low-tech, sci-fi setting: a man gets lost in his memories because the woman he loves has died. I suggest it is because of such movies, and not despite them, that Resnais is one of the few authors from the West who creates a politics that can make us believe in this world. In Resnais's movies, Deleuze (1989, 209) writes, 'feeling' and 'love' are mental functions of creation as flashes of life resisting death, that is the reduction of the world to an uninhabitable place occupied by clichés.

What Resnais calls 'feeling' is akin to what Deleuze (with and without Guattari) more commonly names affect. We know from Deleuze's 1987 talk 'What is the creative act?' that a work of art resists information and communication – and thus resists death, resists destruction (Deleuze 2006, 322–3). And we know from *What is Philosophy?* that art preserves affects, independently of the psychological affections felt by artists, as forces of life resisting death and destruction (Deleuze and Guattari 1994, 163–4). Consequently, I argue that it is by working at creating and preserving affects and the modes of existence they entail that Western cinema can fight the ecological destruction of the Anthropocene/Capitalocene/

Plantationocene from within. After all, if the phrase 'The modern fact is that we no longer believe in this world' has become famous, too little attention is paid to the sentence that directly follows it: 'We do not even believe in the events which happen to us, love, death, as if they only half concerned us' (Deleuze 1989, 171). This sentence is full of pathos, and could be read as sentimentalist by a modernized philosopher who only accept knowable, 'hard' facts (the harder they hit our affects and beliefs, the better, it often seems). And yet, Deleuze has always warned us against the lethal effects of the modern unlearning of belief and of the reign of clichés on our capacities to let ourselves be transformed by affects: 'We mix with all that, even death, even accidents, in our normal life or on holidays. We see, and we more or less experience, a powerful organization of poverty and oppression' (1989, 20). But aesthetic and conceptual clichés shield us from the revolutionary, affective charge those events carry. If we have no choice but to ecologize in order to believe in this world, to invest it with our desire, to deconstruct the Modernization front that has eradicated a myriad of modes of existence and reduced the earth to an uninhabitable place, it is well past time that we cease being afraid of affects as if they were external to the legitimate use of thought. Believing in this world means recognizing in thought a stronger power than mere knowledge: belief, or immanent faith, and the modes of existence and affects it always carries. The political ecology of Western cinema can only rely on the preservation of singular, situated affects that are able to face the bewildering machines of the Anthropocene/Capitalocene/Plantationocene.

Conclusion: The memory of the world as a super-ject

Examined through the lenses of the modern disbelief in this world and of the socially normative assemblage of post-neoliberal mass media, the Anthropoce ne/Capitalocene/Plantationocene appears to be a lot more than a univocal ideology based on the constant, capitalist exploitation of the earth's resources. It is, first and foremost, an ecological disaster depriving terrestrial beings of affective, conceptual, aesthetic and political agency. At both conceptual and aesthetic levels, the spectacular and bewildering shielding of Anthropocene/ Capitalocene/Plantationocene is all the more concerning when it imposes itself as the only representation of what the world is and will/could be – when it posits itself as 'all the memory of the world', to borrow from the title of one of Resnais's short movies that Deleuze often quotes in *The Time-Image* (see, for instance, Deleuze 1989, 122).[7] The danger of accepting the hegemony of the Anthropocene/Capitalocene/Plantationocene as all the memory of the world, thus occulting the devastations it is causing, is to reconduct what Haraway (2016, 214) calls the 'double death', to be understood as the end of ongoingness (of individuals, species and modes of existence) doubled by the lack of memorial resumption of the specific ways of inhabiting the world of those who have disappeared.

By learning how to believe in this world, by making belief a power of thought pragmatically engaging us into situated modes of existence, we can resist the double death the Anthropocene/Capitalocene/Plantationocene both produces and hides. The cinematographic, political ecology described above suggests that affects, as forces of life below and beyond representation, are strong and revolutionary enough to break the repetition of clichés and the dullness of senses and thought it induces. Affects, here, are impersonal entities that disrupt 'signifying projects as well as subjective feelings' (Deleuze and Guattari 1987, 233), critical entities that do not compose an ego (Deleuze 1997, 124) – affects are becomings. And because they initiate becomings, they free us from the normative subjectivation shaped by the clichés and opinions of the Anthropocene/Capitalocene/Plantationocene. Within a political ecology of affects, we no longer subject to the mass media production of bewilderment but we become, according to Whitehead's concept, *super-jects* that thought is aiming for and that are always still to be created against the inertia of social normativity (Deleuze and Guattari 1994, 211). This creation, through immanent belief and affects, resists not only death but also the double death of the Anthropocene/Capitalocene/Plantationocene; it is an ecologization that reclaims the memory of the world not as an already given set of data, but as a *super-ject* we ought to ongoingly create.

Notes

1   See, for instance, Bogue (2003, 179–80), Zabunyan (2006) and Marrati (2008, 78–96).

2   The Cambridge Dictionary of English defines doomscrolling as the activity of spending a lot of time looking at your phone or computer and reading bad or negative news stories.

3   On the Plantationocene, see, for instance, Haraway, Mitman and Tsing (2019).

4   I am thinking here of William James's pragmatist method, which invites us to always (re)connect our abstract ideas – our oxygen – to the concrete milieus of life that are the only places where this oxygen can help us breathe (see James 1907, 127–8).

A Radical Ecology to Believe in this World 141

5   This is a clear allusion to German director Syberberg's *Hitler: A Film from Germany* (1977).

6   It is possible to connect *L'Amour à mort* with Resnais's earlier, more political movies such as *Night and Fog*, since French resistant and writer Jean Cayrol, who wrote the text of *Night and Fog*, has made Lazarus the emblem of people having survived the camps. Deleuze notes that Resnais's cinema demonstrates that thought has something to do with Auschwitz and Hiroshima (1989, 209). Nevertheless, this background is absent for any viewer of *L'Amour à mort* who is not a Resnais scholar: the characters have nothing to do with World War II (one can assume they were born just after the war) and Resnais ([2002] 2008) himself stated it was foremost a new kind of 'musical movie', constructed around an original score by H. W. Henze.

7   *Toute la mémoire du monde* (1956).

References

Bogue, Ronald (2003), *Deleuze on Cinema*, New York and London: Routledge.

Daney, Serge (1983), *La Rampe. Cahier Critique 1970–1982*, Paris: Gallimard.

Daney, Serge (2004), *Itinéraire d'un ciné-fils. Entretiens avec Régis Debray* [filmed interview], Dir. Pierre-André Boutang and Dominique Rabourdin, France: Montparnasse.

Daney, Serge (2015), *La Maison cinéma et le monde. 4. Le moment Trafic, 1991–1992*, Paris: P.O.L.

Deleuze, Gilles (1984), 'Sur le cinéma: l'image-pensée. Cours du 06/11/1984', *Webdeleuze*. https://www.webdeleuze.com/textes/357 (accessed 1 March 2023; English translation forthcoming at https://deleuze.cla.purdue.edu/index.php/seminars/cinema-and-thought/lecture-02).

Deleuze, Gilles (1986), *Cinema I: The Movement-Image*, trans. Hugh Tomlinson and Barbara Habberjam, London: The Athlone Press.

Deleuze, Gilles (1989), *Cinema II: The Time-Image*, trans. Hugh Tomlinson and Robert Galeta, London: Continuum.

Deleuze, Gilles (1995), 'Letter to Serge Daney: Optimism, Pessimism and Travel', in *Negotiations, 1972–1990*, trans. Martin Joughin, 68–79, New York: Columbia University Press.

Deleuze, Gilles (1997), *Essays Critical and Clinical*, trans. Daniel W. Smith and Michael A. Greco, Minneapolis: The University of Minnesota Press.

Deleuze, Gilles (2006), 'What is the Creative Act?', in David Lapoujade (ed.), *Two Regimes of Madness: Texts and Interviews 1975–1995*, trans. Ames Hodges and Mike Taormina, New York: Semiotext(e).

Deleuze, Gilles and Félix Guattari (1987), *A Thousand Plateaus. Capitalism and Schizophrenia*, trans. Brian Massumi, Minneapolis: The University of Minnesota Press.

Deleuze, Gilles and Félix Guattari (1994), *What is Philosophy?*, trans. Hugh Tomlinson and Graham Burchill, London and New York: Verso.

Guattari, Félix (2000), *The Three Ecologies*, trans. Ian Pindar and Paul Sutton, London and New Brunswick: The Athlone Press.

Haraway, Donna (2016), *Staying with the Trouble. Making Kin in the Chthulucene*, Durham and London: Duke University Press.

Haraway, Donna, Gregg Mitman and Anna Tsing (2019), 'Reflections on the Plantationocene: A Conversation with Donna Haraway and Anna Tsing', *Edge Effects*, 12 October. https://edgeeffects.net/haraway-tsing-plantationocene/ (accessed 28 February 2023).

James, William (1907), *Pragmatism: A New Name for Some Old Ways of Thinking*, New York: Longmans, Green, and Co.

Kant, Immanuel ([1787] 1998), *Critique of Pure Reason*, ed. and trans. Paul Guyer and Allen W. Wood, Cambridge: Cambridge University Press.

Latour, Bruno (2013), *An Inquiry into Modes of Existence: An Anthropology of the Moderns*, trans. Catherine Porter, Cambridge, MA and London: Harvard University Press.

Latour, Bruno (2018), *Down to Earth: Politics in the New Climatic Regime*, trans. Catherine Porter, Cambridge: Polity.

Marrati, Paola (2008), *Gilles Deleuze: Cinema and Philosophy*, trans. Alisa Hartz, Baltimore: John Hopkins University Press.

Massumi, Brian (2015), *Ontopower: War, Powers, and the State of Perception*, Durham and London: Duke University Press.

Pisters, Patricia (2012), *The Neuro-Image: A Deleuzian Film-philosophy of Digital Screen Culture*, Stanford: Stanford University Press.

Resnais Alain ([2002] 2008), 'Entretien avec Alain Resnais par Serge Toubiana' [recorded interview], bonus to *L'Amour à mort* DVD in the DVDs box *Alain Resnais. Coffret 6 films*, France: MK2.

Toute la mémoire du monde (1956), [film] Dir. Alain Resnais, France: Les Films de la Pléiade.

Virilio, Paul (1989), *War and Cinema: The Logistics of Perception*, trans. Patrick Camiller, London and New York: Verso.

Zabunyan, Dork (2006), *Gilles Deleuze. Voir, parler, penser au risque du cinéma*, Paris: Presses Sorbonne Nouvelle.

Zourabichvili, François (2012), *Deleuze: A Philosophy of the Event together with The Vocabulary of Deleuze*, trans. Kieran Aarons, ed. Gregg Lambert and Daniel Smith, Edinburgh: Edinburgh University Press.

9

An Infantile-Image in Latin America

A Memory for the World

Marcus Pereira Novaes and Antonio Carlos Rodrigues de Amorim

In this text, we will present how artistic images of a common Latin American event could have the possibility to make us realize, through the inventive forces of creation, the potency of searching for audiovisualities that can friction and promote ruptures with sign regimes that, in the search for expressing the true, could end up reinforcing a danger that neoliberal thoughts bring with them, such as the suspension of democracy and the germination of ideas and discourses that can actualize a past of pain and suffering in the continent, specifically the dictatorial regimes. Through what we call infantile-images[1] we will seek for a relation to the intensities of time with cinema, both through its formations in the midst of an interval and through its filmic dilations and contractions that express thoughts and compositions of other narratives and give us different perceptions and sensations.

With this movement, we approach Cangiano's (2022, 31) ponderation about life being permeated by 'multiple forces of all shades, in the multiple externalities and interiorities of the singularities of bodies. Nevertheless, even in the continuous process of territorializations and deterritorializations of the desiring flows, there are repressions that persist and translate the neoliberal univocity'.

Our main argument is to understand the film *The Wolf House* (2018), made in Stop Motion by directors and artists Cristóbal León and Joaquín Cociña, as a line of flight when it is no longer possible to make sense of fascism, since it is intolerable. In other words, it is a work that does not seek to escape from this memory/history, but rather, to seek other meanings when it is inevitable to escape from such a condition/subjugation. A line of flight, that is, a complex of forces, the potential, the invention, the constitution, an opening that allows us to evade or transform the situation at a given moment. In an age of the overwhelming quantity of images, one collaborates to the sense of acceleration that permeates the contemporary. 'Acceleration is not simply a linear succession of innovations, in which each obsolete item is replaced by a new one. Each replacement is always accompanied by an exponential increase in the number of choices and options available' (CRARY 2013, 43).

One film, layers of time in multiplicity

The editing and montage of the chosen film act creatively in activating other possibles in the story being told. And this happens in some directions, such as demonstrating the intersections between the 'real' stories and the fictionalization that the animation invents/produces. One part of the narratives starts from the character – who is a child – and moves to the infantile-image, a concept of 'resistance' or perforation of the structural and reproductive logics of the neoliberal modes of administration (moral, regulatory, control) of life. Another direction that stands out is the set of memory spaces referenced or represented in the film; it operates, in a contrasting way, a continuous and differential expansion in its production that spreads collective traces. Built and realized in different spaces in Chilean territory, as well as in different museums around the world – such as Argentina and Germany – *The Wolf House* leaves traces in these places, in the form of installations that could or still can be visited by the public. While the mode of its production will value this collective way of producing spaces that bet on the potency of art as an affection that values life, and that could work as a fragmented and spatialized memory in the world, the use of sound, as we will see later, will intensify the oppressive and falsifying discourse of fascism, especially in the use of the voice-off, which seeks to enhance the moral appeal of salvation to be performed by an individual in detriment to the power of the collective.

Far from performing a mere binary game, very present in neoliberal discourses that would dispute the validation of the images according to a correct interpretation of their content or according to their degree of realism associated to an idea of truth, which may vary according to 'the political-ideological bias of the receiver and the agreement of a group identified with an identical political-ideological spectrum' (Camarneiro 2019, 31), the whole construction of *The Wolf House* will seek to evidence the crisis of the discourse of truth associated with images, from its construction to its final form, betting more on showing a falsifying narration that seeks to bring to immanence an ethical–aesthetic–political choice as to the artistic power of images.

After a brief presentation of documentary images, *The Wolf House* will be predominantly constructed in animation form and its narrative will introduce us to the character Maria, a young woman of German descent and the main character of the Chilean animation, seeking to escape from the colony where she lived. Maria's escape happens because she let some pigs from the colony escape, an inattention that would earn her the punishment of 'staying a hundred nights and a hundred days without talking to anyone'. Upon escaping from the colony, Maria finds a house, where she will take refuge. There, the girl will have a double encounter, for she will find two pigs she let escape, and the chance to take care of these animals appears to her, without control or supervision from anyone in the colony; and she will be tormented by a wolf, but the figure of the wolf will not actualize itself as the form of an animal, except once, when a wolf appears as a documentary image on a television set; in the rest of the film, the wolf connects to the narrative as a voice-off, besides sometimes constituting itself as the house itself, which does not stop decomposing and recomposing its form, differently. In this way, in relation to the constant appearance of the wolf as a voice-off or as a metamorphic house, one can raise the suspicion that the wolf is not only looking for the girl physically, because the voice of the wolf does not fail to express the power of morality that continues to judge Maria for her competencies and failures, especially in the relationship that the girl starts to establish with the two pigs. Thus, the wolf is constituted as a permanent force that continues to actualize the effects of the colony on the girl, continuing to control her and to tell her what she should or should not do. We could well say that, if Maria escaped from the colony, she escaped only in its form, for the judging power of the colony follows with her, in the visual and sonorous modulations of the wolf, subordinating her to its judgements, saying what is right and what is wrong, that is, the wolf is the moral.

There is a certain relationship of the wolf's fascist discourse to the way Camarneiro (2019, 23) identifies neoliberal discourse works, as it relies on the meta-narrative to fortify an understanding of history not as a collective product, but as the sum of individual efforts. The wolf asserts a discourse that seeks to nullify the possibility of other world affirmations and seeks to materialize itself as a saviour speech and one that emanates from an individual, a bet on the single story to the detriment of other possibilities of collectivities.

This cinema, chosen by us, similarly to other Latin American cinemas, actualizes the past in its affection. And it is in this kind of movement that the Deleuzian critique of classical thought and cinema comes to light, or rather, points to the fact that a new memory can be germinated.

Latin America is constantly the target of usurpers, and art allows us to bring to life the events that create other views of the continent, the events that build a memory for the world. This is why cinema and the arts suffer repression from extremist and conservative governments. These governments seek to impose a moral through hatred, exclusion and the killing of the plurality of worlds, seeking to appropriate the audiovisualities as political propaganda. We have experienced this in some moments in the history of Brazil, and very recently under the ultra-right government of Jair Bolsonaro. The Ministry of Culture was extinguished, the Brazilian cinematheque closed and its collection looted; the organs of care for the preservation of historical memory and culture started to be administered by those who hated cultural plurality, such a significant mark of the country.

But cinema, in its power to proliferate memories and sensations to the world, proposes a creative combat that representations cannot contain. Far from seeking to represent its memory, Latin American cinema could be closer to what Deleuze (2018, 66) put forward in relation to Third World cinema, when he points out that reconstituting a memory would not be of much use to these peoples or countries, since they permanently suffer repressions organized by reactionary forces, in which many of them rely on the false judgement between good and evil to seek to impose a sense of truth to images. For the philosopher, composing oneself as art to the world makes cinema something much more provocative; it is much more annoying, to serve as a memory to the world, to constitute a place in which one can only be a memory of the world (Deleuze 2018, 66), because these places, always haunted by misery and exploitation, fruits of a brutal colonization, have the power to produce a revolutionary act through the creation of images, direct images of time that would serve as a memory of the world, disturbing time-images that can gain an intense political value. Latin American cinema, as in the case of *The Wolf House*, creates images that are preserved in time, in a memory of the world; it creates, beyond personal memories and historical records, a fabulation of an impersonal memory that invents a people to come.

In the case of this text, we refer to the infantile-images that give voices so that different infanthoods can coexist, actualizing various possible ones, germinating new images to the world and affirming a fight that values life and its degrees of potency.

It is through the infantile-image that we can perceive struggles and ruptures with the two forms of subjectivation of life that Deleuze and Guattari discuss regarding the monitoring, maintenance and production of axioms as 'control of the prevailing neoliberal axiomatics' (Cangiano 2022, 91). These forces are social subjection and machinic submission. Subjectivities are subject to a semiotic, linguistic, colloquial macro-rule and manifest themselves in everyday life as watchwords and 'social obligation' on the molar plane.

The infantile-image comes close to a connection with modern philosophy, whereby the concept of truth would not hold up as a universal model. Cinema can show that, in the Latin American continent, the concept of truth only becomes possible when it is reinvented, when it breaks, shatters the false morality of the dominator, and with this, lives are liberated to make rhizomes and creative connections in encounters, on one side, with the feelings that start to perceive differently depraved perspectives; and on the other side, with the perceptions that rise in degrees of potency in order to affect a world. These are the two sides of the coin of time – the affects and the percepts, the forces of the power of the false that allow the work of actualizing and creating a concept, inventing a truth.

The encounter with Chilean film *The Wolf House* makes us realize an infantile-image related to questioning about the concept of truth and, above all, why this would imply a direct connection with time.

But, why time? What is the problem of time in relation to truth and how can this relation between time and truth be powerful for a conceptualization of an infantile-image?

A very simple answer, still reduced to a problem of content, would be that, surely, we can imagine that infanthood, when related to a concept of truth, will suffer variations over time, differing according to the place in which it is actualized. In the same way, a truth could always change when it clashes with a point of view made dominant, or according to a proposition that necessarily better fits a universal model.

The infantile-image connected to time will confront the moral, the moral as truth. Precisely because it is an infantile-image, it is constantly subjected to the judgements of a dominating power of speech and will try to escape the formula that every moral will seek to impose: 'you must!' This is the legislating phrase of the moral, a moral that sometimes reduces the potency of the existent, and in this chapter, we refer to the existences of audiovisual images that present a differently infantile character, who comes to help problematize possible issues that the Chilean film deals with.

The infantile character – Maria – presented on the screen has an inventive force triggered when she is affected by something terrifying, which makes her more or less potent in perceiving a compossibility of worlds. It will teach us to see and hear images – as sound will also give us to perceive the infantile-images – that are in the depths of time and are actualized amidst the powers of the false, among the affects that make the infantile-images conceivable conceptually, singularly constructing a character who intensely feels something absurd in her daily life; and among the percepts that possibly will become perceptible, the forces among unstratified minority formations. The infantile-image is not representing actions and reactions of such or such a character; it can even appear with such movements and derive effects from some actions of infants, but, above all, the infantile-image actualizes itself in the film by providing a new perception, the powers of infanthood in creating the new, for example, in the case of *The Wolf House*, an imagetic combat against fascism.

We propose to find this infantile-image in connection with time, but also with a common event in some Latin American movies. The scenes that bring back a period of horror in the continent, like a cloud that envelops a Latin American memory, show virtualities of an event that flashes among infantile-images and that constantly threatens to return: the dictatorial regimes.

The infantile-image is a possible line of articulation of the discussions of Deleuze's philosophy and neoliberalism, in the sense that Schleusener (2020, 50) discusses in his text, that is, what is at least as important is its diagnostic and pragmatic dimension: its effectiveness in terms of its ability to make visible, relate to and provide answers to contemporary problems. In other words, the task of philosophy is not to solve the problems of the past, but to create concepts that are able to intervene in the problems of the present, that is (in more proper Deleuzian terms), 'the now of our becoming'.

The dictatorial regimes, arbitrarily and violently implemented in some Latin American countries, have influenced and still influence the making of many films that directly or indirectly create images that express an audiovisual infanthood of this period or of possible actualizations of these events in the present. Sometimes, such images seek to serve as a historical record of that time for the construction of an archive that generates a conscience of the past. At other times, there is a filmic bet on inventing a memory for the world, through aberrant movements of experimentation in the image, by creating an infantile-image that lives and witnesses something absurd and intolerable, also making it possible to show that the effects of these dictatorships, these incorporeal effects, can be actualized differently in this territory.

We will approach the second aspect, as we are interested in conceiving an image that invents itself as infanthood, a concept of infantile-image that has a connection with time, is made within the memory because, in this case, memory is time, a non-chronological time, or even, we could say, it is an impersonal memory, within which, the infantile-images are modulated and constituted among series of temporal folds that appear in filmic narratives.

There are moments in which the images fail to present the truth, resorting to knowledge and habitual memories and not finding the correct answer; there is a failure in the organic circuit of images or in habitual recognition that instigates questions about something that a psychological memory, based on sensory-motor movements, would not be able to provide a solution for. In this film, there would be a certain pedagogy of the image through which a psychic character teaches us to see and hear, making us perceive things that are not visible or audible.

According to Neno and Fernández (2018, 81), 'The disagreement between what we see and what we hear is part of the fundamental equation at the moment of provoking a strangeness, which stars in the film, and which is justified both from the point of view of the narrative and from the historical and political contexts to which alludes to the movie.'

In our discussion of the Chilean film, *The Wolf House*, the infantile-image will not give us a way out, since the character will be a kind of seer of a time, in which she experiences something terrifying in her daily life, showing us an exhausting and terrible life, but that, in her impossibility to react to the situations in which she is involved, she has to open gaps to release the powers of metamorphosis, recreating herself imagetically.

The infantile-images teach us the need to exercise our eyes and ears, to perceive differently, because there is no learning that does not pass through the affection and possibility of learning with time, to connect between the modulations of sounds, between noises and silences, and thus be able to create an attentive response to the problem that an event raises, avoiding repeating opinions that justify the loss of power in the bodies.

The Wolf House: An infantile-image among paints, drawings, sculptures and sounds

The film *The Wolf House* presents images of drawings, paintings and sculptures that will prolong a reality in the work of the imagination out of consciousness; a fairy tale is created that actualizes a memory merged into an event through a falsifying narration, with crystalline descriptions that imagetically express a problem that haunts Chile to this day, virtualities of a Germanophilia that envelops the country. For Neno and Fernández (2018), the film appeals, to a large extent through sound, to a real that goes beyond the narration and exceeds the limits of representation, to claim a new aesthetic experience around the cinematographic proposals anchored in Chilean history.

In this animation, the images are constructed together with the narrative and let coexist traces of what they were, at the same time that they create other figures. For example, a drawing figure is modulated into a painting that, soon after, will give way to a sculpture. No figure pre-exists; they all appear in the immanence of the play of forces on the canvas and seek to assert themselves in movements of metamorphosis, waging a struggle for existence, immersed in changing relationships, between intensifications of paint colours that fill and illuminate the canvas by colouring effects of contrasts, but which, in an instant, are erased by other elements present in the image or that will appear in the scene. Soon the new image that has emerged will be cracked by scratches of other colours, and from the cracks created, a new colour will come to take its place. The illusion of the flat screen's spatial perspective is made and undone by the colouring sensations of intensive movements, by contours that open gaps in the image and allow the passage of the new, of a new figure, an eternal return in which the next image will always return with as much difference as possible.

The images would 'slide over each other'. Not only the images, but the points of view begin to displace one on top of the other, in a game in which the hierarchy between one image and the others ends up being always provisional – another reason why the objective point of view required by the epic seems impossible.

There is all this possibility of seeing a figure of an infanthood among the arts that create and recreate it, which leads us to a perception in another temporal dimension. We leave the logical and solid relationship among images for a perspective that can only be made in time, a perspective that can both affect our power to exist, in a Deleuzian approximation to Spinoza, and intensify our ability to perceive. One enters the image from a point of view of the indiscernibility between the real and the imaginary, from the possibility of being affected by the forces of time, or in other words, by the powers of the false.

A series of forces of the visual arts, used in the animation, compose a temporal formation, compete with each other to pass through the gaps in the images and modulate a new figure, a new infantile-image of a girl that coexists with the narration of the story that the film tells. The figure of this character is actualized at every instant; it does not exist before, it can only exist when drawn, painted or sculpted, in the middle of the composition plane of the image on the screen. Nor can it be dissociated from the other elements belonging to the composition of each frame or photogram; each image that appears in this game between different visual relations erases and actualizes the previous image, at the same time that it will be blurred and replaced by the following one. This process of making the figure appear, while erasing the previous image, is constituted more by an intensive relationship between colours and contour with the background of the screen than expressed by a sensory-motor sequence derived from movement-images. A process of description that crystallizes and makes coexist many simultaneous perceptions that will derive its content, and that will be accompanied by a falsifying narration, expressed by sound.

A permanent modulation is created, with a series of crystalline descriptions expressed in the visual images; another connection with time is created when their relationship with sound is analysed. The soundtrack is composed of character voices, ambient sounds and a sound design of voice and other elements. Sometimes the sounds are subordinated to the forms they represent, diegetic sounds; at other times, they do not represent a direct relationship between the visual and the sound, as in the case of the narrator's voice that is present in various ways in the film, a classic example of the voice-off as a non-diegetic sound. There is a third falsifying power of sound in which a logical relationship between the visual and the sound is broken, creating a new connection between them, for example, when the hands of a clock are shown to turn rapidly, the sound will follow a pulsed and marked rhythm, with which we would normally hear it; in other words, an intensive and accelerated visual image comes to inhabit chronological time, breaking a logical association. This sound relationship allied to this process of dissolution of images on the screen, plus the preponderance of the fixed camera, seems to declare an independence of time from regular and uniform movement, describing that what is preserved is time while space is what deteriorates. The logical disconnection between the visual and the sound is a possibility of presentation of the time-image expressed by the cinema, as we directly perceive the intensive play of the forces of creation.

In relation to sound, it is also worth noting the role of music, which will potentiate even more this insubordination of the sound to the visual. As Neno and Fernández (2018, 80) state, music, in *The Wolf House*, will intensify 'the threat of an invisible off-screen and to which we cannot access from the visible (despite the fact that, we insist, it is a permanently disturbing image)'. It thus composes an offstage that helps construct the sinister as something threatening and that borders the images, instigates to destroy the possibility that another life can live in peace and assert itself as possible. The sound modulations interfere with the visual formations that struggle to take effect in the time-image.

In other words, in Chilean animation we can perceive series of sound and visual images that coexist and vary within the form of time; it is time that makes it possible for everything to change and from where there are possibilities of coming out different series, but, for that, the form of time itself cannot change, otherwise it would change to infinity. This was the great inversion that Kantian thought sought to affirm: the insubordination of time to movement. As Elizabeth Grosz (2012, 148) points out, from Kant one could say that 'everything moves or changes, moves or changes in time, but time itself does not move or change, nor does it measure or accompany movement and change'. Following this perspective, Daniel Smith (2013, 383) points out that '[y]et time itself is neither succession, nor simultaneity, nor permanence, since time cannot be reduced to any of its modes, or to what takes place within time (its content)'. So, if what changes is not time, but what is within it, how to guarantee the existence of something necessarily universal and prior to time? Time begins to call into question the concept of truth, or the form of the true, because the only unchanging form is time. Still according to Smith (2013, 382) '[w]e cannot even say that the immutable form of time is permanent, since what is permanent – no less than what is successive or simultaneous – appears and is perceived in time, whereas the immutable form of time itself cannot be perceived'. In this way, we could never perceive the form of time, but cinema could fabulate images that, in the relation with montage and thought, would present themselves as pure time-images, at least this was Deleuze's bet. If on one hand Deleuze approaches Kant to think a pure time, on the other hand, as Grosz (2012) points out, Deleuze also approaches Bergson's thought, for whom: 'time splits into two trajectories: one virtual, the other actual; one that makes the present pass, and the other that preserves itself as past while still part of the present'. We believe that *The Wolf House* can give us some of this coexistence between the virtual and the actual, actualizing us by the coexistence of series of images that provoke us to perceive beyond the usual filmic relations, placing us in a depraved perception of a memory of the world.

The Wolf House could be seen as a long interval, in a filmic memory, being able to make us realize a problem related between time and truth. In relation to this work, it is already possible to open some questionings to help us think. Is it possible to point out which true image will best express the figure of the girl in the animation? What could be the effects derived from the encounters of this work, whereby infantile-images, created by different arts, transmute and compose a child character on the screen? Why is it from within time that these images of an infanthood are constituted, one that seeks more to question an event than to be able to tell the truth about it?

As we pointed out in the introduction of this text, what time will confront will be moral, putting the relations between good and evil in immanence, in the

An Infantile-Image in Latin America   153

games of becoming among relations that metamorphose in time. In this sense, *The Wolf House* composes an interesting intercessor, which will both make us realize the strength of the discourse of morality and how it has a power to penetrate relationships to try to control them; as we will be able to see, in this animation, through an intensive construction by the modulation processes of the arts that compose this film, the form of truth metamorphoses in layers within time, showing us a dispute for the true that can both actualize itself in a praise of fascism that poisons life in a discourse supported by morality; as it can affirm life through the artistic mutations of the infantile character who perceives and provokes us to see the effects of its terrifying politics. Two moves that come close to the three types of falsifier that Deleuze found in Nietzsche to think about the potency of the false. According to Bogue (2003, 150) these would be, precisely, 'the man of truth, who in the name of the ideal judges the world of appearances guilty; the man of vengeance, who no longer believes in the ideal but negates the world of appearances out of self-hatred; and the artist, a joyous forger or falsifier (faussaire) who creates value by affirming the becoming of the world'. Being the figure of the true man the representation found in the classic cinema that no longer sustains itself in modern life, *The Wolf House*, on one hand, actualizes the figure of the wolf as the man of revenge, a kind of monster that, knowing how to play with the power of falsifications, 'betrays the truth' but only out of self-loathing and a hatred of life; and on the other hand, brings all the power of the false in the infantile-image and in the figure of her character Maria, who fully embraces the becoming and metamorphoses herself artistically, insisting on the potential of change that would intensify life and make possible the creation of truth.

Thus, there is in the animation of Cociña and León (2018) the possibility of perceiving time-images by the intensive movements of the images that seek to appear on the screen, one emerging from within the other, constituting itself with the previous one, metamorphosing into another image and composing aberrant affiliations that do not clash with the form of the true, because the form of the true would only work if it existed as an essence, in other words, a figure that was given a priori as truth, according to a universal reason. In the frames that make up the scenes of animation, the images are like larval ideas that germinate, grow and die in immanence. By opening temporality and bringing temporal perspectives through the arts that compose it, freeing the coexistence of diverse possibilities of images, this work also makes it possible to call into question the content of its narrative. Far from being able to be stated as a single logical and necessary interpretation of the film.

A visionary struggle: Creating with concepts, affects and percepts

In a rather inventive way, *The Wolf House* (2018) fictionalizes the effects of the *Colonia Dignidad* (Dignity Colony), located in Chile. The colony was created by former Nazi military officer Paul Schäfer (1921–2007). Although in a first presentation, this place could be seen as an education centre, whose main activity was agronomy, it is known that in reality it constituted a detention centre, where people opposed to the dictatorial regime of Augusto Pinochet (1915–2006) were taken to be interrogated, tortured and often killed.

Cociña (Leon and Cociña 2018) says that their major concern, to create the film, was first technical. The reference to the colony was emerging and being filtered, little by little. But when they had to choose the plot, they ended up, according to Cociña (Leon and Cociña 2019), taking the opportunity to question bases poorly linked to Germanophilia in Chile. Since then, another challenge appeared, as they chose to create the animation as if they themselves embodied feelings and discourses of that place, thus presenting the point of view of the colony, that is, of Paul Schäfer himself.

The encounter with Cociña's lines helps to perceive how the agency of the images with history constructs a falsifying reality in itself, which is not related by opposition to the truth of history, because the history of the colony comes in layers that falsify each other, bringing all levels of falsifiers that seek to pass for truth, including Schäfer himself. In this way, the animation makes us realize the danger of fascism being actualized again, especially through the moralistic discourse and supported by an idea of 'Good', which implies the loss of power and life in the bodies, bodies that continue to be affected by a cloud of virtualities of an event, which can always be actualized again. Above all, the still-present force of the moral is shown, for in the film Maria will end up killing the pigs and returning to the colony, after asking the wolf for help, giving in to the insistent calls of its persuasive power of domination. Therefore, the girl will fail to free herself from a system of judgements and punishments, choosing to return to pain, suffering and the loss of her freedom.

The film also brings the forces to an ethical plane, showing that Maria did not flee the colony because she was confused or because of an error in judgement about the place, and, even if the wolf seduces her again, Maria finds herself with an intensified perception of life. The new images, which appear at every moment in the film, bring the powers of colours and sounds, creating other perspectives that compete with the moral and judgemental discourse of Schäfer, bringing a whole descriptive power by percepts and affects, which dispute with the sentimental and interpretive force that the fascist discourse produces, making coexist an intensified and ephemeral perception that is detached from the form of truth, the latter, related to a solid perspective of seeing and hearing. In *The Wolf House* (2018), the artistic images both create the trap that the house itself composes and help Maria escape it, falsely describing the absurdity that a proposition such as Nazism or Fascism can evoke.

Cociña and León (2018) throw us descriptions that highlight the power of the false, or percepts and affects, in crystalline imagetic formations that potentiate visibilities and sonorities, modulating an infantile-image. Of course, with these descriptions we could raise questions such as: What does it mean to be a child and to be in the midst of a fascism, still so present in Latin America? Or how does Latin America again desire authoritarian governments with segregationist policies that history has tried so hard to denounce and point out the danger of repeating such mistakes?

Today, especially, these issues seem to be repeated in countries that have, with great cost, managed to establish democratic governments, but the form of democracy does not prevent these desires for fascism from returning. The effects of those dictatorial governments are still in time, insisting and being updated here and there. What images can show an infanthood of these places? What do the arts in this animation want us to perceive by deepening the relationship with a historical fact? Why is this artistic animation so interesting to think about an infantile-image that tries to make us perceive among things? Wouldn't it be because it presents us with images and teaches us to see other perspectives?

The artistic compositions of animation teach us to perceive among things, to see worlds, to get out of a solid perception. Of course, animation could teach us that in Chile, at a certain moment, such and such a thing happened, and that it was horrible. But it goes beyond this; it teaches us to see details that eyes and ears, accustomed to seeking the truth in a filmic relationship, are not stimulated to perceive; it teaches us to touch the events amidst the forces of creation that compose themselves in an intensive movement. The figure of Maria is that of an infanthood that has to change, undo and recreate itself all the time. The figure of the wolf is actualized as house, as drawing and as sound. Transversally, an infantile-image is created that always has to metamorphose in order to escape the judgement of the moral, or rather, the traps that a judgement, based on a false principle, creates in order to establish itself as desire and truth.

In this animation, there is a battle for the concept of truth when confronted with percepts and affects present in the arts that make it up. But which truth should be let through? One that diminishes the potency of existence of a place, excluding and subsuming affects that proliferate life, or the truths that value the possibilities of coexistence and that may imply an increase in potency of a set of singular forces that build a common? Isn't there a dispute between a moral form and an ethical formation?

In a direct connection to one of Deleuze's (2018) classes, concerning the powers of time and truth, there is another important placement about the moral and its relation to time and that goes through connecting the moral to a fair feeling, in which there is the idea that there is a true feeling. For Deleuze (2018), the moral is the domain of feeling, and we know that Deleuzian philosophy, attending to its immanent connection, in the differential line with which it ties itself to Spinoza, feels the need to be linked to ethics and not to the moral, because it sees in the potency of existing the possibility of linking ourselves to affects, through which the existent can make choices that increase or decrease its potency of existing. But it is always a matter of being in the midst of relations of forces and in perceiving the forces with which we want to establish links, that is, between percepts and affects. However, the force of the moral is cunning and insistent, in its will to power. We saw, in *The Wolf House*, that the character Maria could not resist meeting with the forces of time and ended up electing Schäfer's camouflaged speech and the false security of the colony again. So, how do we know how to elect the forces with which we bind ourselves? At this point, the ethical choice intervenes, which, for Deleuze (2018), involves learning to become able to feel amidst the forces, amidst the connections between the affects, in a work of auto-affection in which one can affect oneself and raise the degree of one's existence, an intensive path that escapes the habitual and chronological line that standardizes and imposes true feelings.

The Wolf House well showed us that behind every sentiment can dwell the wolf of the moral. And even though we know that, in this animation, the 'evil' will put on his wolf skin and pass as the true pretender to the truth, the film will also present a whole series of other fakes that compete to dispute the role of truth, above all, the modulations of sounds and colours, through artistic creations that give us aberrant and creative perceptions, while undoing possible ties of colours, sometimes, stuck to cataloguing feelings, showing us the power of art.

And we know that in Deleuzian philosophy, this is the task of thought, the work of creation, that in philosophy one creates concepts, while in the arts one creates a block of percepts and affects. An indication of the philosopher to bring the concept to immanence, for as he will point out, the concept, as it was seen in classical philosophy, corresponded to the form of the true (Deleuze 2018, 185). But when we actualize it as potency, the concept will always have a double aspect, the affect and the percept. Thus, Deleuze (2018, 185) will add: 'while the true world refers to a truthful man, the concept does not suffice itself, but refers to the two aspects of potency: the affect and the percept'. In this way, according to Deleuze (2018, 186), the crisis of the notion of truth is the confrontation of the concept with its correlates: affects and percepts, that is, the concept meets time. Since then, when facing a concept, we would have to ask ourselves: 'Does this concept make us fit to perceive more and more things or, on the contrary, does it petrify, coagulate all perspectivism?' (2018, 186).

Finally, the French philosopher will point out that at the same time that 'the concept must be related to the affects and the percepts, [. . .] nothing is possible if the concept is not'. In raising the question that confronts the concept with the affects and the percepts, truth undergoes a fundamental crisis, and the power of time, in its double aspect, becomes itself a power of the false.

The Wolf House helps us think the concept we propose in this text, the infantile-image, from within time. For both image and infanthood are still too attached to representation and linked to a universal, a moral, in many current discourses. Deleuzian philosophy helps us to think ethically and affirm them through artistic experimentation, in films that find their potency in time, as well as move infantile figures beyond logical and standardized forms, not reducing them to representations or story illustrations. Neither infanthood nor image exist prior to the complex media that constitute the film, but they help to actualize a common problem of an event in Latin America, the dictatorships and their effects that continue to hover over the continent differently, problematizing it together with the images that appear on the screen. Maria makes us see the horror of this period, seeking to generate in us a potentialized sensitivity rather than a conscience. The percepts not only help us to discover new things, but also end up giving other orderings to things.

The concept of infantile-image finds in the artistic creations present in *The Wolf House* the possibility of being created when affected by something very singular, that are the once latent effects of fascism on the Latin American continent, and that can expand the possibilities of perceiving them through the different images that are actualized in the encounter of the infantile character with the movements of experimentation of these images.

Instead of seeking to represent what an infanthood was like in periods of dictatorship, Cociña and León experiment with creating infantile-images that teach us to see among things, to perceive temporal perspectives of events, beyond a motif that serves as history. They do not only build a memory of their country, but a memory for the world; they are infantile-images within time and that compose an aesthetic-political field wrapped in revolutionary affects and percepts, or, better put, less than revolution, they express the affirmation of a visionary struggle.

The fascist and moral wolf is always lurking and is actualized in different ways, in different bodies, and its effects are always prowling around, anywhere or in any one place. *The Wolf House* is always showing and imposing watchwords, modulating its discourses, changing its form, sometimes docile, sometimes vengeful. Always telling a child, 'YOU MUST'. Fascism covers itself with the moral and revisits Latin America, provoking it to serve as a memory to the world. It is in the power of the false that this visionary struggle with images can be constituted.

Note

1 Conceptualization originated in the doctoral thesis of Novaes (2021): images individuated by sound and visual experimentations and deriving infantile-figures in their filmic spaces, continuously potentiating them, among the folds that constitute themselves throughout several filmic works studied, among them *The Wolf House* (2018). Folds that affect the infantile-images with other virtualities, intensifying them with sounds and colours.

References

Bogue, Ronald (2003), *Deleuze on Cinema*, New York and London: Routledge.

Camarneiro, Fabio (2019), 'Algumas explosões (e um suspiro): ontologia das imagens digitais na era do neoliberalismo', *Rebeca: Revista Brasileira de Cinema e Estudos Audiovisuais*, 8 (1): 17–34.

Cangiano, Antônio (2022), *A construção da subjetividade no neoliberalismo: Deleuze e Guattari*, Santo Ângelo: Metrics.

Crary, Jonathan (2013), *24/7 - Late Capitalism and the Ends of Sleep*, New York and London: Verso.

Deleuze, Gilles (2018), *Cine III. Verdad y Tiempo. Potencia de lo falso*, trans. Pablo Ires and Sebastián Puente, Buenos Aires: Cactus.

Grosz, Elizabeth (2012), 'Time Out of Joint', in Bernd Herzogenrath (ed.), *Time and History in Deleuze and Serres*, 147–51, London: Continuum.

León, Cristóbal and Joaquín Cociña (2018), *Entrevista a los directores de película 'La Casa Lobo' León & Cociña. Cristóbal León: 'Se hizo evidente que teníamos una pata en el mundo del cine y otra pata puesta en el mundo de arte'*. [Interview] Culturizarte, Santiago.

León, Cristóbal and Joaquín Cociña (2019), *Berlinale Forum: La Casa Lobo León & Cociña*. [Entrevista cedida a] Arsenal – Institute for Film and Video Art, Berlin.

Neno, Carolina Urrutia and Ana Fernández (2018), 'Sound Perturbations, Visual Resonances: Reflections About Sound in Three Experimental Films', *Cuadernos de Música, Artes Visuales y Artes Escénicas* 1 (14): 65–83.

Novaes, Marcus (2021), *Ionizations of Senses and Infanthoods in Latin American Cinematographies*, Campinas: State University of Campinas.

Schleusener, Simon (2020), 'Deleuze and Neoliberalism', *Coils of the Serpent Journal*, 6: 39–54.

Smith, Daniel (2013), 'Temporality and Truth', *Deleuze Studies*, 7 (3): 377–89.

The Wolf House (2018), [Film] Dir. Joaquín Cociña and Cristóbal León, Chile: Diluvio – Globo Rojo Films.

10

Schizoanalysis and Neoliberalism

Philosophy as Revolutionary Praxis
for a People-to-Come

Tony See

Introduction

The connection between mental illness and neoliberal capitalism has become the subject of much concern in recent years. In *The Soul at Work: From Alienation to Autonomy* (2009), Franco 'Bifo' Berardi draws our attention to the subterranean connection between Western capitalism and the current mental health epidemic. In this text, Berardi argued with a deep sense of pessimism that '[t]here are no more maps we can trust, no more destinations for us to reach. Ever since its mutation into semiocapitalism, capitalism has swallowed the exchange-value machine not only for the different forms of life, but also of thought, imagination, and hope. There is no alternative to capitalism' (Berardi 2009, 131). His concept of 'semiocapitalism' refers to the idea of an all-pervading ideological form of capitalism, one that extends well beyond the economic sphere and well into signifying practices, whose 'semiotic regime' subjects citizens to an 'excessive velocity of signifiers' that 'stimulates a sort of interpretative hyperkinesis' (Berardi 2009, 181). The question that haunts us today should not be whether there is a connection between capitalism and mental health, but whether there is a way out of this mental health plague that is linked to semiocapitalist neoliberalism.

Berardi's critique of neoliberal capitalism is echoed by Mark Fisher, whose similar critique of neoliberal capitalism in the British context has been gaining traction in the last decades. Fisher's two major works on this subject, *Capitalist Realism: Is There No Alternative?* (2009) and *Ghosts of My Life: Writings on Depression, Hauntology and Lost Futures* (2014), paint a brutal image of the interrelation between mental illness and capitalism. Fisher argued that there is now an alarming 'epidemic' level of depression and anxiety in contemporary Western societies, most of which are closely related to capitalism. Capitalism in its current neoliberal form is held responsible for the growing rates of mental illness. This is accompanied by a plethora of misguided approaches to tackling mental illness, most of which lead to further complications. These approaches usually begin with the *privatization* of mental disorders, that is, interpreting mental illnesses such as anxiety, depression and burnout as issues of *individual* concern that are unrelated to social formations, and in doing so, these approaches deflect attention from their systemic causations (2009). In Fisher's opinion, these mental health issues are directly caused by imposing the neoliberal doctrines of individual meritocracy on human beings – capitalism's tendency to view people as abstract individuals exercising 'rational choice' in principle rules out the possibility that mental illnesses have systemic causes. Instead of capitalism, they reduce explanations to individual neurology and family backgrounds. Fisher states,

> Capitalist realism insists on treating mental health as if it were a natural fact, like weather [. . .]. In the late 1960s and 1970s, radical theory and politics [. . .] coalesced around extreme mental conditions such as schizophrenia, arguing, for instance, that madness was not a natural, but a political, category. But what is needed now is a politicization of much more common disorders. Indeed, it is their very commonness which is the issue: in Britain, depression is now the condition that is most treated by the NHS. [. . .] [W]e need to ask: how has it become acceptable that so many people, and especially so many young people, are ill? (Fisher 2009, 19)

In response to this, Fisher suggested that we need to reconsider the politicization of psychiatric issues in our own times. Fisher has proposed that we can do this through the denaturalization of capitalism's dominant ideology and a re-politicization of mental illness through psychoanalytic concepts. Fisher argued that these 'involve invoking the Real(s) underlying the reality that capitalism presents to us' (p. 18). He theorized that this could involve the Real of environmental catastrophes, but also what Fisher calls the 'aporias' within the naturalized order presented by capitalist realism. He identifies the 'mental health plague' (p. 19) and its naturalization as an individual biochemical defect as a paradigmatic example.

If Fisher's solution would lead us to believe that he was an optimist, that there is still a way to stand up against neoliberalism capitalism and the harm that it causes, we need to reconsider his deeply pessimistic statement that it is easier for us to imagine the end of the world than the end of capitalism itself (2009, 2014). For Fisher believes that capitalism is now a deeply entrenched ideological form that has become a state of mind of individuals in society (2009). In its current neoliberal form, capitalism immediately affects the mental well-being of large parts of the population through precarious work and insecurity that it produces. The concept of 'capitalist realism' is developed to explain how capitalist modes of thinking and acting in society have pervaded both the imaginary and symbolic orders, becoming so pervasive that the logic of capitalism has rendered alternative concepts of economic and social life almost impossible. In other words, 'Capitalist realism' describes 'the widespread sense that not only is capitalism the only viable system, but also that it is now impossible even to *imagine* a coherent alternative to it' (Fisher 2009, 2). In fact, we have even come to believe that such alternatives are dangerous. In Fisher's words, capitalist realism is 'analogous to the deflationary perspective of a depressive who believes that any positive state, any hope, is a dangerous illusion' (2009, 5). This implies that the resulting mental conditions are not restricted to those of unfortunate individuals in society, but also become part of a '"mental health plague" in capitalist societies', which suggests that 'instead of being the only social system that works, capitalism is inherently dysfunctional, and that the cost of it appearing to work is very high' (Fisher 2009, 19). In fact, what we have now is 'mental health plague'.

Neoliberalism and its discontents

It is interesting to see how neoliberal capitalist social formations, which begin with the assumption that human beings are 'rational' beings, ultimately create a situation which fosters mental illnesses. Neoliberalism's 'rational choice theory' is based on the assumption that human beings are nothing more than beings that make rational calculations in order to maximize their own utility. Needless to say, this is a reductive image of the human being which does not merely simplify but also misrepresents what human beings are. When this liberal idea is writ large, it simply means that corporations as legal 'persons' should also engage in free competition for the sake of maximizing profits in the neoliberal imaginary. This image of the rational subject in neoliberal dogma *seems* to be challenged by the development of Freudian psychoanalysis which says that *our conscious decisions are determined by our unconscious desires*. In other words, such a rational choice subject does not exist. However, this Freudian challenge proves to be an illusion since Freud also theorized that the unconscious is characterized by the Oedipal structure of the father, mother and child, and in doing so it is unable to reach the *true unconscious*.

In Deleuze and Guattari's *Anti-Oedipus* the true unconscious is to be found in the pre-individual and non-personal *socius*, in other words, the social formation that is defined in terms of the materiality of the earth. Deleuze and Guattari's 'schizoanalysis' departs from reductionist interpretations and foregrounds complexity in their new account by seeing it as within this complex materiality where the subject first emerges. As Guattari explains, 'rather than moving in the direction of reductionist modifications which simplify the complex', schizoanalysis 'will work towards its complexification . . . in short towards its ontological heterogeneity' (Guattari 1995 [2006], 61).

To be sure, not all psychoanalytic theories privatize the unconscious. Lacan has theorized that the unconscious is not to be discovered in individual consciousnesses but in the exterior, in institutionalized symbolic and linguistic systems which constitute our symbolic reality. From the Lacanian perspective, even the source of mental illnesses such as perversion, hysteria and narcissistic tendencies was also not simply to be found within subjective individuals but can be located in the language and speech acts found within a linguistic space that together constitute our symbolic reality. The issue with Lacan's theory is that even though it manages to give an account of the unconscious in terms of exteriority, it continues to interpret the unconscious as being organized in terms of the big Other. In doing so, Lacan's subject remains stuck within the logic of desire as lack and is unable to liberate itself from the imaginary order.

Deleuze and Guattari's critique of Lacanian psychoanalysis is that it fails to see that desire as lack only appears when the social formation in which we have invested our libidinal energies comes to suppress desire. In the third chapter of *Anti-Oedipus*, this *socius* is said to evolve in terms of the three registers of territorialism, despotism and capitalism. In the primitive *socius*, there is no familial in the Oedipal sense; the Oedipal is a later development in the consciousness that only appears under despotic forms of power and through the mediation of the imperial state. The task of the despot was mirrored by the role of the father at this later stage. The role of the father undergoes further transformation and becomes independent in modern nuclear families.

Since social formations are the true unconscious that is the primary determinant of our desire, it means that our desire cannot be considered in terms of produced, representational entities. This means that our desires are *transcendental* and impersonal and exterior to personal minds, as it marks a transcendental exteriority. Hence, our conscious will is the product of a real transcendental desire. A real, immanent *synthesis* undergirds this productive unconscious desire. Production here is indeed synthesis, but not the transcendent synthesis of complete objects we associate with a full subject; rather, it is an immanent synthesis of partial objects. If the relation of the *psyche* to the outside is called experience, this experience takes place in terms of *production*. Further, the unconscious experience is the productive site of both the subject and the object of experience. On the one hand, experiencing and constructing the subject are one and the same process. On the other, the process through which the subject is under production is identical to the process through which the outside world is under production.

Guattari in his *The Machinic Unconscious: Essays in Schizoanalysis* gives us a picture of the unconscious as being situated within a social space that casts the future as a screen of possibility. According to Guattari, the unconscious must be seen in the context of a sedimented, materialized past that is, however, open to a reconstruction through deterritorializing enunciations and acts. Here, schizoanalysis is not merely a representation of what things are like but a *productive* way of furthering a becoming through an interpretive and active assemblage of systemic or machinic processes and operations. He writes:

> the unconscious works inside individuals in their manner of perceiving the world and living their body, territory, and sex, as well as inside the couple, the family, school, neighborhood, factories, socius, and universities. . . . In other words, not simply an unconscious of the specialists of the unconscious, not simply an unconscious crystallized in the past, congealed in an institutionalized discourse, but, on the contrary, an unconscious turned towards the future whose screen would be none other than the possible itself, the possible as hypersensitive to language, but also the possible hypersensitive to touch, hypersensitive to the socius, hypersensitive to the cosmos. . . . Then why stick this label of 'machinic unconscious' onto it? Simply to stress that it is populated not only with images and words, but also with all kinds of machinisms that lead it to produce and reproduce these images and words. (Guattari 2011)

This is why Deleuze and Guattari reject the contractarian idea that society emerges from the common needs of individuals when they come together through a contractual agreement. It is not individuals that give rise to the *socius*, rather, it is the *socius* that gave rise to the individual. In 'Jean-Jacques Rousseau: Precursor of Kafka, Celine and Ponge' Deleuze already argued that 'one of Rousseau's constant themes is that need is not a factor which brings people together: it does not unite, it isolates each of us'. This raises the question as to what brings us together, what unites us? First, it is desire that unites. But this desire is not that of individuals, rather it is social desiring-machines that are primarily linked together on the earthly body. Hence, society is not a structure that is derived from pre-existing individuals, rather, individuals are emergent from a pre-existing social structure. Society is a machine that produces individuals. This *socius* is itself not structural but *machinic*.

This means that the real source of my actions does not lie in my conscious will but in the true unconscious which is the *socius*, the social formation. Deleuze and Guattari would emphasize that the unconscious is not a field of representation but a field of *production*, that is desiring-production. This is why they replace the traditional Freudian metaphor of the theatre with that of the factory; the unconscious does not merely represent things like in a theatre but *produces* things like in a factory. Since desire is productive, Deleuze and Guattari would say that the fundamental problem of political philosophy is one that was formulated most clearly by Spinoza: 'Why do people fight for their servitude as stubbornly as though it were their salvation?' (AO 29). In other words, why do people have such a stake in investing in a social system that constantly represses them, persistently thwarts their interests and introduces lack into their lives? Daniel Smith is of the opinion that the answer to this question is because your desire is not your own, but part of the capitalist infrastructure; they are not simply your own individual mental or psychic reality (AO 30). This is obvious in the effects of marketing, which are directed entirely at the manipulation of the drives and affects (Smith 2007, 74). In other words, Deleuze and Guattari's discovery is that your drives have been constructed, assembled and arranged in such a manner that your desire is positively invested in the system.

Thus, Deleuze and Guattari rejected psychoanalysis not simply because it misrepresents the unconscious, but also because it is *complicit* in making one accommodate oneself to capitalism. According to Deleuze and Guattari, psychoanalytic analyses tend to pathologize desire – interpreting it as an issue with the individual and not with the neoliberal society at large, and then attempting to bring the individual back to mental health. This 'mental health' is defined, however, in relation to a norm that sustains capitalism, the very system that produces mental health issues in the first place. Thus, the psychoanalytic approach to mental health is nothing more than an apparatus that is designed for the socio-historical transformation of the desiring-production.

Revolutionary praxis

Deleuze and Guattari's schizoanalysis can be seen as an attempt to undermine the system of capitalism by merging psychoanalysis (libido) with the socio-historical dimensions of Marxism (labour-power). Schizoanalysis accepted that there is an unconscious, but it rejects the idea that this unconscious lies within individual persons. It agrees more with Lacan that this unconscious is *exterior* to the individual and can be found in the symbolic and linguistic structures of society, but it does not believe that desire should be thought in terms of lack. This lack only comes about from the capitalist social formation, a formation that we have invested our energies in itself. More importantly, it emphasizes that this unconscious is productive, a desiring-production. Deleuze and Guattari state that 'The only means of bypassing the sterile parallelism where we flounder between Freud and Marx, is by discovering . . . how the affects or drives form part of the infrastructure itself' (AO 63). This means that our drives and impulses, including the unconscious ones, which seem to be what is most individual about you, are themselves *economic*, they are already part of what the infrastructure (Smith 2007, 71). In *Anti-Oedipus*, Deleuze and Guattari also emphasize that our 'desires' are our drives and impulses, and these drives and impulses are not to be thought in terms of lack, but in terms of production; they are the desiring-machines themselves (AO 35). In other words, our desires are always arranged and assembled by the social formation in which we find ourselves, such as primitive territorial societies, states, capitalism and, later, in *A Thousand Plateaus*, nomadic war machines.

If Deleuze and Guattari's theory of schizoanalysis helps us to gain a better understanding of how individual subjectivities are formed by capitalist formations and vice versa, it is not very obvious how this understanding can lead to effective revolutionary strategies that bring about liberation from capitalism. Guattari, for instance, responded to George Stambolian's question 'What then is the basic difference between schizoanalysis and psychoanalysis?' with the answer that

> Psychoanalysis transforms and deforms the unconscious by forcing it to pass through the grid of its system of inscription and representation. For psychoanalysis, the unconscious is always *already there*, genetically programmed, structured, and finalized on objectives of conformity to social norms. For schizoanalysis, it's a question of *constructing* an unconscious, not only with individuals or relations between individuals, but also with groups, with physiological and perceptual system, with machines, struggles, and arrangements of every nature. There's not a question here of transfer, interpretation, or delegation of power to a specialist. (Guattari 1979a, 59)

The idea is that we should *construct* an unconscious of exteriority, but how can this be done when the constructing subject is constructed by the social formation in the first place?

168   *Deleuze, Guattari and the Schizoanalysis of Post-Neoliberalism*

Deleuze and Guattari have together maintained that they were Marxists in the sense that they remained committed to the critique of capitalism as an immanent system that constantly moves its limits and constantly re-establishes them on an expanded scale (Deleuze 1995b, 171; Pellejero 2009, 102). While this much is clear, it is less clear why Deleuze and Guattari did not subscribe to orthodox Marxist ideas such as dialectics and the ideal of the utopian state. Jean-Francois Lyotard, for instance, even went to the extent of saying that Deleuze and Guattari's *Capitalism and Schizophrenia* may be an implicit critique of Marx's ideas because it does not contain classical Marxist concepts such as the base and superstructure, the proletariat and work-value theory, and the workers' struggle (Lyotard 1972). Instead of these orthodox Marx concepts, Deleuze and Guattari's works contain new and creative ideas such as 'lines of flight', 'minorities' and 'war machines' (Pellejero 2009, 102).

In order to address the complex relationship between Deleuze and Guattari and Marx, it may be worthwhile for us to see how Marx defined 'communism'. In *The German Ideology*, Marx did not define 'communism' as an ideal arrangement or system for ruling society, much less a state-form that needs to be established by revolutionary forces, but as a 'real movement' that abolishes the actual state-form itself. What is this 'real movement?' We can get a glimpse of this from Marx's remark that his own analyses of capitalism are not carved in stone but necessarily include modification in the light of changing conditions. If we take Marx at his words, this throws new light on Deleuze and Guattari's apparent refusal to stick to Marxist orthodoxy while remaining Marxist, to their creation of new concepts which are relevant to the times and intended to bring about some changes in the order of things (Deleuze 1988, 16).

This becomes apparent when Deleuze and Guattari suggest that philosophical concepts must be critical of the present to the extent that they 'connect up with what is real here and now in the struggle against capitalism' (Deleuze and Guattari 1994, 100). From this perspective, Deleuze and Guattari's idea of philosophy as the practice of inventing concepts as tools for social and political change is actually more in keeping with Marx's spirit than with historical Marxist orthodoxies which have become party lines and turned into dogmatic images of thought.

It is quite obvious that Deleuze and Guattari were critical of the events of 1968, that is, they were critical of the French communists, but it is important to note that they did not abandon the idea of revolution. In an interview in the 1980s, Deleuze, in response to an ever-popular accusation against the Left that revolutions turn out badly, that they give birth to 'monsters' who devour their

Schizoanalysis and Neoliberalism

children, stated that 'when you say that revolutions have a bad future, you have still said nothing about the becoming-revolutionary of people' (Deleuze 1988, 24). Here, Deleuze was not criticizing the revolutions per se, but was making an important distinction between the idea of revolution and historical revolutions. The problem with actually existing revolutions is that they are approximations of the idea of revolution, and they thus fall short of the ideal. In other words, actually existing revolutions betray the ideal even as they are instantiated. However, this is no reason for abandoning the idea of revolution itself. The thing to do is to constantly revise revolutionary practices and to expand them further, so that they come to include those that they failed to include previously. It is from this perspective that philosophy plays an important role in society, as a critique of actually existing revolutions in the name of the ideal of a more ideal revolution.

One common criticism against Deleuze and Guattari's recommendation is that in separating Marxism in spirit from Marxism as historical orthodoxies, it becomes unclear how social change may be achieved in practice. In his 1990 interview with Deleuze, Negri, for example, says that even as he celebrates the ideas behind *A Thousand Plateaus*, he could not see how it could be 'effective' and 'institutionalized'. In his words, 'How could resistance become insurrection?' (Deleuze 1990, 234). Schizoanalysis, we are told, does not rest with the assumption that the political economy and the libidinal economy are two separate things but as *one and the same thing*. One possible way of accounting for this is to say that perhaps we might never know the answer to this *theoretical* question, but the Deleuze and Guattari's idea of schizoanalysis in *Anti-Oedipus* may be seen as a *practical solution*. Buchanan, for instance, has stated that schizoanalysis may be intended to draw our attention to the potential for revolution in the realm of everyday life instead of confining revolution to political parties. 'Schizoanalysis as such does not raise the problem of the nature of the socius to come out of the revolution; it does not claim to be identical with the revolution itself' (AO 415/456). This is why it uses the language of revolution in a sense which goes beyond the orthodox Marxist's assumption that it must necessarily involve the taking of power, the overturning of the capitalist regime and the installation of a top-down regime as the Maoists and Leninists demand (Buchanan 1998, 10).

Buchanan states

> Revolution for Deleuze and Guattari means schizophrenizing the existing power structure, making it vibrate to a new rhythm, making it change from within, without at the same time becoming a schizophrenic. But they don't offer a model for a new society, save that it won't replicate the old repressions. Their argument

is that we'll never get to that new society the militants of every persuasion claim their doctrine is leading us towards if we don't first of all shed our old habits, our old love of power, our manifold addictions to the exercise of force, our customary obsequiousness in the face of power, and so on.

The idea that revolution involves the ethical transformation of the subject instead of political reforms seems to be supported by Foucault's statement that Deleuze was in fact writing a book of ethics. In his 'Preface' to Deleuze and Guattari's *Anti-Oedipus*, Foucault states that, 'the major enemy, the strategic adversary is fascism . . . and not only historical fascism, the fascism of Hitler and Mussolini . . . but also the fascism in us all, in our heads and our every day behavior, the fascism that causes us to love power, to desire the very thing that dominates and exploits us' (Deleuze and Guattari 1977 [2000], xiii). One issue with Foucault's interpretation of Deleuze and Guattari's work in terms of 'ethics' is that it runs the risk of turning schizoanalysis into yet another form of personal ethics, one that is exclusively focused on personal transformation instead of social and political engagement.

Schizoanalysis and the financial capitalism of banks

So what would a schizoanalysis of neoliberalism look like today? What would an ethics of schizoanalysis look like in relation to neoliberalism? In *Anti-Oedipus*, Deleuze and Guattari repeatedly reminded us that desiring-production and social production *are one and the same thing*. This means that schizoanalysis in practice should not rest content with the analysis of personal consciousnesses but also include critical engagements with social formations that have a real impact on individuals. There are many social formations that we may engage with. Ian Buchanan has suggested that if we want to understand how desire is induced, managed and channelled into socially sanctioned avenues today, *then we need to understand how banking works, for it is banks that orchestrate this new arrangement of filiation and alliance*. In fact, Deleuze and Guattari have pointed out that if we want to 'return to Marx' today, then one needs to return to his work on banking practice (AO 250/273) (AO 166/178) (Buchanan 1998, 108).

Buchanan has once referred to this as the defining contradiction at the heart of the modern capitalist machine. In a way reflecting what Mark Fisher and Franco 'Bifo' Benardi have said but in a more targeted manner, the 'ultimate obscenity' of capitalism today is that it must constantly try to gloss over the scandalous difference in kind between the money of the wage earner and the money of the financier, between money that functions purely as payment (alliance) and money that functions as finance (filiation) (Buchanan 1998, 108–9). The gross inequalities that we see today have less to do with capitalism itself than with the world of financial reproduction, a reproduction that reaches the zenith of madness. This raises the question of whether the individual cases of mental illness that we see today are but a reflection of the illness in the social formation itself, a formation that demands of us the strictest sanity to such an extent that it reaches insanity. Buchanan states:

> In the one case, there are impotent money signs of exchange value, a flow of the means of payment relative to consumer goods and use values, and a one-to-one relation between money and an imposed range of products ('which I have a right to, which are my due, so they're mine'); in the other case, signs of the power of capital, flows of financing, a system of differential quotients of production that bear witness to a prospective force or to a long-term evaluation, not realisable *hie et nwtc*, and functioning as an axiomatic of abstract quantities. (AO 249/271) (Buchanan 1998, 108–9)

In a word, people are made to chase after signs in a way that the horizon of signs forever remains outside their reach.

This is but the very situation of the Third World, now every so graciously called 'the developing world'. The Third World lives in a dream in which they have been talked into adopting as its own, and the dream is of transforming payment money into finance money. No.

> Integration of the dominated classes could occur without the shadow of this unapplied principle of convertibility – which is enough, however, to ensure that the Desire of the most disadvantaged creature will invest with all its strength, irrespective of any economic understanding or lack of it, the capitalist social field as a whole. (AO 249–50/272) (Buchanan 1998, 109)

Thus, Deleuze and Guattari can say it is the banks that control desire in contemporary society, and if so, this means that it is now even more urgent that we do a schizoanalysis of banks and the financial world, its semiotics of exchange. This is no less true today than it was in 1972, when *Anti-Oedipus* was published; indeed, it is no exaggeration to say that it is truer today than it was then (Buchanan 1998, 109).

On a larger scale, manufacturing has been exported from the First World to the Third World for the same reason: *to maintain the rate of profit*. Yes, it is much cheaper to manufacture goods in the low-wage regions of the Third World, but those cost savings are rarely passed on to the consumer. More usually, they are passed directly to the company directors and shareholders in the form of dividends and an enhanced capitalization of their stock. The tendency towards a falling rate of profit is a continually recurring 'crisis' for capitalism, but not one it has any interest in overcoming. In fact, it is the principal motor powering the system, giving it its restless energy (Buchanan 1998, 110).

So, what is the revolutionary path? What is the solution? Deleuze and Guattari outlined three tasks – one negative and two positive – that will better position us to become revolutionaries in relation to neoliberalism. According to Deleuze and Guattari, the very first task is a negative one; it is to 'Destroy, destroy. The task of schizoanalysis goes by way of destruction – a whole scouring of the unconscious, a complete curettage' (AO 342/371). The object that is to be destroyed is the Oedipus, and to do so, we must neither retreat to a pre-Oedipal phase nor project a post-Oedipal phase as a means of escaping the Oedipal trap. We must rediscover the operation of *desire* – a desiring-production that lies hidden behind and beneath Oedipal representations. Destruction is essentially a practical matter of undoing the complex set of illusions such as political and national territories by means of which we give structure and purpose to our lives. It is to deterritorialize them (Buchanan 1998, 117). This includes the task of eliminating reterritorialization, as it is constantly a threat (120). This is why the second task is a positive one; it consists of 'discovering in a subject the nature, the formation, or the functioning of *his* desiring-machines, independently of any interpretations. What are your desiring-machines, what do you put into these machines, what is the output, how does it work, what are your nonhuman sexes?' (AO 354/384). In order to reach the point of being able to answer these questions, the investigation must push beyond the interpretative realm – the realm in which the question 'what does it mean?' still applies – into what Deleuze and Guattari specify as the functional or machinic realm (Buchanan 1998, 121). Finally, the third task is also a positive one for schizoanalysis; it consists of reaching 'the investments of unconscious desire of the social field, insofar as they are differentiated from the preconscious investments of interest, and insofar as they are not merely capable of counteracting them, but also of coexisting with them in opposite modes' (AO 383/419) (Buchanan 1998, 123). It goes without saying that the answer to this question becomes more apparent in Deleuze and Guattari's last major collaborative work, *What Is Philosophy?* In this text, we are called to maintain the revolutionary potential of philosophy as a discipline that involves *the creation of new concepts* (Deleuze 1988, 16). In *What Is Philosophy?*, philosophy is a critique of the present and with the aim of calling 'for a future form, for a new earth and people that do not yet exist' (Deleuze and Guattari 1994, 108).

Conclusion

Deleuze and Guattari's schizoanalysis can be seen as an attempt to undermine the system of neoliberal capitalism, a system that is becoming increasingly clear that is the cause of mental health issues. Schizoanalysis approaches the issues by the apparent merging of psychoanalysis – which studies the libido – with the socio-historical insights of Marxism. Schizoanalysis agrees with psychoanalysis that the agent is not entirely rational, that conscious decisions are subject to the unconscious, but it rejects the idea that this unconscious belongs to private individuals with desire interpreted in terms of lack. This lack only comes about from the capitalist social formation, a formation that we have invested our energies in itself. Instead, Deleuze and Guattari theorized that the true unconscious is exterior to the private individual, pre-personal and the result of capitalist formations. This means that for Deleuze and Guattari, schizoanalysis does not rest with the assumption that the political economy and the libidinal economy are two separate things but as *one and the same thing*. Deleuze and Guttari's texts suggest many ways by which we may expand the concept of revolution etc. However, the question of practice remains: If the subject's unconscious is constituted by social formations, whence is the subject that is able to reconstitute this social formation productively? The answer to this may lie in a philosophy which no longer reflects, which no longer prides itself on doing representation, but which creates new concepts for a becoming-people, for a people-to-come.

References

Berardi, Franco 'Bifo' (2009), *The Soul at Work: From Alienation to Autonomy*, South Pasadena: Semiotexte(s).

Buchanan, Ian (1998), *Deleuze and Guattari's Anti-Oedipus: A Reader's Guide*, New York and London: Continuum.

Deleuze, Gilles (1988), 'Signes et événements', *Magazine littéraire*, no. 257 (September): 16–25.

Deleuze, Gilles and Félix Guattari (1977), *Anti-Oedipus*, trans. Robert Hurley, Mark Seem and Helen R. Lane, New York: Viking Press.

Deleuze, Gilles and Felix Guattari (1994), *What Is Philosophy?*, trans. H. Tomlinson and G. Burchell, New York: Columbia.

Fisher, Mark (2009), *Capitalist Realism. Is There No Alternative?*, Winchester: Zero Books.

Fisher, Mark (2014), *Ghosts of My Life: Writings on Depression, Hauntology and Lost Futures*, Winchester: Zero Books.

Guattari, Félix (1979a), 'A Liberation of Desire', in George Stambolian and Elaine Marks (eds), *Homosexualities and French Literature*, Ithaca: Cornell University Press.

Guattari, Felix (1979b), *L'fnconscient rnachinique*, Pans: Recherches.

Guattari, Félix (1995 [2006]), *Chaosmosis: An Ethico-aesthetic Paradigm*, Sydney: Power Publications.

Guattari, Félix (2011), *The Machinic Unconscious: Essays in Schizoanalysis*, Los Angeles: Semiotext(e).

Lyotard, Jean-François (1972), 'Energumen Capitalism', *Critique*, 306 (November); English translation in *Semiotext(e)*, 2 (3).

Pellejero, Eduardo (2009), 'Minor Marxism: An Approach to a New Political Praxis', in Dhruv Jain (ed.), *Deleuze and Marx*, 102–18, Edinburgh: Edinburgh University Press.

Smith, Daniel (2007). 'Deleuze and the Question of Desire: Toward an Immanent Theory of Ethics', *Parrhesia*, 2: 66–78.

Index

1977 *Le Monde* op-ed 'Le pire moyen de
   faire l'Europe' 43

Agar, Jon 101, 105 n.14
agroecological movements 13
agroecological war machines 123
agroecology
   agricultural space 118
   author function 110–18
   Brazilian Landless Workers'
      Movement 121
   chemical fertilizers 119
   collective assemblage of
      enunciation 121
   collective assemblages of
      enunciation 110
   corporate food regime 120
   food security 118
   food sovereignty 120
   Green revolution 118
   high coefficient of
      deterritorialization 120
   hybrid seed–chemical fertilizers–
      pesticide nexus 119
   innovations and ideas 120
   minoritarian-majoritarian
      interface 110
   pesticides 119
   political immediacy 110, 120, 121
   processes of dividualization 110,
      118–22
   small farming 119, 123
Amazon 47, 48, 99, 100
Amin, Samir 7
analog and digital power
   analog media 96
   continuation 101–3
   cybernetics 96
   diffusion of 'digital new media' 95

digital capitalism 95, 99
digital Morse telegraph 96
digital symbol scheme 97
discretization 101–3
   examples 97
   history of 94–8
   modulation 98–9
   moulding 98–9
   transition 95
Anthropocene/Capitalocene/Plantatio
      nocene 127, 128, 130, 131, 133,
      134, 136, 138–40
anthropogenic disaster 9
anti-intellectualism 13, 43–5
anti-Marxist *nouveaux philosophes* 44
anti-natural morality 78
Anti-Oedipus (Deleuze and Guattari)
      7–9, 22, 23, 45, 46, 49, 50 n.5, 66,
      68, 164, 167, 169–71
anti-productive colonial mechanisms 3
Aradau, Claudia 43
arboreal locomotion 24
artificial intelligence 35, 59, 80
asambleas populares ('people's
      assemblies') 42
austerity 35, 39, 42
author function 110
   concept of sexuality 112
   corporate authorship 114
   critical-constructive authorship 114
   dividuality 113, 115, 116
   facilitative counselling skills 114
   fictional narrator 112
   individuality 114, 115, 117
   individualized authorial activity 111
   initiators of discursive practices 111
   latency of sexuality 114, 115
   multiplication and attenuation
      111–14

mythical stories/folk tales 111
political axis of individualization 111
principle of rational autonomy 112
principle of 'self-decipherment' 112
rational entity 112
religious bias 111
responsible innovation 114
socio-economic stability 113
virtual-economic identity 115
axiomatization 11, 26
axioms 26, 29, 36, 37, 41, 69, 146

Bacon, Francis 82
Barbarism with a Human Face (Levy) 50 n.5
Baroque operation 78
Becker, Gary 16 n.9
Beckman, Frieda 9, 10
Beller, Jonathan 101
Beniger, James 101, 105 n.14
Berardi, Franco 'Bifo' 161, 170
big data 58, 59
Big Tech 47–9, 99
bioconservatives 80, 83
bio-human 4
biological diversity 25
biological specialization 25, 26
bio-political strategies 4
biopoliticization of humanitarianism 16 n.11
Blake, William 129
Bogue, Ronald 153
Bolivian and Ecuadorian governments 46
Bolsa Família (Portuguese for 'Family Allowance') 38, 46–7
Bolsonaro, Jair 39, 47, 146
Boltanski, Luc 5
Braidotti, Rossi 81
Braun, Bruce 17 n.15
Brazilian Landless Workers' Movement 121
Bricmont, Jean 103 n.1
Broncano, Fernando 82
Brown, Wendy 22
Brusentsov, Nikolai P. 103 n.4
Brusseau, James 47, 48
Buchanan, Ian 169–71
Buen Vivir 46
Bush, Vannevar 103 n.3

Camarneiro, Fabio 145
Canessa, Andrew 38
Cangiano, Antônio 143
Canzutti, Lucrezia 43
Capital Is Dead (Wark) 11, 55
capitalism 4–8, 21–3, 25, 26, 68, 161, 162, 168, 172
anthropocentric conceptualization 69
capitalist realism 163
central capitalism 37
contradictions of 57
definition 55, 57, 69
denaturalization of 162
digital age 96
digital capitalism 95, 99
financial capitalism of banks 170–2
gangster capitalism 3
global capitalism 9
gross inequalities 171
human labour 66
industrial capitalism 27, 32
info-capitalism 57
Keynesian capitalism 113, 117
laissez-faire capitalism 27
mutation of capitalism 39
neoliberal capitalism 1, 14, 15, 113, 120, 161, 162, 173
platform capitalism 30–2, 56
postanthropocentric analysis 70
postcapitalism 56–9, 62
post-industrial capitalism 68
reterritorialization 69
semiocapitalism 161
surveillance capitalism 56
ultimate obscenity 170
Western capitalism 161
Capitalism and Schizophrenia (Deleuze and Guattari) 168
capitalist realism 162, 163
Capitalist Realism: Is There No Alternative? (Fisher) 161
capital-labour conflict 55
capital–labour conflict 55, 59
Cayrol, Jean 141 n.6
cell therapy 2
central capitalism 37
centralization of production 57
Chabot, Pascal 64, 65
Chávez, Hugo 38
Chiapello, Eve 5

Index

cinema   13–14
  cinematographic, political
    ecology   135–9
  classical cinema   135
  death (or murder) of cinema   136
  ecological destruction   138
  mass media   130
  modern cinema   135, 136
  quantitative mediocrity   129
  reign of clichés   129–35, 139
  Resnais's 'cerebral'
    cinematography   138
  'Romantic' approach   129
  social normativity   137
  super-jects   140
  Western classical cinema   137
Cinema 2 (Deleuze)   104 n.8
Clastres, Pierre   46
Claude Shannon's theory   60
Cociña, Joaquín   143, 153–5, 157
Colebrook, Claire   6
commodification   3, 61, 116
Common Programme   36, 37
Compact Disc   96
convergence of struggles   50 n.1
Cool Capitalism   16 n.13
corporate authorship   114
corporate intellectuals   44
corporate oligarchy   5
Covid-19 pandemic   35, 47, 105 n.18,
    118
Covid-19 vaccines   85
Critique of Cynical Reason (Sloterdijk)   9
critique of kinetics   17 n.17
Critique of Pure Reason (Kant)   132
Croissant, Klaus   40, 43
cryptocurrency   32, 33
cultural diversity   25
cultural hegemony   29
cultural posthumanism   12, 80–6, 89
cybernetes   117, 120
cybernetics   96
A Cyborg Manifesto (Haraway)   81

Daney, Serge   135–7
Dardot, Pierre   86
Darwinian evolution   84
da Silva, Luiz Inácio Lula   38, 46
Davies, William   15 n.2, 87
decoding mechanism   7, 8, 23, 27, 68, 69

Deleuze, Gilles   2, 6–15, 21–3, 25, 26, 31,
    32, 35–49, 50 n.1, 50 n.2, 50 n.5, 56,
    63, 66, 67–71, 76–81, 85, 89, 93, 94,
    96–9, 101–3, 103 n.1, 103 n.2, 104
    n.5, 104 n.11, 105 n.14, 105 n.15,
    109, 110, 113, 115–22, 127–39, 141
    n.6, 146, 148, 152, 153, 156, 157,
    164–73
Deleuzean schizoanalysis   14–15
despecialization   10, 11, 23–8, 30
  biological despecialization   25
despecialized technologies   25, 32
deterritorialization   8–10, 23, 29, 69, 70,
    119–21, 123, 143
developing world   171
Diéguez, Antonio   81–3
Differential Analyser   103 n.3
digital age   96
digital capitalism   95, 99, 101
digital images   104 n.6
digitalization   12
digital neoliberalism   116
digital war machine   110, 118
Dillon, Michael   4
Discipline and Punish (Foucault)   21
Dosse, François   45
Down to Earth (Latour)   134
Dufour, Dany-Robert   7

ecological disaster   130, 131, 133, 135,
    136, 139
Eglash, Ron   105 n.17
Eliade, Mircea   25
empresas recuperadas ('recovered
    companies')   42
'engaged misreading,' Deleuze's
    philosophy   7
Epimetheus   24
epistemological ambivalence of
    neoliberalism   15 n.2
exo-Darwinism   24
Extinction, Deterritorialisation and
    End Times: Peak Deleuze
    (Colebrook)   6

Facebook   30, 48
Farías, Mónica   42
Fernández, Ana   149, 151
financial capitalism of banks   170–2
Finkielkraut, Alain   44

Fisher, Mark   161–3, 170
food sovereignty   120
Foucault, Michel   2–6, 16 n.9, 16 n.10, 21, 22, 27, 36, 42, 47, 78, 94, 105 n.15, 110, 111, 116, 123 n.1, 170
Franz Kafka's minor literary war machine   119
Freudian psychoanalysis   15, 163

Galloway, Andrew   6
Gane, Nicholas   87
gangster capitalism   3
The Gay Science (Nietzsche)   77
genetic supermarket   12, 76
geographical evacuation   41
The German Ideology (Marx)   168
Ghosts of My Life: Writings on Depression, Hauntology and Lost Futures (Fisher)   161
Giroux, Henry   3
global 'telecommunications' machine   29
Glucksmann, André   44
Goodman, Nelson   96, 97, 104 n.6
Google   6, 30, 47
governance of suffering   5
Great Acceleration   113, 114, 117
Green revolution   118
Grosz, Elizabeth   152
Grundrisse (Marx)   62, 68
Guattari, Félix   1, 9–11, 14, 15, 22, 23, 25, 26, 31, 33, 35–8, 40–7, 49, 50 n.3, 56, 63, 66–71, 76, 77, 85, 89, 102, 110, 119, 121, 127, 128, 130, 132, 146, 164–73

A Hacker Manifesto   71 n.2
haecceities   3
Hallward, Peter   49
Harari, Yuval Noah   88
Haraway, Donna   13, 81, 127, 128, 140
Hardt, M.   71 n.3
Hartree, Douglas R.   96
Harvey, David   22
Hayek, F.A.   5, 28, 29, 33 n.8, 36, 37, 39
Hitler: A Film from Germany (Syberberg)   141 n.5
Hominescence   32
hominization   24, 25
homo economicus   4, 15
homo oeconomicus   16 n.10

homosexuality   43
Hottois, Gilbert   80, 82, 87
Hui, Yuk   98, 104 n.8
humanism, definition   82
humanity   2, 12, 25, 77, 78, 82, 88, 89
Huxley, Julian   83

Individualism and Economic Order (Hayek)   36
industrial capitalism   27, 32
'infinite life' of zoë   119, 121
info-capitalism   57
information revolution   60
information technologies   11, 47, 67, 70, 71, 119
  asymmetry of information   58
  big data   58
  class antagonism   55
  concept of value   59–63
  emergence of   57
  market economy   55
  mode of production   55, 57–9, 66
  Simondon's concept of information   63–6
  thought experiment   58, 63, 71
institutional neoliberalism   17 n.18
Integrated World Capitalism (IWC) (Guattari)   127
intellectual marketing   44
internationalism   5
Israeli settler-colonialism   41
Israel's settler-colonial state apparatus   41

James, William   140 n.4
Jameson, Fredric   40
Je t'aime, je t'aime (Deleuze)   138
joys of marketing   48

Kafka, Franz   110, 119–21, 123, 165
Kant, Immanuel   132, 133, 152
Kelly, Mark G. E.   94, 95, 98, 99, 101, 104 n.12, 105 n.14
Kennedy, Robert   118
Keynesian capitalism   113, 117
Keynesian economics   36, 113
Kiely, Ray   16 n.6

Lacan, Jacques   97, 99, 164, 167
Lacanian psychoanalysis   164
laissez-faire capitalism   27

Index

laissez-faire economics   86
laissez-faire ethics   8
L'Amour à mort (Love unto death) (Deleuze)   138
L'amplification dans les processus d'information (Simondon)   65
Languages of Art (Goodman)   96
Latin American cinema. *see The Wolf House* (León and Cociña)
Latour, Bruno   13, 87–9, 133, 134, 137
Laval, Christian   86
León, Cristóbal   143, 153, 155
Leroi-Gourhan, André   23
Lévy, Bernard-Henri   44, 50 n.5
liberal democracy   75
libertarian pragmatism   84
Linares Salgado, Jorge E.   82
Linnean taxonomy   24
The Logic of Sense (Deleuze)   109
Luhmann, Niklas   104 n.13
Luhmannian systems theory   100
Lyotard, Jean-Francois   168

Maastricht Treaty   40
machinic surplus value   66–70
The Machinic Unconscious: Essays in Schizoanalysis (Guattari)   165
machinism/transversalism   7
Macri, Mauricio   42
Malinovskiy, Boris N.   103 n.4
Manetti, Giannozzo   82
market economy   1, 55–7, 62
Marrati, Paola   132
Martin, Keir   37–9
Marxism   68, 167, 169, 173
Marxist critical theory   57
Marx's critique of political economy   66
Mason, Paul   11, 55–62, 65, 66, 71 n.1
Massumi, Brian   127
McCarthy, Annie   6
McFalls, Laurence   4, 16 n.4
McGoey, Linsey   15 n.2
McGuigan, Jim   16 n.13
Meca, Diego Sánchez   78
Medien, Kathryn   41
mental illnesses   14–15, 162–4, 171
metastability   64, 65
micropolitics   45, 46
Mirandola, Pico della   82
Mitterrand, François   36

Modernization front   133, 134
modulation technologies   12
monetarism   35
Money–Commodity–Money cycle   31
Money–Money cycle   31
Moore's law   103 n.4
Morales, Evo   38
More, Max   83
The Movement-Image (Deleuze)   129
Movimento dos Trabalhadores Rurais Sem Terra (MST)   121, 122

nanobots technology   2
Nassehi, Armin   100, 101, 105 n.14
naturalism in morality   78
natural resource extraction   46
Nature (Hartree)   96
Negri, A.   71 n.3
Negt, Oskar   44
Neno, Carolina Urrutia   149, 151
neoclassical trends   1
neo-hyper-modernism   88
neoliberal capitalism   1, 14, 15, 113, 120, 161, 162, 173
neoliberal critiques of antitrust law   47
neoliberal-digital economy   117
Neoliberalism's 'rational choice theory'   163
neoliberal paradox   16 n.6
The Net (Winkler)   115
New Atlantis (Bacon)   82
Nicolas de Condorcet (*Tableau historique des progrès de l'esprit humain*, 1793)   82
Nietzschean overman   12, 75–9
Night and Fog (Cayrol)   141 n.6
Nolan, Ryan   71 n.4
nouveaux philosophes ('New Philosophers')   40, 44, 45
Nozick, Robert   84

objective knowledge   13
ontopower (Massum)   127
Operations of continuation   102
Operations of discretization   102
The Order of Things (Foucault)   78, 111

Palestinians' identity and affirmation   41
pandemic Keynesianism   35
Pandolfi, Mariella   4, 16 n.4

patipolitics 5
Patton, Paul 10, 17 n.18
Paulo, São 46
pensée unique 40
perpetual training 36
philosophy, definition 172
Pinochet, Augusto 154
plane of consistency 8
platform capitalism 30–2, 56
   characteristics of 30
   types of 30
political ecology 128, 129, 135–40
political economy 2, 15, 36–40, 45, 46,
   49, 58, 66, 72 n.6, 79, 169, 173
political restructuration 11
politico-economic autarky 45–7
politics of indifference 1, 16 n.3
postcapitalism 56–9, 62
Post-capitalism (Mason) 11, 55
post-Covid-19 deviation 15 n.1
Postero, Nancy 46
posthumanist humanism 81, 89
The Posthuman (Braidotti) 81
post-industrial capitalism 68
post-neoliberal controlling
   mechanisms 13
post-neoliberal interregnum 43
post-neoliberalism 1, 2, 4–6, 9–11, 15,
   22, 32, 35, 41, 42, 49, 75, 93, 102
   axioms of 41
post-neoliberal 'pink tide'
   experiments 35
Postscript on the Societies of Control
   (Deleuze) 9, 21, 32, 36, 39, 40,
   47, 49, 50 n.2, 93, 109, 113. *see also*
   analog and digital power
post-war German political economy 2
post-World War II liberalism 36
predatory states 40, 42–3
price system 28, 55
principle of individuation 63–6
Prometheus 24, 25
pseudo-intellectualism 40
psychologism 87
psychotherapy 45

A Radical Ecology to Believe in This World
   (Wiame) 13
radical intellectualism 15
radical monopolization 57

reactionary propaganda 44
Reagan, Ronald 86
Reid, Julian 4, 16 n.11
reign of clichés 129–35, 139
Resnais, Alain 138
Resnais's 'cerebral' cinematography 138
reterritorialization 8, 9, 69, 70, 172
revolutionary praxis 166–70
Riofrancos, Thea 38, 46
Rolnik, Suely 45
Romer, Paul 60
Rousseau, Jean-Jacques 165
ruling class 59, 60

Saad-Filho, Alfredo 47
Sandberg, Anders 83
'Savages, Barbarians, Civilized Men' 46
Schäfer, Paul 154, 155
schizoanalysis 14, 45, 164–7, 169–72
   vs. psychoanalysis 167
'schizoanalytic' clinics 45
Schleusener, Simon 9, 17 n.16, 50 n.2,
   148
scientific axiomatics 26
scientific posthumanism 80–1
semiocapitalism 161
Serres, Michel 23, 24, 31, 32
Shannon's mathematical theory of
   information 65
Shiva, Vandana 119
Simmel, Georg 85
Simondon, Gilbert 11, 33 n.4, 56, 63–6,
   68, 71, 72 n.11, 98
Simondon's concept of information
   63–6
Simondon's theories of amplification 11
Sloterdijk, Peter 9, 17 n.17
small farming 119, 123
Smith, Adam 27–9
Smith, Daniel 152, 166
smooth spaces 3, 31, 32, 102
Sobering, Katherine 42
social media 44, 100
social reproduction 56, 63, 67–71
society of clichés 128, 131
sociocultural stratification 3
Sokal, Alan 103 n.1
*The Soul at Work: From Alienation to
   Autonomy* (Berardi) 161
Srnicek, Nick 30, 56

Printed in the USA
CPSIA information can be obtained
at www.ICGtesting.com
LVHW011821041124
795688LV00003B/295

Index

Staab, Philipp   99, 100
stable equilibrium   63, 64
Stambolian, George   167
struggles of the Third World   42
surveillance capitalism   56
Syberberg   141 n.5 (AU:Please provide
    initial for "Syberberg")

Taylorization   21
techno-enthusiastic version of
    communism   62
techno-feudalism   55, 72 n.10
technological theory of information   64
technologies of cruelty   43
Thatcher, Margaret   86
A Thousand Plateaus (Deleuze and
    Guattari)   9, 22, 23, 38, 40, 46, 49,
    130, 167, 169
Thus Spoke Zarathustra (Nietzsche)   77
The Time-Image (Deleuze)   131, 135–7,
    139
transhumanism   11, 12
    anthropology   77–86
    assemblage theory   76
    cultural posthumanism   80–6
    vs. cultural posthumanism   12
    definition   75
    Deleuzo-Guattarian concept   76
    inconsistencies   84–5
    Nietzschean overman   12, 75–9
    philosophical framework   76
    post-neoliberal techno-utopia   86–9
    transhumanist movement   76
transmogrification of neoliberalism   40
Trente Glorieuses   40
Trois milliards de pervers:
    Grande encyclopédie des
    homosexualités   43
Turkle, Sherry   116
Twilight of the Idols (Nietzsche)   78

The Use of Knowledge in Society
    (von Hayek)   28
use value   61, 62, 171

Vandenberghe, Frédéric   17 n.14
vectorialists   58, 59, 71 n.2
Via Campesina   110, 118, 123
videoconferencing systems   105 n.18

Virilio, Paul   71 n.2, 135
Vrasti, Wanda   4

Wark, McKenzie   11, 55–63, 65, 66, 71,
    71 n.2, 72 n.6
war machine   6, 15, 22, 23, 38, 39, 41, 42,
    109, 110, 113, 167, 168
    agroecological war machines   123
    digital war machines   110, 118
    Franz Kafka's minor literary war
    machine   119
Washington Consensus institutions   37,
    39, 42
weakening of historicity   41
Wealth of Nations (Smith)   27
Web 2.0   109, 116
Weeks, Samuel   11, 50 n.3
Western capitalism   161
Wiame, Aline   13
Wiener's cybernetic theory   65
Winkler, Irwin   115
Winner, Langdon   85
The Wolf House (León and Cociña)   14
    artistic compositions of
    animation   155
    audiovisualities   146, 147
    Chilean animation   151
    colouring effects   150
    concept of truth   147, 152, 156
    concept to immanence   157
    degree of realism   144
    drawing figure   150
    editing   144
    infantile-image   144, 146–53, 155,
    157, 158, 158 n.1
    montage   144
    neoliberal discourses   144, 145
    period of horror   148
    sound modulations   151
    soundtrack   151
    visionary struggle   154–8
    visual arts   150
worker self-management   38

zero marginal cost   72 n.5
Žižek, Slavoj   6
Zoom   105 n.18
Zourabichvili, François   132
Zuboff, Shoshana   56